About this Participant Guide

This participant guide is designed to complement Cape Project Management's course, *All About Agile: Preparing for the PMI-ACP Exam.*

This guide is not intended to be a standalone artifact in preparing for the PMI-ACP exam. Contained in this guide are the slides, exercises and practice exam questions used in their public training, virtual training and self-paced training.

If you are interested in taking any of these courses, you can contact me at dan@capeprojectmanagement.com or check out links below:

Self-paced training:

http://bit.ly/ACPSelfStudy

Public Virtual Training

https://www.capeprojectmanagement.com/public-agile-training-schedule/

Additional PMI-ACP Exam preparation Resources

Free PMI-ACP Glossary and Study Guide

http://bit.ly/ACPStudyGuide

410 PMI-ACP Practice Questions: Available online

http://bit.ly/practice-pmi-acp

Table of Contents

CAPE PROJECT MANAGEMENT, INC.

All About Agile™
Preparing for the PMI-ACP® Exam
Module 1: Introduction and Knowledge Check

Part of the Agile Education Series™

Dan Tousignant, PMP, PMI-ACP

About Your Instructor: Dan Tousignant

- Agile Coach and Trainer
  - Project Management Professional (PMP)
  - Agile Certified Practitioner (PMI-ACP)
  - Professional Scrum Master I (PSM I)
  - Certified Scrum Professional (CSP)

First Scrum project was with Ken Schwaber, the co-founder of Scrum

About Us

- **Cape Project Management, Inc.**
- **Provides public and onsite training:**
  http://CapeProjectManagement.com/
- **Training Store:**
  https://capeprojectmanagement.learnupon.com/store
- **Contact me:**
  Dan@CapeProjectManagement.com
- **Follow me on Twitter @ScrumDan**

Copyrighted material. 2018

The Agile Education Series™

☐ All About Agile™: PMI-ACP® Agile Exam Preparation
☐ Scrum Master Certification Training
☐ Product Owner and User Story Training
☐ Kanban for Software Development Teams
☐ Achieving Agility – How to implement Agile in your organization
☐ Agile for Team Members
☐ Agile for Executives
☐ Agile Testing and Engineering
☐ Scaling Agile

All of these curriculums are available on Amazon, just search by Author on Dan Tousignant.

CAPE PROJECT MANAGEMENT, INC.

PMI-ACP Course Objectives

☐ Prepare for the PMI-ACP® Exam
☐ Provide a comprehensive review of Agile practices – Learn "All About Agile"

CAPE PROJECT MANAGEMENT, INC.

Taking this Course

- ☐ Participant materials
  - ◘ Slides
  - ◘ Exercises
  - ◘ Practice Questions & Answers
  - ◘ Access to online exams

Course Modules	% of Questions
1: Introduction and Knowledge Check	
2: Agile Principles and Mindset 2-1 Agile Manifesto and Agile Methods Overview 2-2 Scrum 2-3 Extreme Programming 2-4 Kanban 2-5 Lean and More Agile Methods	16%
3: Value Driven Delivery	20%
4: Stakeholder Engagement (4-1, 4-2)	17%
5: Team Performance	16%
6: Adaptive Planning	12%
7: Problem Detection and Resolution	10%
8: Continuous Improvement	9%
9: Study Tips	

Exam & Course Content

- Knowledge & Skills Domains
    1. Agile Principles and Mindset
    2. Value Driven Delivery
    3. Stakeholder Engagement
    4. Adaptive Planning
    5. Team Performance
    6. Problem Detection and Resolution
    7. Continuous Improvement (Product, Process, People)
- Tools and Techniques
    - All of the items in our Study Guide
- Pay attention to the content in the study guide noted with our logo

Exam Eligibility Requirements

Requirement	Description
General Project Experience	2,000 hours working on project teams earned within the last 5 years **Note:** An active PMP® or PgMP® will satisfy this requirement
Agile Project Experience	1,500 hours working on Agile project teams or with Agile methodologies earned within the last 3 years **Note:** These hours are in addition to the hours required above
Training in Agile Practices	21 contact hours in Agile practices

For complete details regarding the PMI-ACP eligibility requirements, please view the PMI-ACP Handbook under *Resources.* There are no changes to this criteria for the new exam.

The Exam Breakdown

- 120 questions
- 3 hours
- 2 domains
  - Agile Tools and Techniques – 50%
  - Agile Knowledge and Skills – 50%
- Score Pass/Fail
  - Proficient = Pass
  - Moderately proficient = Pass
  - Below proficient = Pass

Copyrighted material. 2018

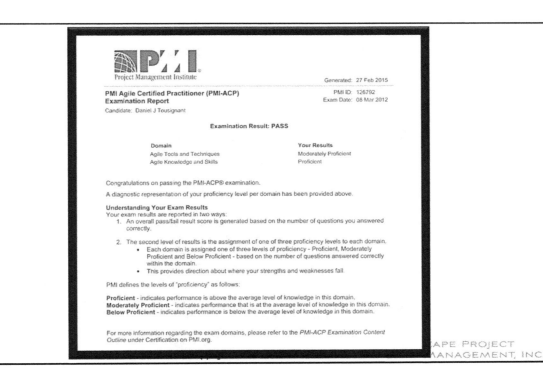

2018 Exam Updates

- Begins March 26, 2018
- See Resources for Links
- No outline changes from 2014
- Common terminology adopted from Agile Practice Guide
- This course has been updated to reflect changes

Copyrighted material. 2018

Copyrighted material. 2018

Module 1 Knowledge Check

Questions

1. Which one is NOT one of the 5 common risk areas mitigated by Agile?

Correct	Choice
	Intrinsic schedule flaw
	Stakeholder apathy
	Specification breakdown
	Personnel loss
	Productivity variation
	Scope creep

2. A key component of Agile software development is:

Correct	Choice
	Requirements should be complete before beginning development
	Change must be minimized
	Risk management is robust
	Requirements are able to evolve during development

3. Which is NOT a Scrum Role?

Correct	Choice
	Product Owner
	Project Manager
	Scrum Master
	Team Member

4. There must be a release every Sprint.

Correct	Choice
	True
	False

5. No one, not even the Scrum Master, tells the development team how to build the product.

Correct	Choice
	True
	False

6. Which one of the following is NOT a Scrum Event?

Correct	Choice
	Retrospectives
	Reviews or Demos
	Daily Stand-ups
	Status Meetings

7. The ultimate goal of _____ is to deploy all but the last few hours of work at any time.

Correct	Choice
	Continuous Integration
	Collective Code Ownership
	Asynchronous Builds
	Synchronous Builds

8. An artifact on an Agile project can best be described as:

Correct	Choice
	A work output, typically a document, drawing, code, or model
	A document that describes how work the work needs to be done
	The Agile model of persona
	The deliverable from a Sprint retrospective

9. Which of the following sets of tools is least likely to be utilized by an Agile team?

Correct	Choice
	Digital camera, task board
	Wiki, planning poker cards
	Smart board, card wall
	WBS, PERT charts

10. In Scrum, who is responsible for managing the team?

Correct	Choice
	Scrum Master
	Development Team
	Product Owner
	Project Manager

11. The Project Leader's primary responsibilities are to "move boulders and carry water." What is this an example of?

Correct	Choice
	Servant leadership
	Leadership by example
	The leadership metaphor
	Command and control leadership

12. On Agile teams, conflict is to be avoided at all cost.

Correct	Choice
	True
	False

13. Incremental delivery means:

Correct	Choice
	Deliver nonfunctional increments in the iteration retrospectives.
	Release working software only after testing each increment.
	Deploy functional increments over the course of the project.
	Improve and elaborate our Agile process with each increment delivered.

14. Scrum is a software development methodology.

Correct	Choice
	True
	False

15. What is a product roadmap?

Correct	Choice
	A list of reports and screens
	Instructions for deployment
	A backlog prioritization scheme
	A view of release candidates

Agile Manifesto and Agile Methods Overview

All About Agile: Module 2-1

Version 4.0

Module Objectives

- ☐ Gain an understanding of the Agile Manifesto:
  - ◻ Values
  - ◻ Principles
- ☐ Define Project Management Lifecycles
- ☐ Review the most common Agile Methods
  - ◻ Scrum
  - ◻ XP
  - ◻ Kanban
  - ◻ Lean

Agile Manifesto History

☐ The Agile Manifesto was written February 11-13, 2001, at The Lodge at Snowbird ski resort in the Wasatch mountains of Utah.

☐ Seventeen people met to talk, ski, relax, and try to find common ground in software development project management.

☐ Included representatives from Extreme Programming, SCRUM, DSDM, Adaptive Software Development, Crystal, Feature-Driven Development, Pragmatic Programming, and others.

☐ All were actively offering solutions to documentation driven, heavyweight software development processes and a way for companies to respond to disruptive technologies.

Copyrighted material. 2018

CAPE PROJECT
MANAGEMENT, INC.

Disruptive Technologies

Historically:

☐ The (PC) displaced the typewriter and forever changed the way we work and communicate.

☐ The Windows user-friendly interface was instrumental in the rapid development of the personal computing industry in the 1990s.

☐ Email transformed the way we communicating, largely displacing letter-writing and disrupting the postal and greeting card industries.

☐ Cell phones made it possible for people to call us anywhere and disrupted the telecom industry.

More recently

☐ Cloud computing has displacing many resources that would conventionally have been located in-house or provided as a traditionally hosted service.

☐ Social networking has had a major impact on the way we communicate and -- especially for personal use -- has disrupted telephone, email, instant messaging and event planning.

☐ One-demand printing has changed the way book and print publication occurs making everyone a potential author or marketer.

☐ Virtual conferencing like Skype and Google hangouts has changed how companies work with a growing number of virtual employees throughout industry.

Copyrighted material. 2018

CAPE PROJECT
MANAGEMENT, INC.

The Agile Manifesto:
A statement of values

We are uncovering better ways of developing software by doing it and helping others do it.

Through this work we have come to value:

Individuals and interactions	over	Process and tools
Working software	over	Comprehensive documentation
Customer collaboration	over	Contract negotiation
Responding to change	over	Following a plan

That is, while there is value in the items on the right, we value the items on the left more.

Source: www.agilemanifesto.org

CAPE PROJECT
MANAGEMENT, INC.

We value:

"Individuals and interactions over processes and tools"

☐ The right people are more valuable than tools or methods

☐ New solutions and resolutions to problems are found through interactions and discussions

CAPE PROJECT
MANAGEMENT, INC.

We value:

"Working software over comprehensive documentation"

- ☐ The primary focus for software development teams must be on delivering something that works for the customer
- ☐ Documentation, though often necessary, needs to be prioritized to those artifacts that provide value to the customer

Copyrighted material. 2018

We value:

"Customer collaboration over contract negotiations"

- ☐ Listening to what the customer wants is more critical than meeting the language of a contract.
- ☐ Software development needs to be a collaboration between the user and the developer.

Copyrighted material. 2018

We value:

"Responding to change over following a plan"

- Plans are notoriously out of date as soon as they are written.
- By embracing change as opposed to trying to prevent it will deliver products that the customer is actually wanting.

CAPE PROJECT
MANAGEMENT, INC.

12 Principles of the Agile Manifesto

1. Our highest priority is to satisfy the customer through early and continuous delivery of valuable software.
2. Welcome changing requirements, even late in development. Agile processes harness change for the customer's competitive advantage.
3. Deliver working software frequently, from a couple of weeks to a couple of months, with a preference to the shorter timescale.
4. Business people and developers must work together daily throughout the project.
5. Build projects around motivated individuals. Give them the environment and support they need, and trust them to get the job done.
6. The most efficient and effective method of conveying information to and within a development team is face-to-face conversation.
7. Working software is the primary measure of progress.
8. Agile processes promote sustainable development. The sponsors, developers, and users should be able to maintain a constant pace indefinitely.
9. Continuous attention to technical excellence and good design enhances agility.
10. Simplicity—the art of maximizing the amount of work not done—is essential.
11. The best architectures, requirements, and designs emerge from self-organizing teams.
12. At regular intervals, the team reflects on how to become more effective, then tunes and adjusts its behavior accordingly.

CAPE PROJECT
MANAGEMENT, INC.

The Principles

Our highest priority is to satisfy the customer through early and frequent delivery of valuable software.

- Early delivery allows for quick wins and early feedback.
- The paradigm, "fail sooner," is a valuable benefit as well.
- Competition in the marketplace is often driven by innovation and frequent releases.

CAPE PROJECT
MANAGEMENT, INC.

The Principles

Welcome changing requirements, even late in development. Agile processes harness change for the customer's competitive advantage

- The Agile approach strives to accommodate change as easily and efficiently as possible.
- Changes in technology, regulations, resources and requirements are a reality of software development projects.

CAPE PROJECT
MANAGEMENT, INC.

The Principles

Deliver working software frequently, from a couple of weeks to a couple of months, with a preference for the smaller time scale.

☐ It is more rewarding to deliver frequently.

☐ Feedback that occurs after shorter delivery cycles is a key advantage of iterative development

The Principles

Business people and developers work together daily throughout the project

☐ There can no longer be an "us" and "them" between business and IT.

☐ Involve the customer every step of the way

The Principles

Build projects around motivated individuals. Give them the environment and support they need, and trust them to get the job done

☐ One of the cornerstones of Agile is the focus on the value of the motivated team.

☐ Trust first is a major shift in leadership style.

 CAPE PROJECT MANAGEMENT, INC.

The Principles

The most efficient and effective method of conveying information to and within a development team is face-to-face conversation.

☐ Non-verbal communication is only possible face-to-face.

☐ Informal communication often leads to creativity and relationship building.

CAPE PROJECT MANAGEMENT, INC.

The Principles

Working software is the primary measure of progress

☐ Many well run projects often fail because the focus is removed from the actual deliverable.

☐ This is the number one principle and measurement of a successful Agile team.

CAPE PROJECT
MANAGEMENT, INC.

The Principles

Agile processes promote sustainable development. The sponsors, developers, and users should be able to maintain a constant pace indefinitely.

☐ Software development is a creative process.

☐ Burnout and decreased productivity are the outcomes of a long hours and mandatory overtime.

CAPE PROJECT
MANAGEMENT, INC.

The Principles

Continuous attention to technical excellence and good design enhances agility

- ☐ Don't ignore quality in the rush to deliver more quickly.
- ☐ Nothing can replace a clean design and architecture.

  CAPE PROJECT MANAGEMENT, INC.

The Principles

Simplicity—the art of maximizing the amount of work not done—is essential

- ☐ This is a key Lean principle as well – minimize waste.
- ☐ Focusing on delivering business value is an important part of this principle.

  CAPE PROJECT MANAGEMENT, INC.

The Principles

The best architectures, requirements, and designs emerge from self-organizing teams

☐ This is a combination of some other principles: it is almost impossible to have a high-quality product without a motivated, inspired and skilled team.

CAPE PROJECT
MANAGEMENT, INC.

The Principles

At regular intervals, the team reflects on how to become more effective and then tunes and adjusts its behavior accordingly

☐ The commitment to continuous improvement is a foundation of most Agile practices.

☐ This can only occur if there is an environment of trust and honesty.

CAPE PROJECT
MANAGEMENT, INC.

Activity: Agile Manifesto Sounds Bites

Directions:
1. Create a 3-5 word "sound bite" to simplify each principle to its most basic intent.
2. Document your answers on the back and be prepared to share with the class.
3. This activity should take 20 minutes.

		Sound Bite
1.	Our highest priority is to satisfy the customer through early and continuous delivery of valuable software.	
2.	Welcome changing requirements, even late in development. Agile processes harness change for the customer's competitive advantage.	
3.	Deliver working software frequently, from a couple of weeks to a couple of months, with a preference to the shorter timescale.	
4.	Business people and developers must work together daily throughout the project.	
5.	Build projects around motivated individuals. Give them the environment and support they need, and trust them to get the job done.	
6.	The most efficient and effective method of conveying information to and within a development team is face-to-face conversation.	
7.	Working software is the primary measure of progress.	
8.	Agile processes promote sustainable development. The sponsors, developers, and users should be able to maintain a constant pace indefinitely.	
9.	Continuous attention to technical excellence and good design enhances agility.	
10.	Simplicity--the art of maximizing the amount of work not done--is essential.	
11.	The best architectures, requirements, and designs emerge from self-organizing teams.	
12.	At regular intervals, the team reflects on how to become more effective, then tunes and adjusts its behavior accordingly.	

Activity

Agile Sound Bites

Download the Sound Bites Exercise Under *Resources*

CAPE PROJECT
MANAGEMENT, INC.

A Project Management Life Cycle

□ A Project Management Life Cycle (PMLC) is a sequence of processes that include these phases:
  ◘ Scoping
  ◘ Planning
  ◘ Launching
  ◘ Monitoring & Controlling
  ◘ Closing
□ Every valid project management life cycle must include each of these processes one or more times.

CAPE PROJECT
MANAGEMENT, INC.

The Five PMLC Models

- **Linear** – This management approach is a simple model based on the Traditional Project Management(TPM) approach. The five phases are completed in order sequentially from Scope to Plan to Launch to Monitor and Control and then to Project Closeout.

- **Incremental** – This approach is very similar to the Linear approach and is also a TPM approach, however, an Incremental approach releases solutions as they are completed.

- **Iterative** – This model is based on the Agile Project Management (APM) approach and is a system that delivers solutions on every iteration.

- **Adaptive** – This model is another form of the APM approach, however, unlike the Iterative model, this model has minimal information that is known about the solution and also is missing the functional aspect of searching for a solution.

- **Extreme** – This model is most appropriately used on research and development projects. It involves heavy client involvement and is a process used when the goals nor the solutions are known and are very high risk and high change type projects,

Robert Wysocki *Effective Project Management: traditional, agile, extreme.*

CAPE PROJECT
MANAGEMENT, INC.

Project Approaches

- Traditional Project Management (TPM) – This management approach is based on knowing both the goal and solution.

- Agile Project Management (APM) – This management approach is based on knowing well defined goals but not the means for a solution.

- Extreme Project Management (xPM) – This management approach is when neither a goal or solution is clearly defined.

- Emertxe Project Management (MPx) – This management approach in which the solution is well defined, however, the goal is not defined.

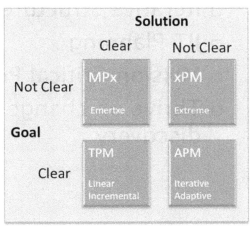

Robert Wysocki *Effective Project Management: traditional, agile, extreme.*

CAPE PROJECT
MANAGEMENT, INC.

Agile Project Management

- Iterative and Adaptive PMLC Models are those that proceed from iteration to iteration based on very limited specification of solution.
- Each iteration learns from the preceeding ones and redirects the next iteration in an attempt to converge on an acceptable solution. At the discretion of the client an iteration may release a partial solution.

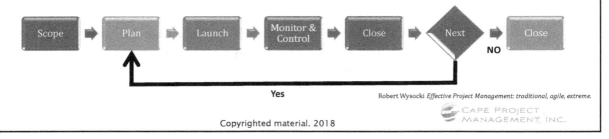

Yes

Robert Wysocki *Effective Project Management: traditional, agile, extreme.*

CAPE PROJECT MANAGEMENT, INC.

Copyrighted material. 2018

Characteristics of an Adaptive PMLC Model

- Iterative Structure
- JIT Planning
- Mission Critical Projects
- Thrive on change through learning and discovery

Robert Wysocki *Effective Project Management: traditional, agile, extreme.*

CAPE PROJECT MANAGEMENT, INC.

Copyrighted material. 2018

Strengths of Adaptive PMLC Model

- Does not waste time on non-value-added work
- Avoids all management issues processing scope change requests
- Does not waste time planning uncertainty
- Provides maximum business value within the given time and cost constraints

Robert Wysocki *Effective Project Management: traditional, agile, extreme.*

 CAPE PROJECT MANAGEMENT, INC.

Copyrighted material. 2018

Weaknesses of Adaptive PMLC Model

- This model requires more client input
- Cannot identify what will be delivered at the end of the project
- Recommends co-located teams

Robert Wysocki *Effective Project Management: traditional, agile, extreme.*

CAPE PROJECT MANAGEMENT, INC.

Copyrighted material. 2018

Terminology Update

Predictive	Definable Linear • Car production • Appliances • Most construction • Automated
Adaptive	High-uncertainty Exploratory High rate of change, complexity & risk • Clinical • Product design • Feasibility studies

Characteristics of Project Lifecycles

Characteristics				
Approach	Requirements	Activities	Delivery	Goal
Predictive	Fixed	Performed once for the entire project	Single delivery	Manage cost
Iterative	Dynamic	Repeated until correct	Single delivery	Correctness of solution
Incremental	Dynamic	Performed once for a given increment	Frequent smaller deliveries	Speed
Agile	Dynamic	Repeated until correct	Frequent small deliveries	Customer value via frequent deliveries and feedback

Selecting a Project Lifecycle

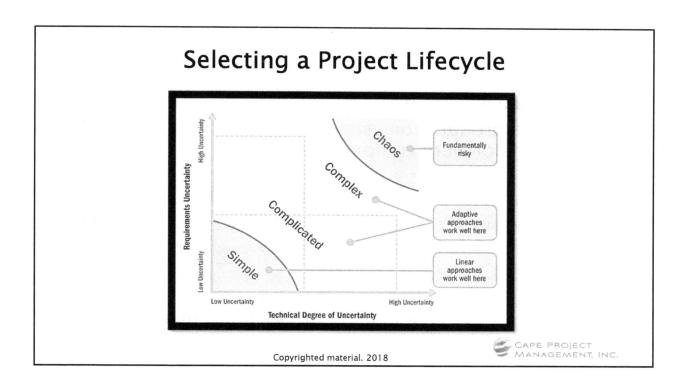

Requirements Stability vs. Development Approach

- Selecting a PMLC depends upon the stability of the requirements:
  - A predictive team can report exactly what features and tasks are planned for the entire length of the development process.
  - Adaptive methods focus on adapting quickly to changing realities. When the needs of a project change, an adaptive team changes as well.

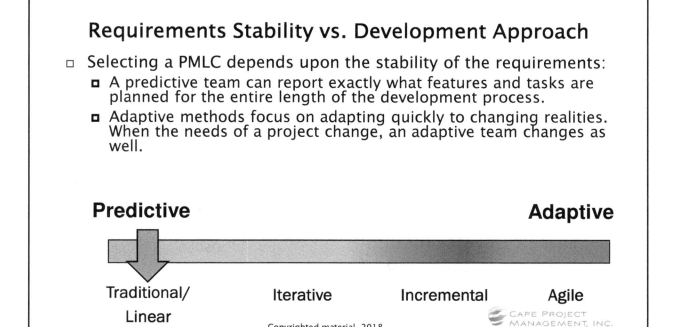

Hybrid Approaches

Predictive + Adaptive

☐ The product consists of (equally important) hardware and software components

☐ The product is a piece of software which has legacy back-end and newer front-end technology

☐ The product has a single delivery requirement like a new drug, but interim reviews

Blended Agile

☐ A software product built using extreme programming engineering practices and Scrum framework

CAPE PROJECT
MANAGEMENT, INC.

Agile Project Management Methodologies

☐ Agile is an umbrella term that encompasses many processes or methodologies.

☐ Common practices include Scrum, Extreme Programming, Agile Unified Process, DSDM, Feature Driven Development, Kanban, Crystal and more...

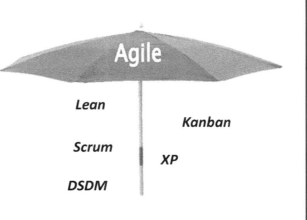

CAPE PROJECT
MANAGEMENT, INC.

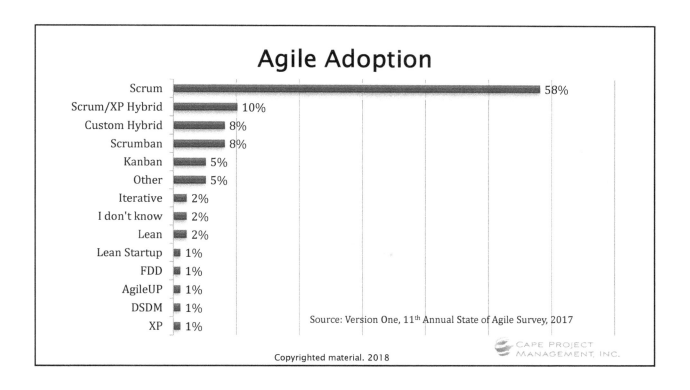

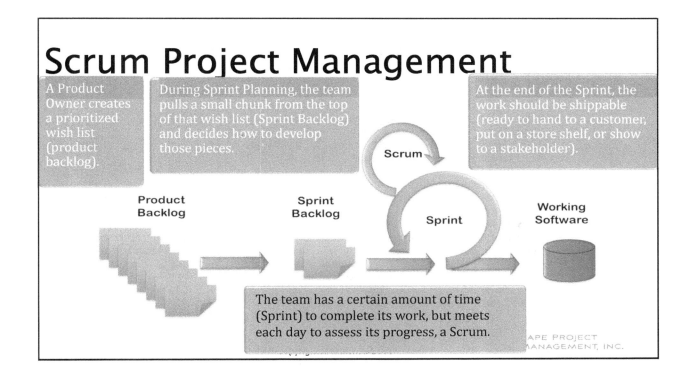

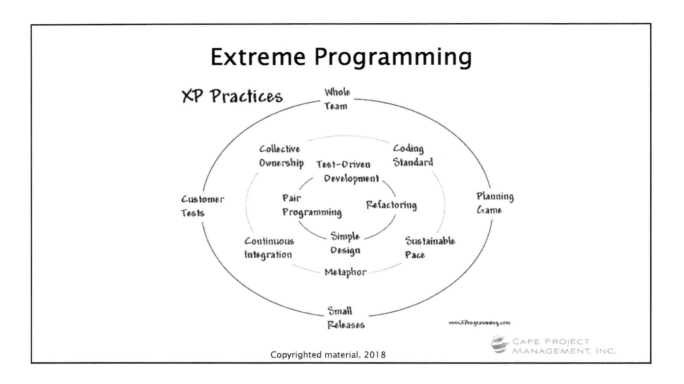

Extreme Programming Practices

Business Practices:
Whole Team, Planning Game, Small Releases, Customer Tests, Sustainable Pace
- Every contributor to the project is an integral part of the Whole Team.
- The team forms around a business person called the Customer, who sits with the team and works with them daily.
- A simple form of planning called a Planning Game occurs to decide what should be done next and to predict when the project will be done.
- Focused on business value, the team produces the software in a series of small fully-integrated releases that pass all the tests the Customer has defined.
- Everyone works at a pace that can be sustained indefinitely.

Technical Practices
Metaphor, Simple Design, Pair Programming, Test-Driven Development, Design Improvement
- The team shares a common and simple picture of what the system looks like called the Metaphor.
- Extreme Programmers work together in pairs and as a group, with simple design and obsessively tested code, improving the design continually to keep it always just right for the current needs.

Collective Code Ownership, Coding Standards, Continuous Integration
- Extreme programmers share the code base and code in a consistent style so that everyone can understand and improve all the code as needed.
- The team keeps the system integrated and running all the time.

Copyrighted material. 2018

CAPE PROJECT
MANAGEMENT, INC.

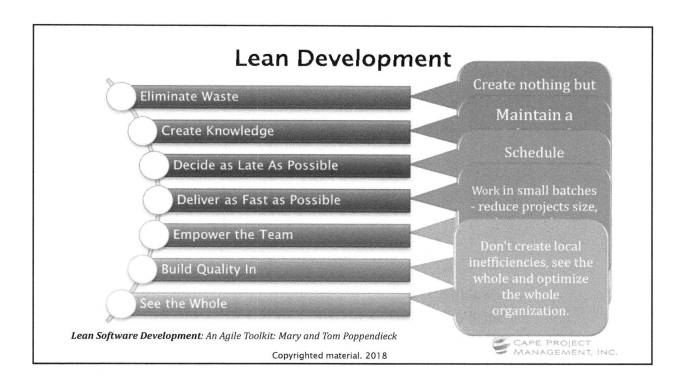

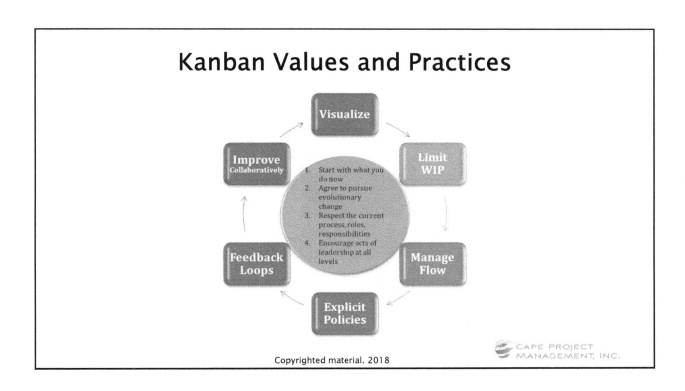

Kanban – Flow Based Approach

Backlog	Design		Develop		Test		Done
	In Progress	Ready	In Progress	Ready	In Progress	Ready	
Story 1 6/1							Story 1
Story 2 6/1	Story 1						6/7
Story 3 6/2	6/3						Lead Time= 6 days
Story 4 6/3							Cycle Time = 4 days
Story 5 6/5							
Story 6 6/7							
WIP Limit	20 hrs		80 hrs		40 hrs		

1. Visualize Flow
2. Set Work in Progress (WIP) Limits
3. Manage Cycle Time

Copyrighted material. 2018

CAPE PROJECT MANAGEMENT, INC.

How it all fits together

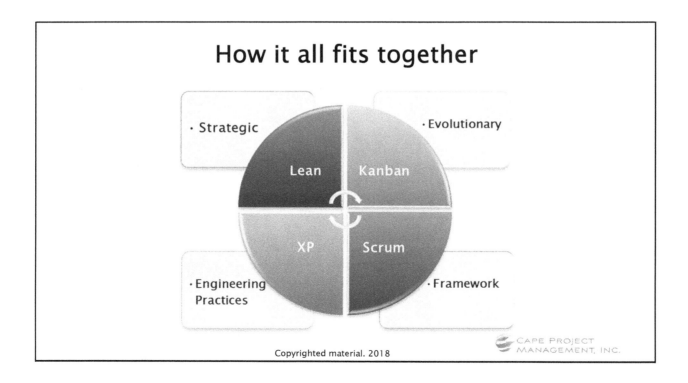

- Strategic
- Evolutionary
- Engineering Practices
- Framework

Lean Kanban XP Scrum

Copyrighted material. 2018

CAPE PROJECT MANAGEMENT, INC.

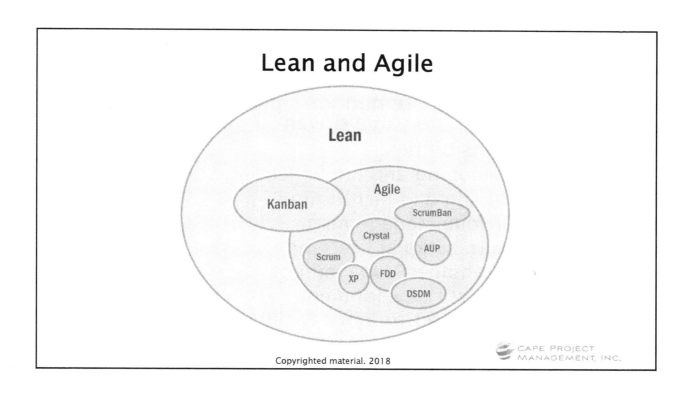

Agile Roles

Role	Description
Team facilitator	The generic term used for Scrum Master or leader of an Agile team. The focus of the role is on servant leadership.
Product owner	The same definition as defined by Scrum. Owns the backlog, vision and value driven delivery.
Cross-functional team member	As with most Agile frameworks, each team member is a "generalizing specialist." Team member are "T-shaped" versus "I-shaped" meaning that they have a primary specialization but have the skills and aptitude when necessary to help other people on the team.

Agile PMOs

- Agile PMOs are multidisciplinary, invitation oriented and value driven
- Responsibilities:
  - Developing and Implementing Standards
  - Training and Mentoring
  - Portfolio Management
  - Organizational Learning
  - Stakeholder Management
  - Resource development
  - Specialized support: Facilitation of retrospectives

Copyrighted material. 2018

ONLINE ACTIVITY

Module 2-1 Knowledge Check

Take a 20 question practice exam to test your understanding of the Agile Manifesto and Agile Methods.

Copyrighted material. 2018

Module 2-1 Knowledge Check

Questions

1. Which of the following is does NOT relate a principle of the Agile Manifesto?

Correct	Choice
	Working software is delivered frequently
	Close, daily co-operation between business people and developers
	Projects built around motivated individuals, who should be trusted
	Daily team meetings are necessary to review progress and address impediments

2. Pick three attributes of an Agile PM0

Correct	Choice
	Value Driven
	Invitation Oriented
	Multidisciplinary
	Functional
	Process Oriented

3. It is important to select a single project lifecycle for a project. "Hybrid" lifecycles can be confusing and counterproductive.

Correct	Choice
	True
	False

4. Match the project lifecycle to its characteristics:

Correct	Choice
Predictive	Dynamic requirements, single delivery, correctness
Iterative	Dynamic requirements, frequent smaller delivery, value driven
Incremental	Fixed requirements, single delivery, cost control
Agile	Dynamic requirements, frequent smaller delivery, speed

5. Agile techniques have become critical for large organizations whose competitors are embracing disruptive technologies. Which of the following are example of a more recent disruptive technology?

Correct	Choice
	Cloud computing
	Google hangouts
	On-demand printing
	Server farms
	Desktop computing

6. Which of the following projects would typically require involve high-uncertainty work?

Correct	Choice
	Automated
	Construction
	Product Design
	Electrical Appliances
	Clinical Studies
	Feasibility Studies

7. Match the Agile practice on the left to the high-level description on the right.

Correct	Choice
XP	Framework
Kanban	Engineering Practices
Lean	Evolutionary
Scrum	Strategic

8. The Agile Manifesto principle, "Our highest priority is to satisfy the customer through early and continuous delivery of valuable software," is achieved through which Scrum practice?

Correct	Choice
	Daily Scrum
	Release Planning
	Sprint Planning
	Sprints

9. Which of the following is a weakness of an Adaptive PMLC Model?

Correct	Choice
	Does not waste time on non-value-added work
	Avoids all management issues processing scope change requests
	Does not waste time planning uncertainty
	Cannot identify what will be delivered at the end of the project

10. Simplicity - the art of _____ - is essential

Correct	Choice
	Maximizing the amount of work not done
	Maximizing the customer collaboration
	Minimizing contract negotiation
	Minimizing the amount of work done

11. This approach includes a visual process management system and an approach to incremental, evolutionary process changes for organizations.

Correct	Choice
	Kanban
	Scrum
	Agile Unified Process
	Extreme programming

12. This management approach is based on knowing well defined goals but not the means for a solution.

Correct	Choice
	Traditional Project Management
	Agile Project Management
	Extreme Project Management
	Emertxe Project Management

13. The best architectures, requirements, and designs emerge from:

Correct	Choice
	Hand-picked teams
	Co-located teams
	Self-organizing teams
	Cross-functional teams

14. Continuous attention to _____ and good design enhances agility.

Correct	Choice
	Best architectures
	Robust plans
	Change control
	Technical excellence

15. This Emertxe Project Management (xPM) approach is when neither a goal nor solution is clearly defined.

Correct	Choice
	True
	False

16. Which is NOT a principle of Lean?

Correct	Choice
	Eliminate waste
	Deliver fast
	Delay commitment
	Time-box events

17. Simple Design, Pair Programming, Test-Driven Development, Design Improvement are all practices of which Agile methodology?

Correct	Choice
	Scrum
	Extreme Programming (P)
	Dynamic Systems Development Method (DSDM)
	Rational Unified Process (RUP)
	Agile Unified Process (AgileUP)
	Crystal Clear
	Feature Driven Development (FDD)

18. Pick the two PMLC models that are based upon the Agile Project Management (APM) approach:

Correct	Choice
	Linear
	Iterative
	Incremental
	Adaptive

19. Which of the following is NOT a principle from the Agile Manifesto?

Correct	Choice
	Our highest priority is to satisfy the customer through early and continuous delivery of valuable software.
	Business people and developers must work together daily throughout the project.
	Working software is the primary measure of progress.
	Continuous creation of technical debt and good design enhances agility.

20. In Agile, _____ is the primary measure of progress:

Correct	Choice
	A Burndown chart
	Increased customer satisfaction
	Working software
	Reduced risk

21. Which of the following is NOT a characteristic of an Adaptive PMLC Model?

Correct	Choice
	Iterative Structure
	JIT Planning
	Clear up front requirements
	Mission Critical Projects

22. What Scrum event or artifact is the set of items that the Team selects to work on during a Sprint?

Correct	Choice
	Product Backlog
	Definition of Done
	Sprint Backlog
	Burndown Chart

23. The Agile Manifesto states we value some items over others. Match the items in the columns below so each item on the left is valued over the corresponding item on the right.

Correct	Choice
Working Software	Following a Plan
Customer Collaboration	Comprehensive Documentation
Individuals and Interactions	Contract Negotiation
Responding to Change	Processes and Tools

24. In Agile project management, responding to change is valued over _____.

Correct	Choice
	Contract negotiation
	Customer collaboration
	Processes and tools
	Following a plan

25. Every Project Management Life Cycle (PMLC) has a sequence of processes that include these phases:

        Scoping

        Planning

        Launching

        Monitoring & Controlling

        Closing

Correct	Choice
	True
	False

CAPE PROJECT
MANAGEMENT, INC.

Agile Methods:
The Scrum Framework

All About Agile: Module 2-2

Version 4.0

Scrum

□ Scrum (n): A framework within which people can address complex adaptive problems, while productively and creatively delivering products of the highest possible value.

Source: Schwaber, Sutherland: *A Scrum Guide*

CAPE PROJECT
MANAGEMENT, INC.

Scrum Resources

☐ Exploring Scrum the Fundamentals

☐ The Scrum Guide (scrumguides.org)

☐ The Agile Practice Guide

Replaced:

☐ Agile Product Management with Scrum (2004)

Scrum

Origins of the idea

"The... 'relay race' approach to product development...may conflict with the goals of maximum speed and flexibility. Instead a holistic or 'rugby' approach—where a team tries to go the distance as a unit, passing the ball back and forth—may better serve today's competitive requirements."

Hirotaka Takeuchi and Ikujiro Nonaka, "The New New Product Development Game", *Harvard Business Review*, January 1986.

CAPE PROJECT MANAGEMENT, INC.

Sequential vs. overlapping development

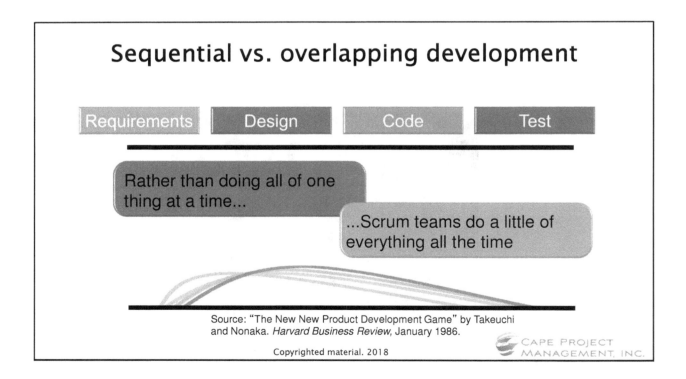

| Requirements | Design | Code | Test |

Rather than doing all of one thing at a time...

...Scrum teams do a little of everything all the time

Source: "The New New Product Development Game" by Takeuchi and Nonaka. *Harvard Business Review*, January 1986.

CAPE PROJECT MANAGEMENT, INC.

History of Scrum

□ Ken Schwaber and Jeff Sutherland developed the Scrum method in the early 1990's.

□ In 2002 "Agile Software Development with Scrum" was written by Ken Schwaber & Mike Beedle

□ The Scrum method has evolved somewhat over the years.

□ 2002 – Present, organic growth due to its anecdotal successes, grass roots adoption and an aggressive training approach have made it the most common Agile methodology

□ The definitive guide to the rules of Scrum, The Scrum Guide, is maintained by Ken Schwaber and Jeff Sutherland. http://www.Scrumguides.org

CAPE PROJECT
MANAGEMENT, INC.

Scrum is:

□ Scrum is a lightweight, simple to understand (but difficult to master) agile process framework.

□ Scrum is one of several agile software development methods.

□ Scrum and Extreme Programming (XP) are probably the two best-known Agile methods. XP emphasizes technical practices such as pair programming and continuous integration. Scrum emphasizes management practice such as the role of Scrum Master.

□ Many companies use the management practices of Scrum with the technical practices of XP.

CAPE PROJECT
MANAGEMENT, INC.

Scrum is Agile

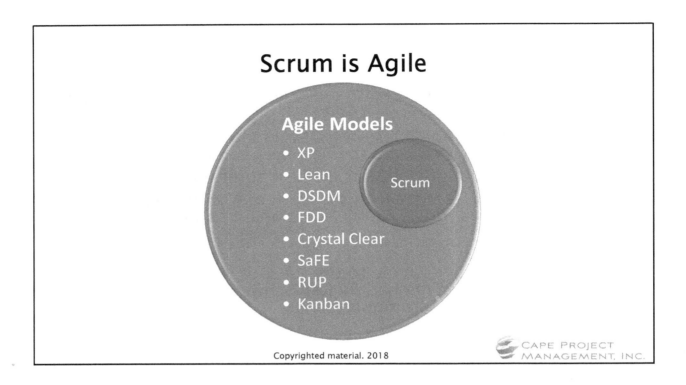

Agile Models

- XP
- Lean
- DSDM
- FDD
- Crystal Clear
- SaFE
- RUP
- Kanban

Scrum

CAPE PROJECT
MANAGEMENT, INC.

Specific Scrum Terminology

"Scrum is Immutable" – Scrum Guide	Alternatives
Scrum Events	Ceremonies, Meetings, Rituals
Backlog Refinement	Backlog Grooming, pre-planning
Daily Scrums	Daily Standups
Scrum Rules	Best Practices
Sprint	Iteration, Container
Requirements, Product Backlog Items (PBIs)	User Stories
Work Remaining	Burndown Charts, etc.
Mandatory Timebox	Recommendations
No Project Manager	Agile Project Manager
No Gantts	Iterative Gantts
Cross Functional Team	Specialties such as QA often exist

CAPE PROJECT
MANAGEMENT, INC.

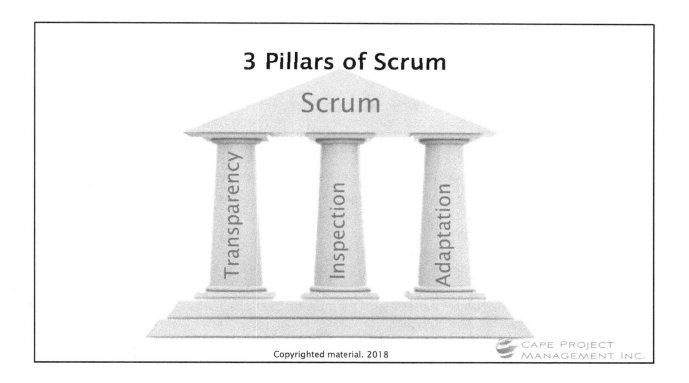

3 Pillars of Scrum

Transparency

☐ ALL relative aspects of the process must be visible to those responsible for the outcome.

Inspection

☐ There is frequent inspection of the artifacts and progress to identify and correct undesirable variances. Inspection occurs during the Sprint Planning Meeting, Daily Scrum, Sprint Review and Sprint Retrospective.

Adaptation

☐ After inspection, adjustments should be made to the processes and artifacts to minimize further deviation.

5 Core Values of Scrum

1. **Commitment** – When we, as a team, value the commitment we make to ourselves and our teammates, we are much more likely to give our all to meet our goals.

2. **Focus** – When we value Focus, and devote the whole of our attention to only a few things at once, we deliver a better quality product, faster.

3. **Openness** – When we value being Open with ourselves and our teammates, we feel comfortable inspecting our behavior and practices, we can adapt them accordingly.

4. **Respect** – When we value Respect, people feel safe to voice concerns and discuss issues, knowing that their voices are heard and valued.

5. **Courage** – When we value Courage, people are encouraged to step outside of their comfort zones and take on greater challenges, knowing they will not be punished if they fail.

Copyrighted material. 2018

Scrum Project Management

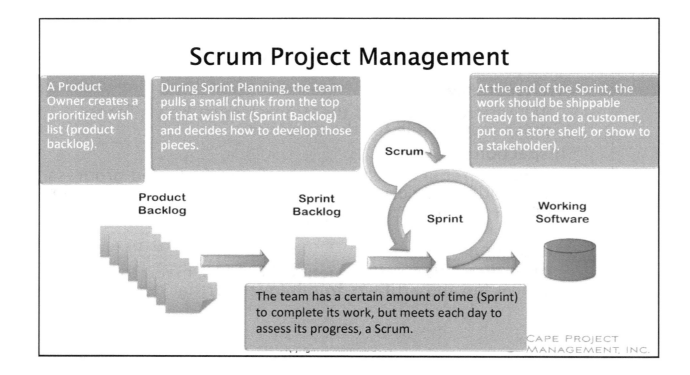

A Product Owner creates a prioritized wish list (product backlog).

During Sprint Planning, the team pulls a small chunk from the top of that wish list (Sprint Backlog) and decides how to develop those pieces.

At the end of the Sprint, the work should be shippable (ready to hand to a customer, put on a store shelf, or show to a stakeholder).

Scrum

Product Backlog

Sprint Backlog

Sprint

Working Software

The team has a certain amount of time (Sprint) to complete its work, but meets each day to assess its progress, a Scrum.

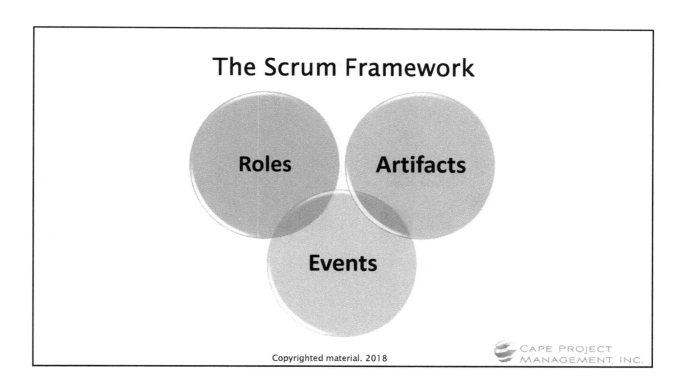

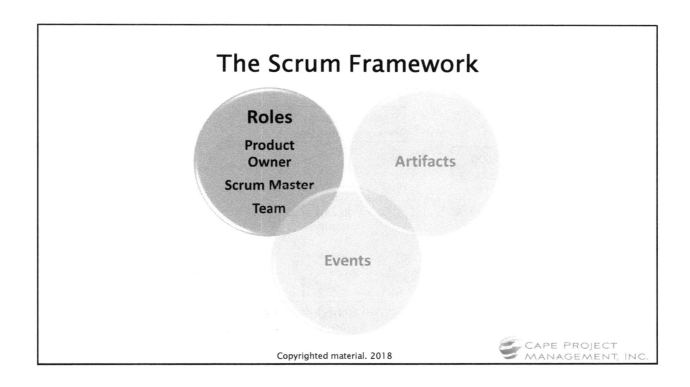

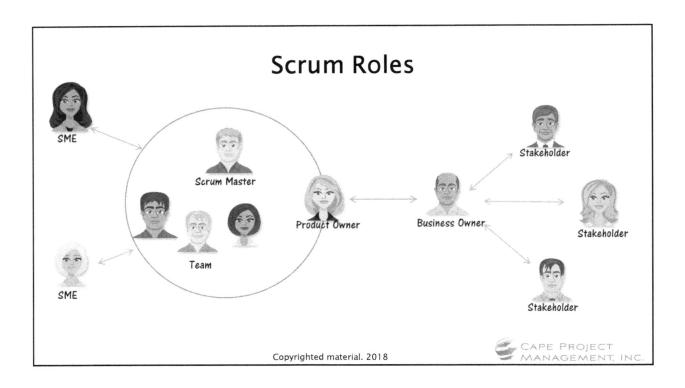

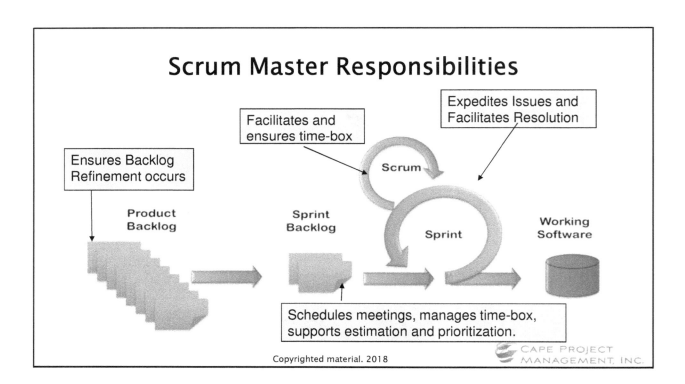

The Scrum Master Do's

- Represents management to the project
- Responsible for enacting Scrum values and practices
- Removes impediments
- Ensure that the team is fully functional and productive
- Enable close cooperation across all roles and functions
- Shield the team from external interferences

Copyrighted material. 2018

Scrum Master Don'ts

- Own the product decisions on Product Owner's behalf
- Make estimates on team's behalf
- Make the technology decisions on team's behalf
- Assign the tasks to the team members
- Try to manage the team

Copyrighted material. 2018

Scrum Master – Top 5

1. Coach team members
2. Manage conflict
3. Facilitate decision making
4. Remove team impediments
5. Increase organizational awareness of Scrum

Product Owner Responsibilities

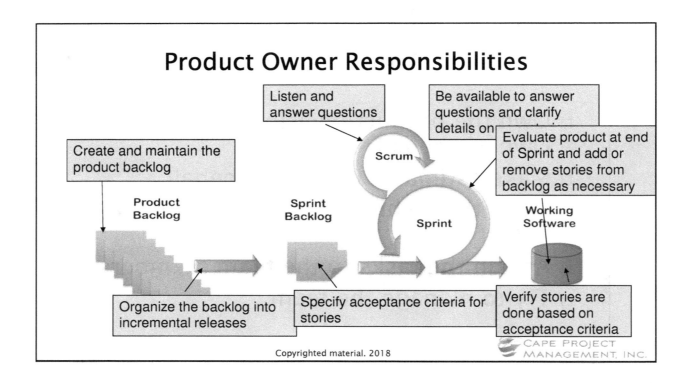

The Product Owner Is a:

- Subject Matter Expert
  - Understand the domain well enough to envision a product
  - Answer questions on the domain for those creating the product
- End User and Customer Advocate
  - Describe the product with understanding of users and its use.
  - Understand the needs of the business and select a mix of features valuable to the customer
- Business Advocate
  - Understand the needs of the organization paying for the software's construction and select a mix of features that serve their goals
- Communicator
  - Capable of communicating vision and intent – deferring detailed feature and design decisions to be made just in time
- Decision Maker
  - Given a variety of conflicting goals and opinions, be the final decision maker for hard product decisions
- The Product Owner role is generally filled by a single person supported by a collaborative team

CAPE PROJECT
MANAGEMENT, INC.

Product Owner Interactions

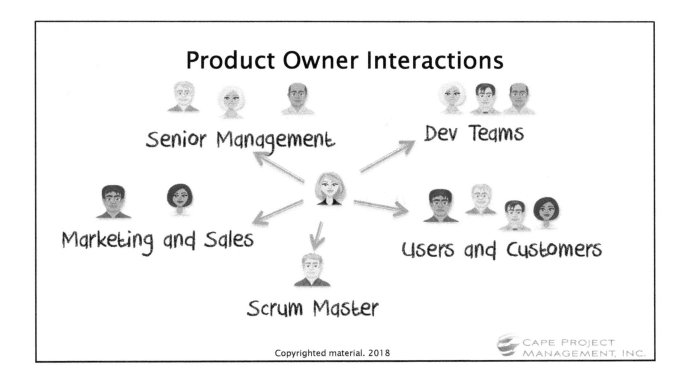

CAPE PROJECT
MANAGEMENT, INC.

Product Owner Do's

- □ Define the features of the product
- □ Decide on release date and content
- □ Be responsible for the profitability of the product (ROI)
- □ Prioritize features according to market value
- □ Adjust features and priority every Sprint, as needed
- □ Should spend three hours with the team each day

Product Owner Don'ts

- □ Choose how much work will be accomplished in the Sprint – the team will do this, based on the priorities
- □ Change anything within the Sprint once it has started and don't add items unless the Sprint will end early

Product Owner – Top 5

1. Create and maintain product backlog
2. Represent the customer in Scrum events
3. Ensure the team is adapting to change
4. Inspect product progress
5. Accept or reject work results

Product Owner vs Scrum Master

- □ Two different roles that complement each other
- □ If one is not played properly, the other suffers.
- □ The Product Owner is responsible for the *product success*
- □ The Scrum Master is responsible for *project success*

Team Responsibilities

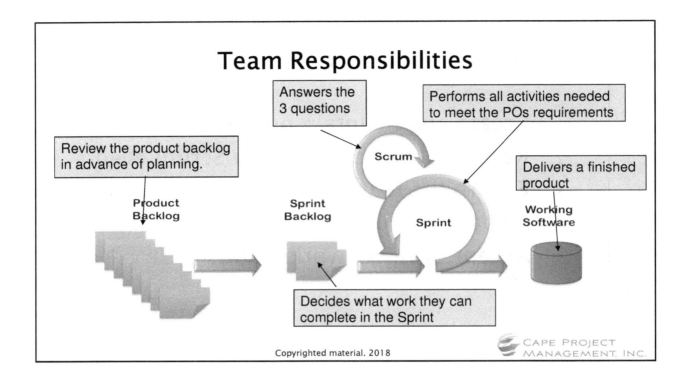

Answers the 3 questions

Performs all activities needed to meet the POs requirements

Review the product backlog in advance of planning.

Delivers a finished product

Scrum

Product Backlog

Sprint Backlog

Sprint

Working Software

Decides what work they can complete in the Sprint

CAPE PROJECT MANAGEMENT, INC.

The Team Do's

- Typically 6 ± 3 people
- Teams are self-organizing
- Cross-functional:
  - Programmers, testers, user experience designers, etc.
- Members should be full-time
  - May be exceptions (e.g., database administrator)
- Membership should change only between Sprints

CAPE PROJECT MANAGEMENT, INC.

The Team Don'ts

□ Skip Scrum Meetings

□ Stop working when there is a roadblock or not enough information

□ Increase technical debt in order to meet the velocity

□ Individuals on a Scrum team should not do excessive individual overtime, or in any other way try to be the "hero" of the team.

Copyrighted material. 2018

CAPE PROJECT
MANAGEMENT, INC.

Team Swarm (or Swarming)

□ Working on one or more stories until they are done

□ Each story has a "TeamLet"

□ Each TeamLet has:

  ◘ A **Coordinator** who is in charge of the story and stays with it until it is complete

  ◘ A **Swarmer(s)** brings their expertise to the story. A Swarmer may be on multiple TeamLets.

Copyrighted material. 2018

CAPE PROJECT
MANAGEMENT, INC.

The Team Top 5

1. Self-organizing team members have to be more creative
2. Have to have a strong discipline and work ethic
3. Must be committed to the project's goals
4. Respect each other
5. Share a genuine conviction that the "we"—the potent concept behind every team—will succeed or fail together

Copyrighted material. 2018

Traditional versus Agile Teams

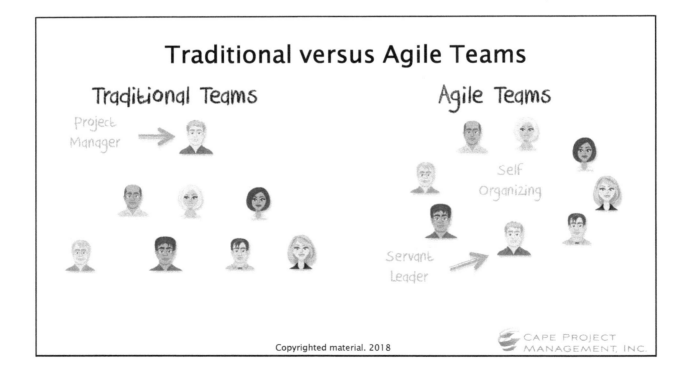

Copyrighted material. 2018

Other Scrum Roles

- Business Owner
- Stakeholders
- Subject Matter Experts (SMEs)

Scrum Business Owner

- Project sponsor and champion
- Controls the budget
- Obtains resources
- Helps Scrum Master remove impediments
- Two types:
  - Lead stakeholder
  - Product Owner of Product Owner

Stakeholders

☐ External to the Team

☐ Provide information for planning and prioritization

☐ Help to create vision and roadmap

☐ Provide meaningful feedback for inspect and adapt

Subject Matter Experts

☐ Considered a type of stakeholder

☐ Fill the skill gaps of the Scrum Team

☐ Often only needed periodically

☐ Examples
  - ☐ Architects
  - ☐ DBAs
  - ☐ Business Domain Experts
  - ☐ BAs

Scrum RASCI Matrix

Responsible	Team members are responsible doing the work that was agreed to with the Product Owner
Accountable	The Product Owner is accountable to business for the product that the Team builds
Supportive	The Scrum Master is supportive to the team by facilitating self-organization and removing impediments.
Consulted	Subject Matters Experts are consulted by the Team if necessary.
Informed	External Stakeholders and the Business Owner are informed of the Team's decisions and progress.

Copyrighted material. 2018

Activity

Scrum Ownership

Link to activity in *Resources*

Copyrighted material. 2018

Exercise: Scrum Ownership

	Team	Product Owner	Scrum Master
Provides Estimates			
Prioritizes Backlog			
Creates User Stories			
Commits To The Sprint			
Performs User Acceptance			
Facilitates Meetings			
Champion Of Scrum			
Volunteers For Tasks			
Makes Technical Decisions			
Designs Software			
Removes Impediments			
Defines Done			
Assign Tasks			

Scrum Ownership

	Team	Product Owner	Scrum Master
Prioritizes Backlog			
Provides Estimates			
Creates User Stories			
Commits To The Sprint			
Performs User Acceptance			
Makes Technical Decisions			
Champion Of Scrum			
Volunteers For Tasks			
Removes Impediments			
Designs Software			
Facilitates Meetings			
Defines Done			
Assign Tasks			

Copyrighted material. 2018

The Scrum Framework

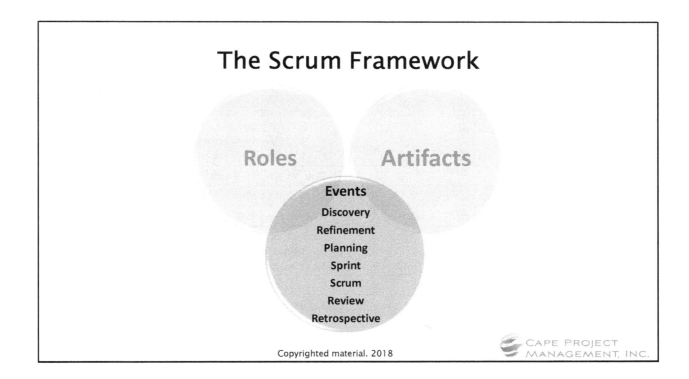

Roles

Artifacts

Events

Discovery

Refinement

Planning

Sprint

Scrum

Review

Retrospective

Copyrighted material. 2018

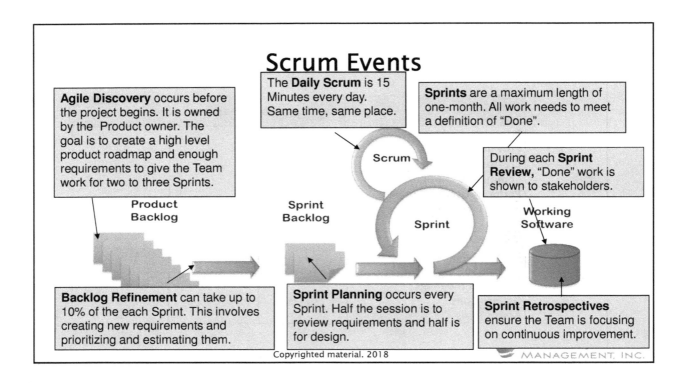

Scrum Events

Agile Discovery occurs before the project begins. It is owned by the Product owner. The goal is to create a high level product roadmap and enough requirements to give the Team work for two to three Sprints.

The **Daily Scrum** is 15 Minutes every day. Same time, same place.

Sprints are a maximum length of one-month. All work needs to meet a definition of "Done".

During each **Sprint Review**, "Done" work is shown to stakeholders.

Product Backlog

Sprint Backlog

Scrum

Sprint

Working Software

Backlog Refinement can take up to 10% of the each Sprint. This involves creating new requirements and prioritizing and estimating them.

Sprint Planning occurs every Sprint. Half the session is to review requirements and half is for design.

Sprint Retrospectives ensure the Team is focusing on continuous improvement.

Copyrighted material. 2018

MANAGEMENT, INC.

The Scrum Events

Events	Timebox
Sprint Planning	8 hours for a one-month sprint • 1 hour/week of Sprint on requirements • 1 hour/week of Sprint on design
Sprints	One-month maximum
Daily Scrum	15 minutes daily
Backlog Refinement (grooming)	2 hours per week
Sprint Review	4 hours for a one-month sprint • 1 hour/week of Sprint • 1 hour prep
Sprint Retrospectives	3 hours for a one-month sprint
Scrum of Scrums	2-3 times per week for 30 minutes

Copyrighted material. 2018

CAPE PROJECT
MANAGEMENT, INC.

Why all the "rituals"?

- These "rituals" are essential to the success of Scrum
- There is a reason that the Scrum team should set aside 10% of their total Sprint time on these meetings. They are not simple "overhead administrative" events. They are part of the work and work needs to get done in those meetings.
- The reason these meetings are rigidly scheduled and enforced is to provide the structure and rhythm for work to be done.
- Structure allows teams to self organize around the "real work" and they trust the rituals and Scrum Master to make sure that everyone is moving along in the same direction.
- The meetings allow the project and the team to regulate and redirect itself.

Why Timeboxing?

- Eliminates the risk of schedule slippage
- Time is the fixed constraint
- Creates a sense of urgency
- Forces Team to focus on first things first
- Increases motivation
- Stops procrastination
- Creates a working rhythm
- Common to most Agile methods

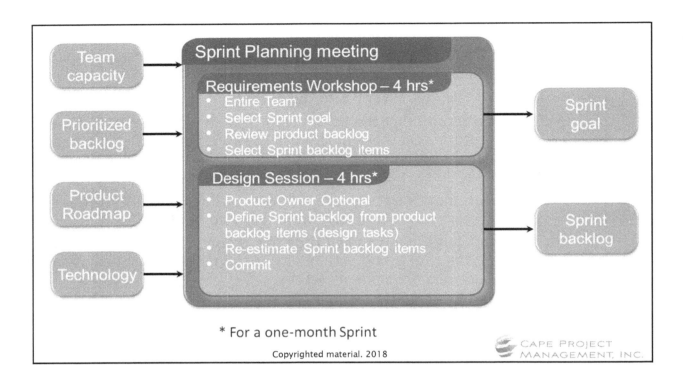

* For a one-month Sprint

The Sprint Goal

□ A short statement of what the work will be focused on during the Sprint

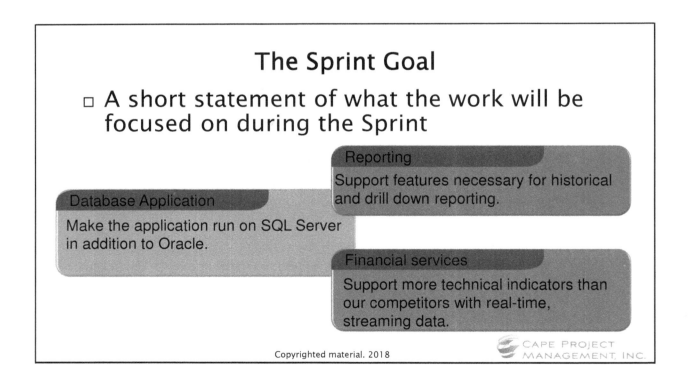

Backlog Refinement (Grooming)

- ☐ Typically two hours per week – no more than 10% of time spent during Sprint
- ☐ Reprioritize every Sprint
- ☐ Product Owner, Scrum Master, and Team are included
- ☐ Critical to the success of the next Sprint
- ☐ User Stories in the backlog should be estimated to cover the next couple of Sprints

Copyrighted material. 2018

 CAPE PROJECT MANAGEMENT, INC.

Backlog Refinement Tips

- ☐ Try to never schedule refinement during the first or last 20% of the Sprint.
- ☐ Treat the backlog refinement meeting just like the first part of the Sprint Planning Meeting
- ☐ The Product Owner should present enough work to next 2 Sprints beyond the current Sprint.
- ☐ Allow Story Splitting and Sizing to occur
- ☐ Make sure everyone understands that estimates are not final until Sprint Planning is performed

Copyrighted material. 2018

 CAPE PROJECT MANAGEMENT, INC.

The Sprint

- Scrum projects progress via a series of Sprints. Sprints are timeboxed to no more than one month.
- During a Sprint, the Scrum team takes a small set of features from idea to coded and tested functionality.
- At the end of the Sprint, these features are done; coded, tested and integrated into the evolving product or system.

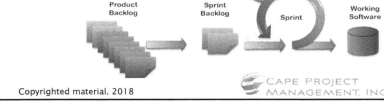

Copyrighted material. 2018

What is the Definition of Done?

- Defined by Product Owner and Team
- Ensures product is ready for release
- Considerations
  - Functionality, Quality, Coding standards, Test coverage, Integration testing, Documented
- Risks of unclear definition of done
  - Inaccurate Velocity
  - Technical debt
- 0/100% Rule (if it is not done, it doesn't count)

Copyrighted material. 2018

No changes during a Sprint

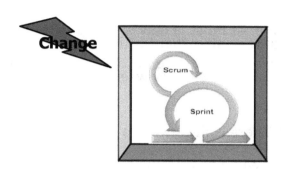

☐ Plan Sprint durations around how long you can commit to keeping change out of the Sprint

Four-week Sprint

Pros:

☐ **Very easy to roadmap.** Long-term, one-year roadmaps are much easier when you only have to plan 12 iterations.

☐ **Low process load.** The key Scrum meetings only once per month, your team is spending less time in meetings and more time building.

Cons:

☐ **Long turnaround time.** A new idea that comes in the day after a Sprint kickoff can't be started for a month and wouldn't be demoed until a month after that. Two months turnaround time from request to demo can feel interminable.

☐ **Mini-waterfall.** There is a risk on a four-week Sprint to break up the weeks into design, develop, test, integrate.

One-week Sprint

Pros:

- **Fast turnaround time.** At most, a new idea has to wait just a week to start development and a week after that for the first product output.
- **High energy.** One-week Sprints are fun. The energy is high because the deadline is always this Friday. Every week is an end-of-Sprint rush to the finish line.

Cons:

- **Minimal feedback.** There isn't time for a lot of customer feedback before delivering code.
- **Lack of a roadmap.** When your horizon is a week it is difficult planning out a year.
- **Story sizing.** It can be difficult to size all Stories to fit into a week.
- **Relatively heavy...or no process.** A one-week Sprint still needs estimation, tasking, demo, grooming, etc. Relative to the size of the Sprint those fixed time costs will now be high.

The Daily Scrum

- Parameters
  - Daily
  - Same time
  - 15-minutes
  - Stand-up
- Not for problem solving
  - Whole world is invited
  - Only team members and Scrum Master can talk
- Helps avoid other unnecessary meetings

Purpose of the Daily Scrum

- ☐ To help start the day well
- ☐ To support improvement
- ☐ To reinforce focus on the right things
- ☐ To reinforce the sense of team
- ☐ To communicate what is going on

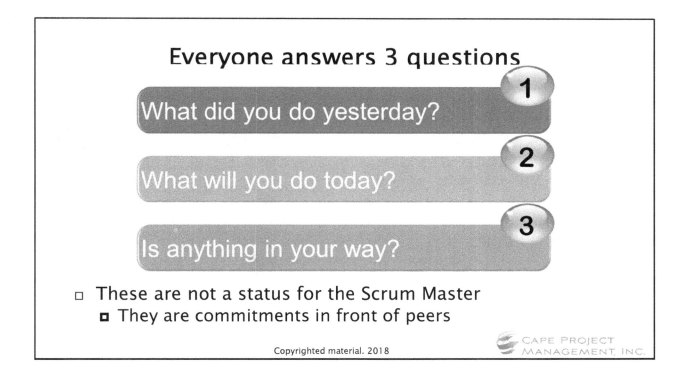

Copyrighted material. 2018

Everyone answers 3 questions

1 What did you do yesterday?

2 What will you do today?

3 Is anything in your way?

- ☐ These are not a status for the Scrum Master
  - ☐ They are commitments in front of peers

Copyrighted material. 2018

Intraspectives

- ☐ Typically occurs immediately after the Daily Scrum
- ☐ Can be an ad-hoc meeting by the Agile team to review on the team practices or teamwork during the sprint, often called for when something went wrong.

Sprint Review Meeting

- ☐ Time-boxed: one-hour per each week of Sprint
- ☐ One-hour prep
- ☐ Only "done" items are demonstrated
  - ☐ Done versus done-done
- ☐ Opportunity for "inspect and adapt"
- ☐ Primary audience are stakeholders
- ☐ Feedback is encouraged

Goals of the Sprint Review

☐ Prove to the stakeholders that the team is moving in the right direction

☐ Get feedback from the stakeholders

☐ Discuss the objective of the next Sprint

☐ Incorporate feedback into release plan, roadmap, etc.

Copyrighted material. 2018

Sprint Review Do's and Don'ts

Do's

☐ Show the progress against the Product Roadmap

☐ Make sure stakeholders are present

☐ Prepare in advance for the Sprint Review meeting

☐ Ensure it becomes the Product Owner's meeting

Don'ts

☐ The Product Owner acts as customer (they should not be seeing anything for the first time)

☐ Allow Sprint Reviews to become boring meetings

☐ Not showing working and tested software

Copyrighted material. 2018

Demonstrations/Reviews Exam Notes

☐ Product Owner sees and accepts or declines the product at the demonstration (This is an anti-pattern in real life)

☐ At least once every 2 weeks

Sprint Retrospective

☐ Takes place at the end of each Sprint
☐ Time-boxed: 3 hours for a one month Sprint
☐ Team, Scrum Master, Product Owner
☐ Use a neutral facilitator
☐ Periodically take a look at what is and is not working
☐ Inspects how the last Sprint went in terms of people, relationships, process, and tools
☐ Important to have open feedback and to incorporate feedback into next Sprint

Start / Stop / Continue

☐ Whole team gathers and discusses what they'd like to:

Start doing

Stop doing

Continue doing

This is just one of many ways to do a Sprint Retrospective.

Sample end of Sprint agenda – The "Planning Day"

Time	Item (two week Sprint)
9:00–9:15	Daily Scrum • Last Scrum of prior Sprint–discuss status of any incomplete stories
9:15–10:30	Sprint Review: • Demo of stories delivered over the course of last Sprint
10:30–11:30	Sprint Retrospective • Focus both on product and process opportunities
11:30–12:30	Lunch
12:30 – 2:30	Sprint Planning Requirements Session: • Review roadmap, discuss sprint goal, review each story in priority order and estimate until velocity is met
2:30–4:30	Sprint Planning Design Session: • Team reviews stories, creates tasks for each
4:30–4:45	Team commits to the Sprint Backlog • Ready to start with a daily Scrum the next day

ONLINE ACTIVITY

Module 2-2 Knowledge Check
Take a 35 question practice exam to test your understanding of the Scrum Framework.

CAPE PROJECT
MANAGEMENT, INC.

Module 2-2 Knowledge Check

Questions

1. Which is NOT a Scrum Role?

Correct	Choice
	Product Owner
	Team Member
	Scrum Master
	Project Manager

2. In which meeting do you capture lessons learned?

Correct	Choice
	Sprint Planning
	Sprint Review
	Daily Status Meeting
	Sprint Retrospective

3. What Scrum event or artifact is the set of items selected for the Sprint, plus a plan for delivering the product Increment and realizing the Sprint Goal?

Correct	Choice
	Sprint Planning
	Definition of Done
	Sprint Backlog
	Increment

4. What Scrum event or artifact supports daily inspection and adaptation?

Correct	Choice
	Sprint Planning
	Daily Scrum
	Sprint Review
	Sprint Retrospective

5. How long is the time-box for the daily Scrum?

Correct	Choice
	It depends
	5 minutes per person on the Development Team
	Whatever the Team decides
	15 minutes

6. Pick which 3 activities are the responsibilities of the Scrum Master in Scrum.

Correct	Choice
	Provide Estimates
	Commit to the Sprint
	Perform user acceptance
	Facilitate meetings
	Volunteer for tasks
	Make technical decisions
	Remove impediments
	Champion Scrum
	Prioritize the backlog

7. Which one is NOT a Pillar of Scrum?

Correct	Choice
	Transparency
	Inspection
	Empiricism
	Adaptation

8. What is the purpose of the Sprint Review? (Choose three)

Correct	Choice
	To collaborate with stakeholders
	To provide status on the Sprint
	To demonstrate what is "Done"
	To inspect and adapt

9. Select the statements that are TRUE about the Product Owner. (Choose two)

Correct	Choice
	The Product Owner defines the Sprint Goal before the Sprint Planning meeting
	The Product Owner prioritizes the Product backlog
	The Product Owner can clarify the backlog during the Sprint
	The Product Owner estimates the size of the Sprint backlog

10. Pick which 4 activities are the responsibilities of the Product Owner in Scrum.

Correct	Choice
	Provides Estimates
	Create User Stories
	Commit to the Sprint
	Perform user acceptance
	Champion Scrum
	Perform release planning
	Design software
	Facilitate meetings
	Prioritize the backlog

11. If the Development Team doesn't like the time of the daily Scrum, what should the Scrum Master do?

Correct	Choice
	Ask the Team to try the existing time for one Sprint
	Tell them that Scrum is immutable and that they need to stick to it
	Let the Development Team come up with a new time
	Find a time that is open on everyone's calendar

12. Your team is running three-week Sprints. How much time should you schedule for Sprint Review sessions?

Correct	Choice
	45 minutes
	3 hours
	6 hours
	1 hour, 15 minutes

13. In Scrum, who is responsible for managing the team?

Correct	Choice
	Scrum Master
	Project Manager
	Product Owner
	Development Team

14. Match each of the following items with its associated time-boxed duration for a one-month Sprint.

Correct	Choice
Sprint Review	3 hours
Sprint Retrospective	8 hours
Daily Scrum	15 minutes
Sprint Planning	4 hours

15. During which meeting do team members synchronize their work and progress and report any impediments to the Scrum Master for removal?

Correct	Choice
	Sprint Planning meeting
	Sprint Retrospective
	Weekly Status meeting
	Daily Scrum

16. Who is responsible for change management in Scrum projects?

Correct	Choice
	Project Manager
	Scrum Master
	Product Owner
	Project Sponsor

17. Match the activity (on the right) to the Scrum event (on the left).

Correct	Choice
Sprint Planning	Inspect and adapt
Sprint Retrospective	Demonstrate Functionality
Sprint Review	Sprint Goal creation
Daily Scrum	Create Improvement Plans

18. When we use the term "container" in Scrum what are we referring to?

Correct	Choice
	A Sprint or Iteration
	Development team room
	A vertical slice of functionality
	Source code repository

19. Who tracks work remaining in the Product Backlog?

Correct	Choice
	The Development Team
	The Scrum Master
	Senior Executives
	The Product Owner

20. Who is responsible for managing ROI in Agile projects?

Correct	Choice
	The Project Sponsor
	The Agile Project Manager
	The Scrum of Scrums Master
	The Product Owner

21. When is a Sprint finished?

Correct	Choice
	When the definition of "Done" is met
	When the Product Owner accepts the increment
	When the work remaining is zero
	When the time-boxed duration is met

22. Pick 5 activities that are the responsibility of the development team in Scrum.

Correct	Choice
	Provides estimates
	Creates User Stories
	Commits to the Sprint
	Performs user acceptance
	Champions Scrum
	Volunteers for tasks
	Makes technical decisions
	Designs software
	Facilitates meetings
	Prioritizes the backlog

23. When does Adaptation occur in Scrum?

Correct	Choice
	At the Sprint Review
	During Sprint Planning
	As Part of the Sprint Retrospective
	In the daily Scrum
	At all four formal Scrum events

24. A cross-functional team in Scrum consists of which types of team members?

Correct	Choice
	A specialist in QA
	A release manager
	Anyone with the skills to accomplish the work
	An architect

25. The purpose of a Sprint Retrospective is for the Scrum Team to:

Correct	Choice
	Review stories planned for the next Sprint and provide estimates.
	Demonstrate completed User Stories to the Product Owner.
	Individually provide status updates on the User Stories in progress.
	Determine what to stop doing, start doing, and continue doing.

26. What is the best definition of "Done"?

Correct	Choice
	Whatever will please the Product Owner
	It is determined by the Scrum Master
	The product has passed QA and has all of the required release documentation
	The one that would allow the development work to be ready for a release

27. With multiple Scrum teams, you should have a separate product backlog.

Correct	Choice
	True
	False

28. Which one of the following is NOT a Scrum Event?

Correct	Choice
	Sprint
	Daily Scrum
	Weekly Status
	Sprint Review

29. The optimum size of the Scrum Team is:

Correct	Choice
	It depends
	Between 3 and 9
	5
	7

30. **The product owner should spend at least 3 hours per day with the development team?**

Correct	Choice
	True
	False

31. **Match the following roles on the right to the RASCI on the left:**

Correct	Choice
Responsible	Product Owner
Accountable	Stakeholders and Business Owner
Supportive	Scrum Master
Consulted	Subject Matter Experts
Informed	Team Members

32. **The behavior where the Scrum Team focuses on one or more stories until they are done is called:**

Correct	Choice
	Collaboration
	Sprinting
	Swarming
	Pair-programming

33. Which role is external to the Scrum Team but provides a skills the does not exist on the Team?

Correct	Choice
	Subject Matter Expert
	Project Manager
	Scrum Master
	Team Member

34. This role champions the products, provides the budget and supports the Scrum Master in removing impediments.

Correct	Choice
	Subject Matter Expert
	Project Manager
	Business Owner
	Product Owner

Agile Methods: Extreme Programming (XP)

All About Agile: Module 2-3

Version 4.0

Extreme Programming (XP)

- Developed by Kent Beck
- XP is "a light-weight methodology for small to medium-sized teams developing software in the face of vague or rapidly changing requirements."
- Alternative to "heavy-weight" software development models (which tend to avoid change and customers)

"Extreme Programming turns the conventional software process sideways. Rather than planning, analyzing, and designing for the far-flung future, XP programmers do all of these activities a little at a time throughout development."
-- *IEEE Computer , October 1999*

CAPE PROJECT
MANAGEMENT, INC.

A Lightweight (Agile) Process:

- Minimal documentation
- Identify what customer wants up front
- Provide plenty of opportunity for feedback
- Embrace change
  - Iterate often, design and redesign, code and test frequently, keep the customer involved
- Deliver software to the customer in short (2 week) iterations
- Eliminate defects early, thus reducing costs
- Thrives in an Open Space environment

Copyrighted material. 2018

Why Extreme?

XP takes commonsense principles and practices to extreme levels:

- If code reviews are good, we'll review code all the time (pair programming).
- If testing is good, everybody will test all the time (unit testing).
- If design is good, we'll make it part of everybody's daily business (refactoring).
- If integration testing is important, then we'll integrate and test several times a day.
- If short iterations are good, we will make the iterations really, really short – seconds, minutes and hours, not weeks, months and years.

Copyrighted material. 2018

XP Life Cycle

1. Exploration Phase – pre-concept
2. Planning Phase – system design
3. Iterations to release – incremental development, constant integration
4. Productionizing – get a formal release out
5. Death Phase – when there are no additional features needed, document the system before the team disbands

XP Life Cycle

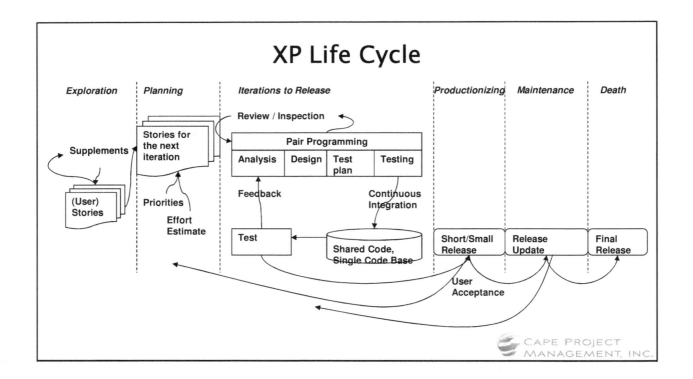

Four Basic Activities of XP

- **Coding**: You code because if you don't code, at the end of the day you haven't done anything.
- **Testing**: You test because if you don't test, you don't know when you are done coding
- **Listening**: You listen because if you don't listen you don't know what to code or what to test
- **Designing**: You design so you can keep coding and testing and listening indefinitely

Copyrighted material. 2018

Four Core Values of XP

- XP is a values-based methodology
  - Communication
  - Simplicity
  - Feedback
  - Courage
- XP's core values are best summarized in the following statement by Kent Beck: "Do more of what works and do less of what doesn't."

Copyrighted material. 2018

Communication

- Communication is accomplished by:
  - Collaborative workspaces
  - Co-location of development and business space
  - Paired development
  - Frequently changing pair partners
  - Frequently changing assignments
  - Public status displays
  - Short standup meetings
  - Unit tests, demos and oral communication, not documentation
- XP employs a coach whose job is noticing when people aren't communicating

Copyrighted material. 2018

Simplicity

- Simplicity encourages:
  - Delivering the simplest functionality that meets business needs
  - Designing the simplest software that supports the needed functionality
  - Building for today and not for tomorrow
  - Writing code that is easy to read, understand, maintain and modify
  - "Just Enough" Documentation
- YAGNI principle ("You ain't gonna need it")
  - Avoid the temptation to write code that is not necessary at the moment

Copyrighted material. 2018

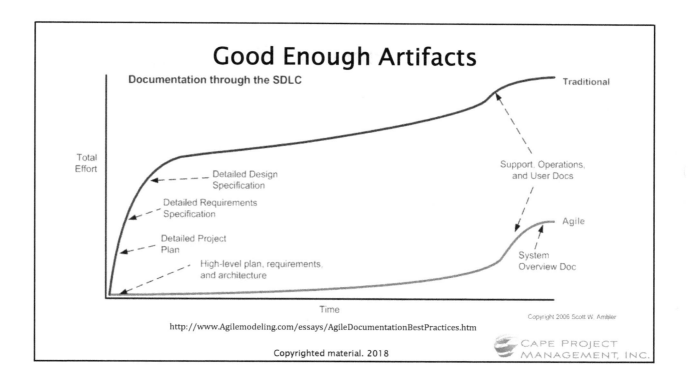

Good Enough Artifacts

Documentation through the SDLC

Total Effort

Detailed Design Specification

Detailed Requirements Specification

Detailed Project Plan

High-level plan, requirements, and architecture

Traditional

Support, Operations, and User Docs

Agile

System Overview Doc

Time

http://www.Agilemodeling.com/essays/AgileDocumentationBestPractices.htm

Copyright 2006 Scott W. Ambler

Copyrighted material. 2018

CAPE PROJECT
MANAGEMENT, INC.

Feedback

□ Feedback is provided by:
- ◻ Aggressive iterative and incremental releases
- ◻ Frequent releases to end users
- ◻ Co-location with end users
- ◻ Automated unit tests
- ◻ Automated functional tests

Copyrighted material. 2018

CAPE PROJECT
MANAGEMENT, INC.

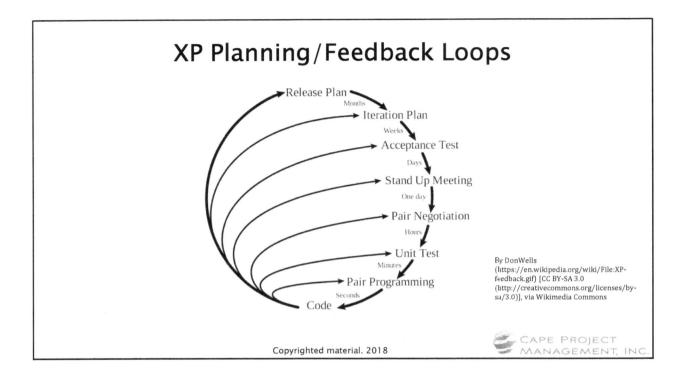

XP Planning/Feedback Loops

Release Plan
Months
Iteration Plan
Weeks
Acceptance Test
Days
Stand Up Meeting
One day
Pair Negotiation
Hours
Unit Test
Minutes
Pair Programming
Seconds
Code

By DonWells
(https://en.wikipedia.org/wiki/File:XP-
feedback.gif) [CC BY-SA 3.0
(http://creativecommons.org/licenses/by-
sa/3.0)], via Wikimedia Commons

CAPE PROJECT
MANAGEMENT, INC.

Courage

- ☐ The courage to communicate and accept feedback
- ☐ The courage to throw code away (prototypes)
- ☐ The courage to refactor the architecture of a system
- ☐ The courage to do the right thing in the face of opposition
- ☐ The courage to do the practices required to succeed

CAPE PROJECT
MANAGEMENT, INC.

Extreme Programming Practices

> **Key:**
> **Blue Ring – Developer Practices**
> **Green Ring – Dev Team Practices**
> **Red Ring – Whole Team Practices**

Twelve XP Practices

1. The Planning Game
2. Small Releases
3. Simple Design
4. System Metaphor
5. Test-driven Development
6. Refactoring
7. Pair Programming
8. Collective Code Ownership
9. Continuous Integration
10. Sustainable Pace
11. On-site Customer
12. Coding Standards

1. The Planning Game

- A joint planning meeting between development team and business stakeholders.
- Business comes up with a list of desired features for the system. Each feature is written out as a User Story.
- Development estimates how much effort each story will take, and how much effort the team can produce in a given time interval (the iteration).
- Business then decides which stories to implement in what order, as well as when and how often to produce production releases of the system.

Copyrighted material. 2018

2. Small Releases

- Start with the smallest useful feature set
- Release early and often, adding a few features each time
- Releases can be date driven or user story driven

Copyrighted material. 2018

3. Simple Design

- Always use the simplest possible design that gets the job done
- The requirements will change tomorrow, so only do what's needed to meet today's requirements (remember, YAGNI)

4. System Metaphor

- "The system metaphor is a story that everyone – customers, programmers, and managers – can tell about how the system works."
  ~Kent Beck, Extreme Programming Explained
- Common Vision: Enables everyone to agree on how the system works. The metaphor suggests the key structure of how the problem and the solution are perceived.
- Shared Vocabulary: The metaphor helps suggest a common system of names for objects and the relationships between them.
- Analogous Descriptions: The analogies of a metaphor can suggest new ideas about the system (both problems and solutions).

5. Test-driven development

- ☐ Test first: before adding a feature, write a test for it
- ☐ When the complete test suite passes 100%, the feature is accepted
- ☐ Two Test Types:
  - ◘ Unit Tests automate testing of functionality as developers write it
  - ◘ Acceptance Tests (or Functional Tests) are specified by the customer to test that the overall system is functioning as specified
- ☐ Common to many other Agile methods and is considered a methodology in itself

6. Refactoring

- ☐ Refactoring is removing redundancy, eliminating unused functionality, and rejuvenating obsolete designs.
- ☐ Refactor mercilessly to keep the design simple
- ☐ Keep your code clean and concise, it will be easier to understand, modify, and extend.
- ☐ Make sure everything is expressed once and only once.

Copyrighted material. 2018

7. Pair Programming

- ☐ Two programmers collaborate on the same design, algorithm, code or test case
- ☐ Driver enters code; navigator critiques it
- ☐ Periodically switch roles
- ☐ Research results:
  - ☐ Pair programming increases productivity
  - ☐ Higher quality code (15% fewer defects) in about half the time (58%)

Copyrighted material. 2018

8. Collective Code Ownership

- Any team member may add to the code at any time
- Everybody takes responsibility for the whole system
- Encourages simplicity:
  - Prevents complex code from entering the system
- Increases individual responsibility and personal power
- Reduces project risk:
  - Spreads knowledge of the system around the team

Copyrighted material. 2018

9. Continuous Integration

- Code is integrated and tested after a few hours
- Daily builds are not enough:
  - Build, end-to-end, at every check-in
  - Check in frequently
  - Put resources on speeding build time
  - Put resources on speeding test time
- Reduces project risk:
  - You'll never spend days chasing a bug that was created some time in the last few weeks

Copyrighted material. 2018

10. Sustainable Pace

- Limit work week to 40 hours
- Programmers go home on-time and are "fresh and eager every morning, and tired and satisfied every night"
- In crunch mode, up to one week of overtime is allowed
- Excessive overtime is a definite sign that there is something wrong with the process

11. On-Site Customer

- A real customer sits with the team full time.
- The on-site customer enables an XP team to explore business requirements as it needs to and gives direct access to someone who can make key decisions quickly.
- Provides value to the company by contributing to the project, thus reducing project risk.
- In XP, if the system isn't worth the time of one customer, maybe it's not worth building.

12. Coding Standards

- Programmers write all code in accordance with rules adopted voluntarily by the team
- Ideally, you should not be able to tell who on the team has touched a specific piece of code

- Typical Constraints
  - No duplicate code
  - System should have the fewest possible classes
  - System should have the fewest possible methods
  - Comments should be minimized

CAPE PROJECT
MANAGEMENT, INC.

The 13th XP Practice: Daily Standup Meeting

- Goal: Identify items to be accomplished for the day and raise issues
- 15 minute duration
- Everyone attends, including the customer
- Not a discussion forum
- Take discussions offline
- Everyone gets to speak

CAPE PROJECT
MANAGEMENT, INC.

XP Roles

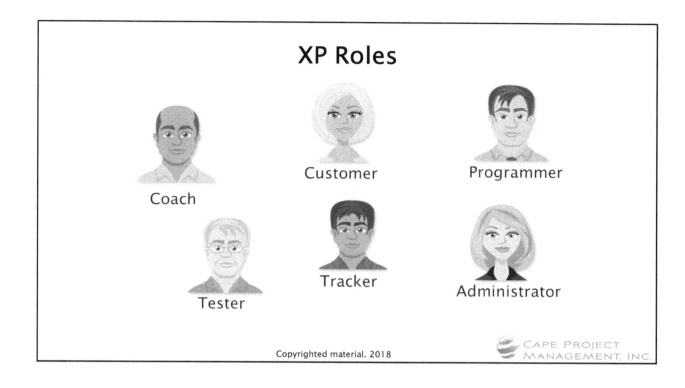

Coach

Customer

Programmer

Tester

Tracker

Administrator

Copyrighted material. 2018

CAPE PROJECT
MANAGEMENT, INC.

XP Coach

- Advocate for the XP values
- Helps a team stay on process and helps the team to learn
- Brings an outside perspective
- Balances the needs of delivering the project while improving the use of the practices
- A coach or team of coaches supports:
  - Customer team
  - Developer team
  - Organization

Copyrighted material. 2018

CAPE PROJECT
MANAGEMENT, INC.

XP Customer

- Defines the right product to build
- Determines the order in which features will be built
- Ensures the product actually works
- Writes system features in the form of user stories that have business value

Copyrighted material. 2018

CAPE PROJECT MANAGEMENT, INC.

Other XP Roles

Role	Responsibility	
XP Programmer	Implements the code to support the user stories	
XP Administrator	Establishes the physical working environment	
XP Tracker	Tracks the release plan (user stories), the iteration plan (tasks) and the acceptance tests	
XP Tester	Helps the customer define and implement acceptance tests for user stories	

Copyrighted material. 2018

CAPE PROJECT MANAGEMENT, INC.

Project Managers in XP

- Most project managers lack the technical expertise to coach XP's programming practices.
- Project managers help the team work with the rest of the organization.
- Project managers may also double as customers.

CAPE PROJECT
MANAGEMENT, INC.

Activity

XP or not XP?

Link to activity in *Resources*

CAPE PROJECT
MANAGEMENT, INC.

	XP	NOT XP
Collaborative Ownership		
Test Driven Development		
Persona		
Planning Poker		
Pair Programming		
Spontaneous Integration		
Simple Design		
Sample Releases		
Collective Code Ownership		
Business Prioritization		
Agile Coach		
Product Owner		
Daily Scrum		

XP or not XP

114

ONLINE ACTIVITY

Module 2-3 Knowledge Check

Take a 15 question practice exam to test your understanding of Extreme Programming

CAPE PROJECT
MANAGEMENT, INC.

Module 2-3 Knowledge Check

Questions

1. In Pair Programming, one programmer is responsible for all the coding in an iteration then the programmers switch for the next iteration.

Correct	Choice
	True
	False

2. Which of the following is NOT one of the 12 core practices of XP?

Correct	Choice
	Visualize the flow
	Coding Standards
	System Metaphor
	On-site Customer

3. On XP teams, what is expected from the Project Manager?

Correct	Choice
	Coach the team on Agile practices
	Help the team work with the rest of the organization
	Design the software
	Provide domain expertise to the team

4. Which is NOT a role on an XP team?

Correct	Choice
	Coach
	Customer
	Programmer
	Product Owner

5. Which 5 roles are defined by Extreme Programming?

Correct	Choice
	Scrum Master
	Coach
	Stakeholder
	Programmer
	Tracker
	Tester
	Product Owner
	Customer

6. Which XP practice promotes the restriction on overtime?

Correct	Choice
	Sustainable Pace
	Servant Leadership
	Small Releases
	Pair Programming

7. In XP, what is the practice of creating a story about a future system that everyone - customers, programmers, and managers - can tell about how the system works?

Correct	Choice
	Extreme persona
	System metaphor
	Simple design
	Wireframe

8. Which of the following is NOT one of the 12 core practices of XP:

Correct	Choice
	Simple Design
	Vertical Slicing
	Refactoring
	Continuous Testing

9. What is the role of the XP Coach?

Correct	Choice
	Defines the right product to build
	Determines the order to build
	Helps the team stay on process
	Ensures the product works

10. In XP, the practice that any developer can change any line of code to add functionality, fix bugs, improve designs, or refactor demonstrates:

Correct	Choice
	Collective Code Ownership
	Pair Programming
	Continuous Integration
	Source Code Control

11. The ultimate goal of _____ is to deploy all but the last few hours of work at any time.

Correct	Choice
	Continuous Integration
	Synchronous Builds
	Asynchronous Builds
	Collective Code Ownership

12. Extreme Programming (XP) defines four basic activities that are performed during the software development process. These include designing, coding, testing and ...?

Correct	Choice
	Collaborating
	Communicating
	Listening
	Leveling

13. Which of the following is an Agile practice promoted by XP that is often used in conjunction with other Agile methods?

Correct	Choice
	Dynamic Systems Development Method (DSDM)
	Adaptive Software Development (ASD)
	Test Driven Development (TDD)
	Feature Driven Development (FDD)

14. Which of the following describe the roles in pair programming?

Correct	Choice
	Pilot and the navigator
	Coder and the planner
	Leader and the second chair
	Driver and the navigator

15. Extreme Programming (XP) includes which of the following 3 practices?

Correct	Choice
	Simple Design
	Coding standards
	Burndown charts
	Sustainable Pace

Agile Methods: Kanban

All About Agile: Module 2-4

Version 4.0

Kanban Principles and Practices

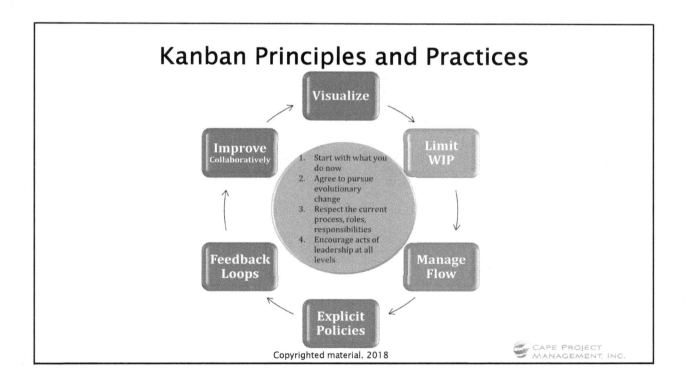

Kanban – Flow-based Agile

- Kanban literally means "visual card," "signboard," or "billboard"
- Developed by Taiichi Ohno when he saw the demand-based inventory management of grocery stores in the U.S. in the 1940s.
- Toyota originally used Kanban cards to limit the amount of inventory tied up in work in progress (WIP) on a manufacturing floor.
- Kanban is part of an overall Lean approach to eliminate waste in a system and focus production on high-value work.
- Using a Kanban approach in software drops time-boxed iterations in favor of focusing on continuous flow.
- Kanban for software development typically has little or no prescriptive "rules" and allows organizations to evolve from where they are today.

CAPE PROJECT MANAGEMENT, INC.

Kanban Board

Backlog	Design		Develop		Test		Done
	In Progress	Ready	In Progress	Ready	In Progress	Ready	
Story — Stor — Stor — Stor — Story 6	Stor — Story 1	Story 2 Story 3	Story 4 Story 5		Story 6		Story — Stor — Stor — Story 1
WIP Limit	20 hrs		80 hrs		40 hrs		

CAPE PROJECT MANAGEMENT, INC.

5 Values of Kanban

- Respect
- Courage
- Focus on Value
- Communication and Collaboration
- Holistic Approach to Change

http://www.infoq.com/articles/open-kanban-introduction

1. Respect

- At the core of Lean is respecting people. Respect for people also means assuming responsibility for your actions, and empowering others to take those actions.
- Respect for people allows for delegation and the demand-pull that is crucial to Kanban. When any developer is able to take a story from the backlog and pull it to development or QA, he is able to do so because we respect him, we respect his skills, and we give him the ability to do so.
- Respect for people also aligns with sustainable pace in Agile, or Muri in Lean.

2. Courage

- It takes courage to reflect and present mistakes or new ideas
- In order to improve or even correct mistakes we need courage.
  - Courage may mean knowing when to throw code away: courage to remove source code that is obsolete, no matter how much effort was used to create that source code.
  - Courage means persistence: A programmer might be stuck on a complex problem for an entire day, then solve the problem quickly the next day, but only if they are persistent.
- Courage combined with respect for people enables teamwork, proper demand-pull and continuous improvement.

3. Focus on Value

- One of the key purposes of Kanban is the creation of value. In software development value means the creation of working, quality code.

- Value implies customer satisfaction, and that is ultimately the purpose of our efforts.

- Value is at the center of Lean and TPS, but frequently it is mentioned as the reverse side of the coin: eliminate waste. By eliminating waste, we optimize the creation of value.

4. Communication and Collaboration

☐ Communication, and collaboration are at the center of teamwork. One value does not work without the other. To succeed we need to make ourselves heard but also we need to be able to work with others to create value.

☐ Without teamwork Kanban fails. Any business that does not communicate and collaborate properly will fail.

5. Holistic Approach to Change

☐ We need to take a holistic view of the system and understand it.

☐ A key part of the system is people, not just as resources, but also as individuals who make the system work.

☐ Kanban aims to drive improvement where it counts. An understanding of the whole is fundamental to arrive at steady, successful change.

Four Basic Principles

1. Start with what you do now
2. Agree to pursue incremental, evolutionary change
3. Respect the current process, roles, responsibilities and titles
4. Encourage acts of leadership at all levels in your organization

Source: Kanban: Successful Evolutionary Change for Your Technology Business. David Anderson

1. Start with what you do now

☐ The Kanban method does not prescribe a certain setup or procedure.

☐ You can overlay Kanban properties on top of your existing workflow or process to bring your issues to light so that you can introduce positive change over time.

2. Agree to pursue incremental, evolutionary change

☐ The Kanban method is an approach to change management that is designed to meet minimal resistance.

☐ It encourages continuous small incremental and evolutionary changes to your current system.

☐ Sweeping changes are discouraged because they generally encounter increased resistance due to fear or uncertainty.

3. Respect the current process, roles, responsibilities and titles

☐ Kanban recognizes that there may be value in the existing process, roles, responsibilities and titles.

☐ Kanban doesn't prohibit change, but it doesn't prescribe it either.

☐ If you do make changes, Kanban encourages incremental change. Incremental change doesn't create the level of fear that impedes progress.

4. Encourage acts of leadership at all levels in your organization

□ You don't need to be a team lead or an executive to be a leader.

□ Some of the best leadership comes from everyday acts from people on the front line of their respective teams.

□ Everyone needs to be fostering a mindset of continual improvement (kaizen) to reach optimal performance.

General Practices of Kanban

1. Visualize the workflow
2. Limit WIP
3. Manage flow
4. Make processes explicit
5. Implement feedback loops
6. Improve collaboratively

Source: Kanban: Successful Evolutionary Change for Your Technology Business. David Anderson

1. Visualize the Workflow

□ Visualizing workflows supports proper understanding of changes planned and helps to implement them according to this plan.

□ A common way to visualize the workflow is to use a card wall with cards and columns.

□ The columns on the card wall represent different states or steps in the workflow.

CAPE PROJECT MANAGEMENT, INC.

Kanban Board										
Story Backlog	Requirements		Design / Architecture		Development		Testing		In Production
	In Progress	Ready	In Progress	Ready	In Progress	Ready	In Progress	Ready	
				Story 3		Story 2			Story 1
Story 6	Story 5		Story 4						

CAPE PROJECT MANAGEMENT, INC.

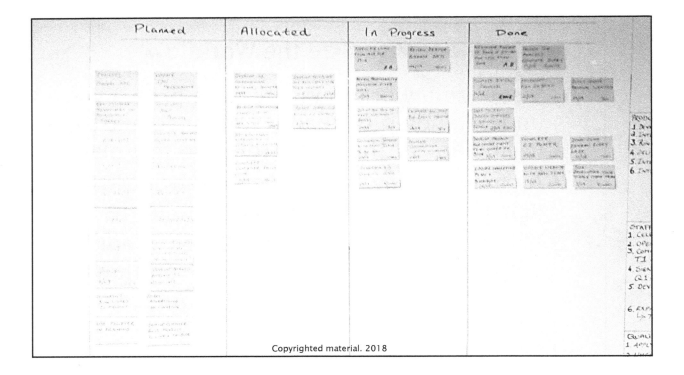

Kanban Cards

□ In manufacturing, a Kanban card is defined as "a card containing a set of manufacturing specifications and requirements, used to regulate the supply of components."

□ In software, it serves a similar function.

□ The card shows a backlog item written as a requirement or user story. As a task is completed, it is moved through the Kanban board to show progress and regulate work.

□ Kanban does not prescribe a format for the card. The following pages show Kanban Cards using User Stories.

CAPE PROJECT
MANAGEMENT, INC.

A Kanban Card with User Story Format – Front

Priority:		Size:
As a:		
I want to:(what)		
So that: (why)		
Started:	Due:	Competed:

Classes of Service

- Kanban Cards are often prioritized by risk determinations called Classes of Service.
- Typical Classes of Service Include:
  - Urgent: Drop everything and work on it
  - Expedited: As soon as possible
  - Scheduled: Deadline driven
  - Standard: Based upon the SLA to the customer
  - Others: Defects, Intangibles, Enhancement Requests

A Kanban Card with User Story Format – Back

Key Tasks	Revised Estimate:
Analysis:	
Design:	
Develop:	
Deploy:	

---

2. Limit Work in Progress (WIP)

☐ Limiting work-in-progress implies that a pull system is implemented on parts or all of the workflow.

☐ Work-in-progress at each state (column) in the workflow is limited and new work is "pulled" into the activity when there is available capacity.

☐ The pull system acts as one of the main constraints and therefore promotes continuous, incremental and evolutionary changes to the system.

The Kanban Pull System

- In a pull system, work items are pulled into the queue by the people doing the work as they complete tasks in order of priority.
- Kanban enables the delivery of work as it becomes available and as part of a Minimum Viable Product (MVP) that is sometimes defined in the business requirements.
- Another term for Minimum Viable Product (MVP) is Minimum Marketable Features (MMF), a term used to describe the work that can be delivered which meets the business requirements without exceeding them.

Copyrighted material. 2018

 CAPE PROJECT MANAGEMENT, INC.

The Kanban Pull System

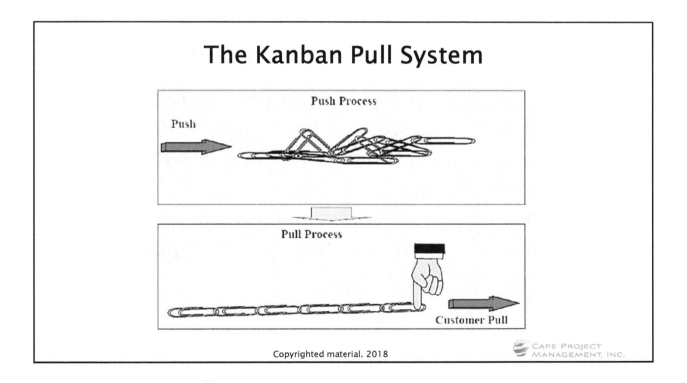

Push Process

Push

Pull Process

Customer Pull

Copyrighted material. 2018

CAPE PROJECT MANAGEMENT, INC.

3. Manage Flow

- Each transition between states in the workflow is monitored, measured and reported.
- Ideally we want fast smooth flow.
- Fast smooth flow means our system is both creating value quickly, which is minimizing risk and avoiding (opportunity) cost of delay, and is also doing so in a predictable fashion.

Cumulative Flow Diagrams

- Is an "information radiator" providing a visual display of development progress over time
- Shows the different states that are defined in the Kanban board columns
- Tracks the completion progress either by number of items, story points, hours, etc.
- Can show cycle time

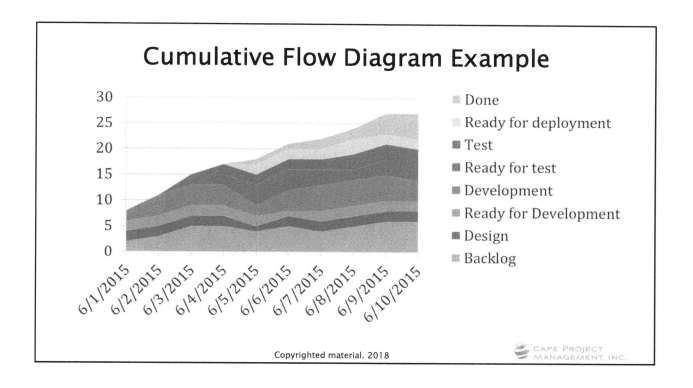

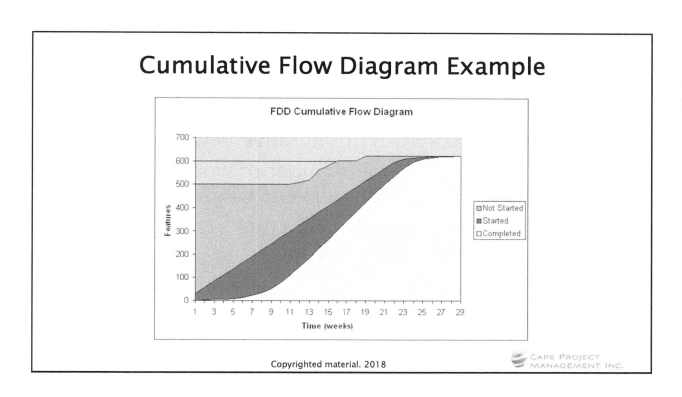

Lead Time & Cycle Time

- The Lead time is the time from when an item is requested until an item is delivered.
- Lead time is often dependent on the business value and/or the service level agreement (SLA) with a customer.
- The Cycle Time is the amount of time that the team spent working on the item.

Throughput

- Measure of the productivity of a Kanban Team
- Similar to velocity in iterative development
- Throughput is the number of work items that the team is capable to deliver in a given time period
- Can be calculated using Little's Law:

$$Throughput = \frac{Work\ in\ Progress}{Lead\ Time}$$

- Throughput also allows evaluating the resources needed for completing work

CAPE PROJECT
MANAGEMENT, INC.

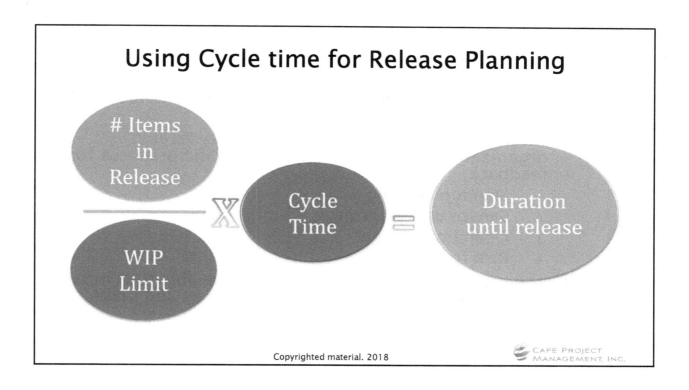

Using Cycle time for Release Planning

---

4. Make Processes Explicit

- ☐ Make the Kanban board reflect the actual flow
- ☐ Adhere to the WIP limits
- ☐ Document how issues will be resolved
- ☐ And more...

5. Implement Feedback Loops

- An evolutionary process cannot work without feedback loops.
- When implemented at a service delivery level in organizations, Kanban, uses four specific practices for feedback:
  1. Standup meeting
  2. Service delivery review
  3. Operations review
  4. Risk review.
- The purpose of feedback loops is to be able to compare expected outcomes with actual outcomes and make adjustments.

6. Improve Collaboratively

- The Kanban method encourages small continuous, incremental and evolutionary changes that stick.
- When teams have a shared understanding of the product, workflow, process and risk, they are more likely to be able to suggest improvements which can be agreed to by consensus.
- Experiments and analysis can change the system to improve the team's effectiveness.

Theory of Constraints

- The Theory of Constraints views systems as chains. The weakest link is the constraint that keeps the chain from doing any better at achieving its goal.
- The Theory of Constraints is essentially about change:
  - What to change? (Where is the constraint?)
  - What to change to? (What should we do with the constraint?)
  - How to cause the change? (How do we implement the change?)
- It is a system philosophy.
  - It poses these questions at the system-level.
  - It requires that at least someone knows what the ultimate goal of the system is.
  - It then helps to establish the necessary conditions for reaching the goal.

Theory of Constraints

The 5 Focusing Steps

1. Identify the system constraint
2. Decide how to exploit the constraint
3. Subordinate everything else
4. Elevate the constraint
5. Go back to step 1, repeat

Kanban Katas

□ Based upon the Toyota kata concept, "a routine for moving from the current situation to a new situation in a creative, directed, meaningful way"

□ Katas or routines for this improvement approach are as follows:

  ◘ Daily Standup Meeting

  ◘ Improvement Kata

  ◘ Operations Review

Standup Meeting – Flow-based Agile

□ Focuses on opportunities for Improvement – "Kaizen"

□ Different questions than iterative development

1. What do we need to do to advance this piece of work?

2. Is anyone working on anything that is not on the board?

3. What do we need to finish as a team?

4. Are there any bottlenecks or blockers to the flow of work?

Improvement Kata

- A mentor-mentee relationship
- Usually (but not always) between a superior and a subordinate
- A focused discussion about system capability
- Discussion of counter-measures and actions taken to improve the capability

Operations Review

- Meets monthly
- Reflect on quantitative performance measures including:
  - WIP (work-in-progress)
  - Cycle time/Lead time
  - Throughput
  - Quality
  - Issues & blocked work
- Considered important part of the Kaizen approach for a project

Kanban Implementation

1. Define a work process flow
2. Lay out a Kanban board
3. Decide on limits for items in queue and work in progress
4. Document Release Goal
5. Place prioritized stories or features in queue
6. Move features through the process flow as work is completed and calculate Cycle Time
7. Manage the flow

Source: http://jpattonassociates.com/kanban_oversimplified/

1. Define a Work Process Flow

☐ Look at the typical flow for features, stories, or work packages and describe typical process steps.
  ▪ Analysis
  ▪ Design
  ▪ Develop
  ▪ Test

2. Lay Out a Kanban Board

Backlog	Design		Develop		Test		Done
	In Progress	Ready	In Progress	Ready	In Progress	Ready	

- Create a work queue or backlog on the left, the process steps, and a final "done" column to the right.

Copyrighted material. 2018

3. Decide on WIP Limits

Backlog	Design		Develop		Test		Done
	In Progress	Ready	In Progress	Ready	In Progress	Ready	
WIP Limit	20 hrs		80 hrs		40 hrs		

- Limit is typically in hours. Put limit on the bottom of each column

Copyrighted material. 2018

Setting WIP Limits

- First of all, when setting Kanban WIP limit you should ask two critical questions:
  - How many people do we have in our team?
  - How many things do we want them to work on at a time?
- WIP Limits are initially a guess, you should change them as often as necessary.
- WIP limits can be defined by team or by column.
- Having a WIP limit that is too high reflects people are multi-tasking and work is not getting completed quickly.
- Having a WIP limit that is too low results in workers sitting idle while waiting for their next task.

Copyrighted material. 2018

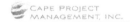

---

4. Document Goal

Backlog	Design		Develop		Test		Done
	In Progress	Ready	In Progress	Ready	In Progress	Ready	Goal: New Web Interface
WIP Limit	20 hrs		80 hrs		40 hrs		

A good goal describes the outcome we hope to achieve after software ships. Goals help keep a focus on the larger outcome.

Copyrighted material. 2018

5. Start the Board by Placing Features in Queue

Backlog	Design		Develop		Test		Done
	In Progress	Ready	In Progress	Ready	In Progress	Ready	
Story 1 6/1							
Story 2 6/1							
Story 3 6/2							
Story 4 6/3							
Story 5 6/5							
Story 6 6/7							
WIP Limit	20 hrs		80 hrs		40 hrs		

Mark on the story or feature card the date it entered the queue. This is the start date. This begins our measurement of lead time.

6. Move Features thru the Flow as Work Completes

Backlog	Design		Develop		Test		Done
	In Progress	Ready	In Progress	Ready	In Progress	Ready	
Story 1 6/1							
Story 2 6/1	Story 1 6/3						Story 1 6/7 Lead Time= 6 days Cycle Time = 4 days
Story 3 6/2							
Story 4 6/3							
Story 5 6/5							
Story 6 6/7							
WIP Limit	20 hrs		80 hrs		40 hrs		

As the story enters the first process step, mark that date on the card. As it's finished, write the number of days it took to complete, then calculate lead time and cycle time.

7. Manage the flow

Backlog	Design		Develop		Test		Done
	In Progress	**Ready**	**In Progress**	**Ready**	**In Progress**	**Ready**	
	Story 1	Story 2 Story 3	Story 4 Story 5		Story 6		
WIP Limit	20 hrs		80 hrs		40 hrs		

Use average cycle time to set wait times from different points on the board. Pay attention to flow and bottlenecks; relieving bottlenecks as quickly as possible.

Kanban Management – Flow based Agile

- ☐ Keep regular time-boxes for product inspection
- ☐ Evaluate the quality of the growing product from a functional, engineering, and user experience perspective
- ☐ Evaluate the pace of development:
  - ◘ Look at the number of development items completed relative to goals
  - ◘ Look at the average cycle time per development item
  - ◘ Adjust the development plan as necessary
  - ◘ Evaluate and adjust the process being used
  - ◘ Use a process reflection session to identify changes to make to improve your product or pace

ONLINE ACTIVITY

Module 2–4 Knowledge Check
Take a 17 question practice exam to test your understanding
of Kanban

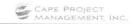

CAPE PROJECT
MANAGEMENT, INC.

Kanban for Project Management Knowledge Check

Questions

1. Which is the first step in setting up Kanban?

Correct	Choice
	Place prioritized goals on the left column of the board
	Map your current workflow
	Lay out a visual Kanban board
	Decide on limits for items in queue and work in progress

2. This approach includes a visual process management system and an approach to incremental, evolutionary process changes for organizations.

Correct	Choice
	Extreme programming
	Lean
	Kanban
	Scrum

3. Kanban means _____ in Japanese?

Correct	Choice
	User Story
	Vertical Slices
	Production Line
	Signal card

4. At minimum, all Kanban boards should have the following columns:

Correct	Choice
	Backlog, Design, Develop, Unit Test, Acceptance Test, Ready-to-ship
	The Kanban board columns are determined by the team
	To-Do, Doing, Done
	Analysis, Design, Develop, Test, Deploy

5. What are the 5 values of Kanban?

Correct	Choice
	Communication, Simplicity, Feedback, Courage, Humility
	Communication, Simplicity, Feedback, Adaptation, Continuous Improvement
	Respect, Courage, Value, Collaboration, Holistic Approach to Change

6. Setting up development work in a way that the team can figure out what to do net is called:

Correct	Choice
	A pull system
	Push system
	Critical path
	Sprint backlog

7. Sequence the core practices of Kanban in order of execution.

Correct Order
Implement Feedback Loops
Limit WIP
Improve collaboratively
Visualize the workflow
Manage the flow
Make process policies explicit

8. The number of days needed between feature specification and production delivery is called:

Correct	Choice
	Cycle time
	Calendar time
	Ideal time
	Real time

9. The number of days needed between customer request and production delivery is called:

Correct	Choice
	Cycle time
	Lead time
	Ideal time
	Real time

10. Classes of Services in Kanban are used to:

Correct	Choice
	Support estimation for Kanban Cards
	Prioritize the queue by risk
	Ensure WIP limits are realistic
	All of the above

11. The purpose of Work in Progress (WIP) limits is to prevent the unintentional accumulation of work, so there isn't a bottleneck.

Correct	Choice
	True
	False

12. The following is a picture of which of the following Information Radiators?

Correct	Choice
	Kanban Tracking System
	Burnup Chart
	Cumulative Flow Diagram
	Burndown Chart

13. The measure of productivity of a Kanban team is:

Correct	Choice
	Velocity
	Throughput
	Cycle time
	Lead Time
	Work in Progress

14. Kanban cards should always be written using User Stories.

Correct	Choice
	True
	False

15. A term used to describe the work that can be delivered which meets the business requirements without exceeding them. (Choose Two)

Correct	Choice
	Epic
	Minimum Viable Product
	Theme
	User Story
	Minimum Marketable Features

16. Order the 5 focusing steps of the Theory of Constraints.

Correct Order
Decide How to Exploit the Constraint
Elevate the Constraint
Go Back to Step 1, Repeat
Identify the System Constraint
Subordinate Everything Else

17. Pick the 3 common Kanban Katas.

Correct	Choice
	Daily Standup Meeting
	Iteration Demo
	Weekly Status
	Operations Review
	Sprint Retrospective
	Improvement Kata

18. In what type of Agile approach would you ask the following questions at the Daily Stand-up?

What do we need to do to advance this piece of work?

Is anyone working on anything that is not on the board?

What do we need to finish as a team?

Are there any bottlenecks or blockers to the flow of work?

Correct	Choice
	Iterative Agile
	Flow-based Agile
	None of the above

Agile Methods:
Lean and More Agile Methods
All About Agile: Module 2–5

Version 4.0

Lean Software Development Principles

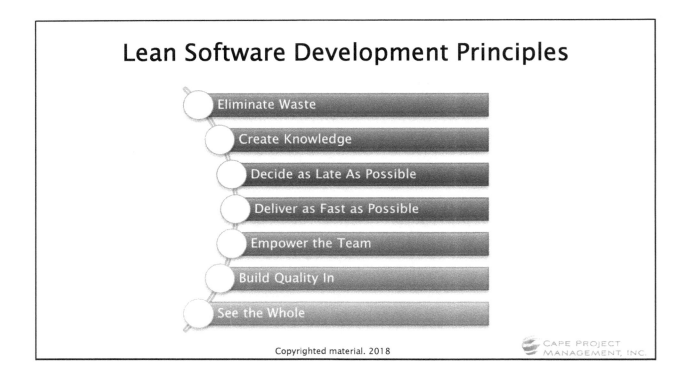

What is Lean Development?

- ☐ Implementation of lean manufacturing principles into a software development model
- ☐ Goal: Reduce the waste in a system and produce a higher value for the final customer

Copyrighted material. 2018

Goals of Lean Development

- ☐ Reduce "Muda"
  - ◘ A Japanese term for an activity that is wasteful and doesn't add value or is unproductive
- ☐ Ensure value
  - ◘ Build what the customer wants
- ☐ Create a value stream
  - ◘ Identify all valuable actions required to bring project from creation to completion
- ☐ Require a process that flows
  - ◘ Ensure product is in motion at all time
- ☐ Implement a pull methodology
  - ◘ No product is made until the customer requests it

Copyrighted material. 2018

Values of Lean Development

1. Pursue perfection
2. After a project flows, keep improving it
3. Balance long-term improvement and short-term improvement

Origins of Lean Software Development

- Lean manufacturing originated at Toyota
- Original author : Taiichi Ohno
    - Inventor of Just-In-Time manufacturing
    - "Costs do not exist to be calculated. Costs exist to be reduced."
- Adapted by Mary and Tom Poppendieck
    - Lean Software Development: An Agile Toolkit

Principle 1: Eliminate Waste

- Remove all wastes that do not add value to project
- Three types of waste; waste in
  - Code development
  - Project management
  - Workforce potential

Wastes in Code Development

- Partially completed work
  - Can become outdated and unusable
  - Solution: Iterative cycle with modular code
- Defects
  - Correction and retesting
  - Solution: Up-to-date test suite, customer feedback

Wastes in Project Management

- Extra processes
  - Wasteful/ Unnecessary documentation
  - Solution: Documentation review
- Code handoffs
  - Loss of knowledge
  - Solution: Don't handoff code
- Extra functions
  - The customer doesn't want or need a feature
  - Solution: Continuous interaction with customer

Wastes in Workforce Potential

- Task switching
  - The danger of multi-tasking
  - Solution: Focus on a task each iteration
- Waiting for instructions or information
  - Developers are too expensive to be sitting around
  - Allow developers to make decisions, access to information

Principle 2: Create Knowledge

- A development process focused on creating knowledge assumes the requirements and design to evolve over time.
- Disciplined experimentation avoids predictions and increases knowledge.
- Process improvement is the responsibility of the development team as they are the ones closest to the process.

Principle 3: Decide as late as possible

- Decisions are often made on incomplete or incorrect information
- Delay until the last responsible moment
- Benefits:
  - More knowledge for decisions
  - Leaves options open

Principle 4: Deliver Fast

- Customers change their mind
  - Solution: Deliver so fast, they don't have time to
- Short release cycles
  - About two weeks
- Requirements:
  - Don't overload developers with requests
  - No partially completed work

Principle 5: Empower the Team

- Often termed, "Respect People"
- Promotes moving decisions as "low" as possible
- Benefits:
  - Increased buy-in and commitment to agreements when they arise from participatory decision making.
  - Reward team members for working together by giving them the power to own their decisions.
  - Engage team members in ownership of their decisions, we move them through the dysfunctions of low standards and artificial harmony into very high standards and high trust.
  - Encourage teams to engage in constructive conflict that leads to better and better decisions

Principle 6: Build Quality In

- Build quality in from the start
- Avoid creating defects in the first place
    - Inspection to prevent defects is required
    - Inspection to find defects is a waste
- If you can't prevent defects – inspect often
- When you find a defect
    - Fix it immediately
    - Put in a test so that it doesn't come back

Principle 7: See the Whole

- Optimize the entire product, not just parts
- Short delivery cycles can lead to optimized parts, sub-optimized whole
- Don't worry about scope
    - By focusing on what customers want, scope will handle itself

The Value Stream

- Understanding the Value Stream is a key component of Lean
- Similar to a Six-Sigma approach, but identifies value, not just efficiencies
- The Value Stream is the entire set of activities across all parts of the organization involved delivering the product or service.
- It is the end-to-end process that delivers the value to the customer.
- Once you understand what your customer wants the next step is to identify how you are delivering (or not) that to them.

Copyrighted material. 2018

Value Stream Mapping

- Pre-requisite to an effective Kanban implementation
- Aims to map and visualize each individual step e.g. in product development from customer request to completed product.
- The target is to identify the steps and actions that create customer value and the steps and actions that can be considered as waste.
- Plan concrete actions for removing the waste.
- Even though the focus is on optimizing the whole, value stream mapping can be applied to smaller processes as well.

Copyrighted material. 2018

Value Stream Mapping Process

□ Four general steps:
1. Choose a particular product or product family as the target for improvement.
2. Draw a current state map of the process.
3. Gather data and assess the current state by focusing on eliminating waste.
4. Create a future state map. This is a picture that depicts how the system should look like when wastes have been removed.

□ Value Stream Mapping is not a process conducted just once, it is part of the continuous improvement philosophy of Lean.

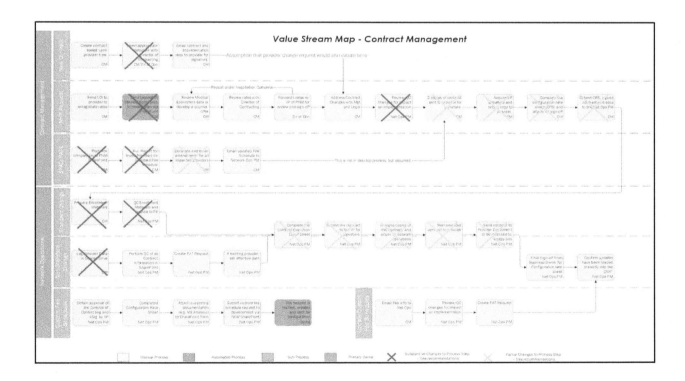

Guidelines for Implementing Lean

□ Map your Value Streams per product family, to visualize wastes within value streams.

□ Start with the low hanging fruit, for instance a department or process where results can be shown relatively quick.

□ When something has improved, improve it again. Continuous means never ending, so keep on looking for the next improvement.

□ 2 steps forward followed by 1 step backward is normal. Lean has everything to do with the way people behave. It is not uncommon for people to fall back into the old behavior. Do not give up when this happens.

□ Adjust Lean tools to your own situation. Do not blindly copy Lean tools from books or other companies, but think about how each tool can or cannot add value to your specific situation in eliminating waste.

□ Train employees in solving problems and root cause analysis to make sure everybody can eliminate waste.

Comparison of Lean and Agile

1. Eliminate waste
   □ Simplicity is essential
   □ Satisfy customer through early and continuous delivery
   □ Working software is the primary measure of progress

2. Create knowledge
   □ Regular reflection
   □ Close collaboration

3. Decide as late as possible
   □ Welcome changes

4. Deliver fast
   □ Deliver fast and frequently
   □ Satisfy customer through early and continuous delivery

5. Build quality in
   □ Working software is the primary measure of progress

6. Empower the Team
   □ Self-Organizing Teams

7. See the whole
   □ Value Driven Delivery

	Deliver Value	Customer Driven	Short Releases	Leave options open	Self organizing	Test possible solutions	Documentation Review
Eliminate Waste							
Empower Team							
Deliver Fast							
See the Whole							
Build Integrity							
Delay Commitment							
Amplify Learning							

Activity

Lean and Agile

Link to activity in *Resources*

Copyrighted material. 2018

CAPE PROJECT
MANAGEMENT, INC.

Agile Project Management

☐ Agile is an umbrella term that encompasses many processes and practices, such as Scrum, Extreme Programming, Adaptive System Development, DSDM, Feature Driven Development, Kanban, Crystal and more...

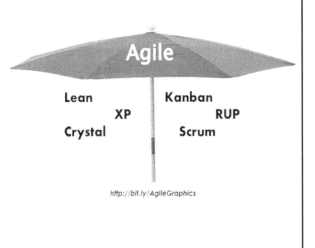

Lean   Kanban
   XP   RUP
Crystal   Scrum

http://bit.ly/AgileGraphics

Copyrighted material. 2018

CAPE PROJECT
MANAGEMENT, INC.

Lean and Agile

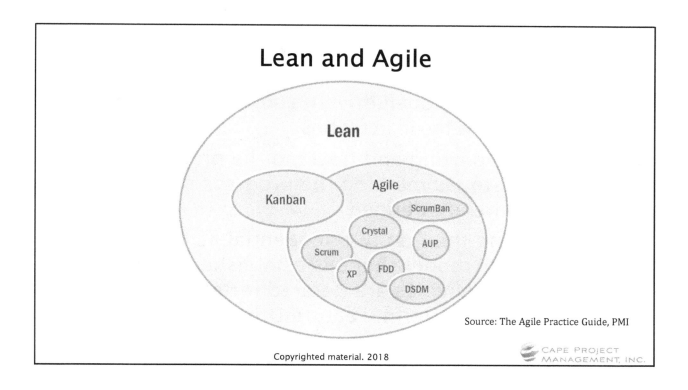

Source: The Agile Practice Guide, PMI

Copyrighted material. 2018

CAPE PROJECT
MANAGEMENT, INC.

Feature Driven Developemnt– FDD

- Feature Driven Development arose before Agile
- FDD arose out of a Singapore project for a large commercial lending organization.
  - Project was using Waterfall and was in deep trouble.
- Major changes were effected such as incremental development and solid engineering techniques (like domain modeling) to resurrect the effort.
- Project was turned around. Its success was attributed to FDD.

Copyrighted material. 2018

CAPE PROJECT
MANAGEMENT, INC.

Feature Driven Development

- FDD is a model-driven, short-iteration process with five basic activities.

- For reporting and tracking the project, milestones marking the progress made on each feature are defined.

- During the first two sequential activities, an overall model shape is established. The final three activities are iterated for each feature (hence the term, Feature Driven Development).

Copyrighted material. 2018

Feature Driven Development Process

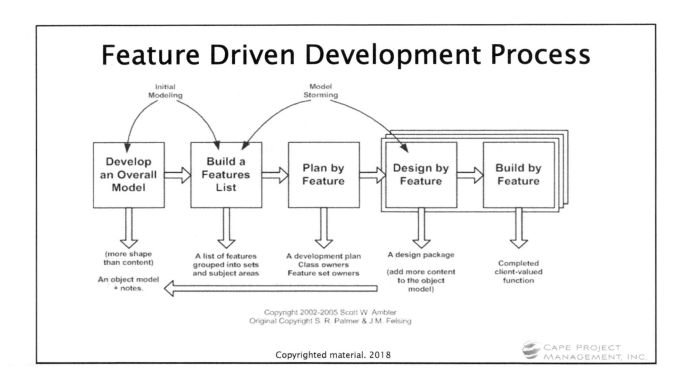

Copyrighted material. 2018

Dynamic System Development Method (DSDM)

Phase	Key Purpose
1: Feasibility Study	Assess whether or not the DSDM approach is correct for the anticipated project
2: Business Study	Gain understanding of the business and technical constraints
3: Functional Model	Create functional specification expressed using an executable prototype with some documentation support
4: Design and Build	Refine the functionality to reflect requirements, the detailed designs are as executable prototypes supported by essential documentation
5: Implement	Applying the product within a series of systems trials ultimately being accepted in the operational environment

Copyrighted material. 2018

The Eight Principles of DSDM

The principles are actively managed at all times because if a principle becomes compromised it represents a risk to the successful execution and completion of a project.

1. Focus on the business need
2. Deliver on time
3. Collaborate
4. Never compromise quality
5. Build incrementally from firm foundations
6. Develop iteratively
7. Communicate continuously and clearly
8. Demonstrate control

Copyrighted material. 2018

DSDM Constraint Driven Delivery

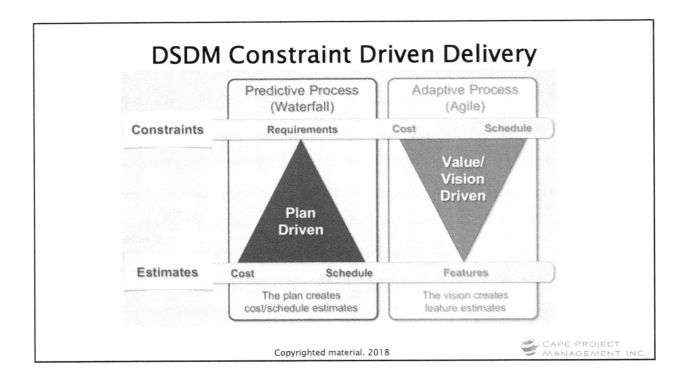

CAPE PROJECT
MANAGEMENT, INC.

Agile Unified Process (AUP)

Philosophies of the AUP

- ☐ Your staff knows what they're doing. People aren't going to read detailed process documentation, but they will want some high-level guidance and/or training from time to time.
- ☐ Simplicity. Everything is described concisely using a handful of pages, not thousands of them.
- ☐ Agility. The Agile UP conforms to the values and principles of the Agile Alliance.
- ☐ Focus on high-value activities. The focus is on the activities which actually count, not every possible thing that could happen to you on a project.
- ☐ Tool independence. You can use any toolset that you want with the Agile UP.
- ☐ You'll want to tailor AUP to meet your own needs.

CAPE PROJECT
MANAGEMENT, INC.

Agile Unified Process (AUP)

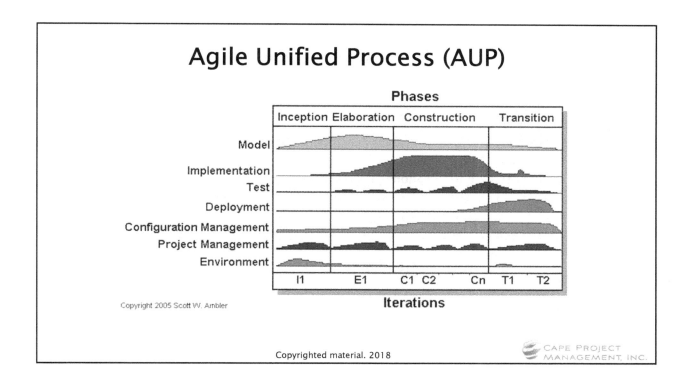

Copyright 2005 Scott W. Ambler

Crystal Methodologies

- Alistair Cockburn created the Crystal Family of Agile Methods whose names contain colors of quartz crystals.
- Different methods(colors) to suit teams of different team sizes and/or criticality:
  - Small projects: Crystal Clear, Crystal Orange or Crystal Yellow
  - Mission-critical ones where human life could be endangered: Crystal Diamond or Crystal Sapphire would be used.

Crystal Methodologies

Cooperative Game Mindset:

- Software Development is a series of resource-limited cooperative games of communication and invention.

Properties:

- **Frequent Delivery:** every month or two
- **Osmotic Communication:** sit next to each other
- **Reflective Improvement:** do reflection workshop monthly
- **Personal Safety:** speak freely without fear of punishment
- **Focus:** Know what is most critical, have time to work on it
- **Easy Access to Expert Users**
- **Technical Environment** with
  - Frequent integration: hourly, daily, 3 times per week
  - Automated testing: unit tests, acceptance tests
  - Configuration management: check-in, versioning

http://alistair.cockburn.us/7+Properties+of+Highly+Successful+Projects+from+Crystal+Clear

Copyrighted material. 2018

---

7 Properties of Successful Crystal Projects

1. Frequent Delivery
2. Osmotic Communication
3. Reflective Improvement
4. Personal Safety
5. Focus
6. Easy Access to Expert Users
7. Technical Environment with:
   - Frequent integration
   - Automated testing
   - Configuration management

Increased Success

Copyrighted material. 2018

Enterprise Agile – Scaling Agile

Disciplined Agile Delivery (DAD®)	Fills in the process gaps that are (purposely) ignored by Scrum, and one that is capable of enterprise-level scale. Adopts Agile Modeling, Kanban and others.
Scale Agile Framework (SAFe®)	Addresses architecture, integration, funding, governance and roles at scale. Includes the terminology of other methods such as Scrum and XP.
Large-Scale Scrum (LeSS®)	General techniques for scaling Scrum and Agile Development which works for up to around 8 teams.
Enterprise Scrum	Written by the author of Scrum. Designed to apply the Scrum method on a more holistic organizational level rather than a single product development effort.
Scrum of Scrums	A scrum-oriented approach for scaling Agile using the simple terms and techniques.

Key Concepts of Scaling

□ Single Product Backlog
□ Single Product Owner
□ Scrum of Scrums
□ Integration Approaches

Single Product Backlog

- When multiple teams are working on the same product it is important to keep only one common Product Backlog for all teams.
- The Product Backlog shall be maintained and prioritized by a single Product owner often called the Chief Product Owner. It can be updated by all Product Owners.
- It is important that all items in the Product Backlog are estimated using the same benchmark for estimation so that the velocity of each team can be rolled up to a release plan.
- If Feature Teams are used it is important that members of all teams participate in the estimation to ensure that all efforts are covered.
- Details, tasks, and acceptance tests are elaborated at the individual team level
- The backlog can be organized by feature, layer, location, etc.

CAPE PROJECT
MANAGEMENT, INC.

Single Product Backlog Option 1

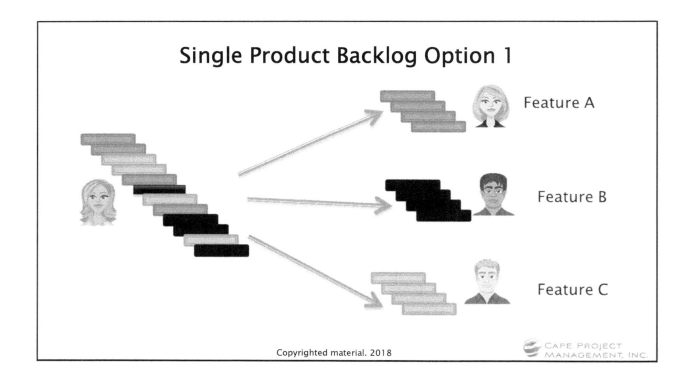

Feature A

Feature B

Feature C

CAPE PROJECT
MANAGEMENT, INC.

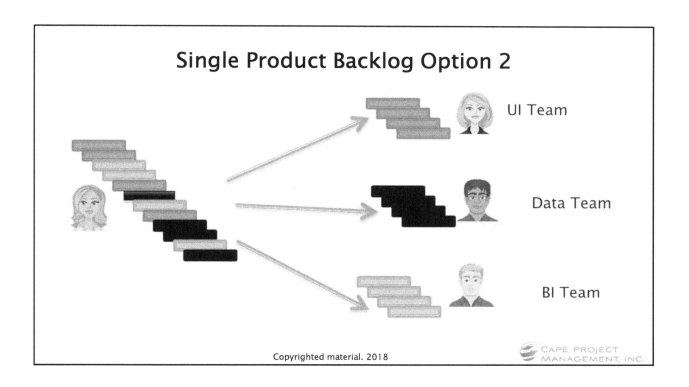

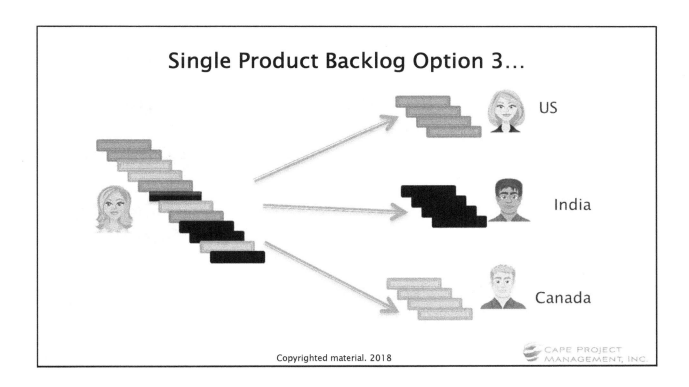

Single Product Owner

- Typically, a Product Owner cannot look after more than two – three teams.
- The solution is to introduce a Chief Product Owner who delegates to others.
- A Chief Product Owner is responsible for the overall product, guides the other Product Owners, and facilitates product decisions.

Copyrighted material. 2018

Chief Product Owner Governance Model

- The Chief Product Owner is responsible for quarterly roadmap updates
- The Product Owner "team" coordinates the release plan monthly
- They hold weekly backlog review meetings to support backlog refinement and Sprint Planning
- The Chief Product Owner needs to approve the Sprint goal for each Scrum Team

Copyrighted material. 2018

Scrum of Scrums

- □ Supports multiple teams working on the same product with the intent to address dependent issues
- □ Each team identifies one person who attends the Scrum of Scrums. Does not have to be the Scrum Master.
- □ A Scrum of Scrums meets two or three times a week for 30 minutes (or every day)

Copyrighted material. 2018

Scrum of Scrums cont'd

- □ The Scrum of Scrums team maintains a backlog of issues and problems to address
- □ There needs to be a "Scrum of Scrums Master"
  - ◘ Can be a shifting role each iteration or a permanent role
  - ◘ Responsible for managing the issues backlog
- □ Scrum of Scrums Questions:
  - ◘ What has your team done since we last met?
  - ◘ What will your team do before we meet again?
  - ◘ Is anything slowing your team down or getting in their way?
  - ◘ Are you about to put something in another team's way?
- □ There can also be a Scrum of Scrum of Scrums

Copyrighted material. 2018

Scaling through the Scrum of Scrums

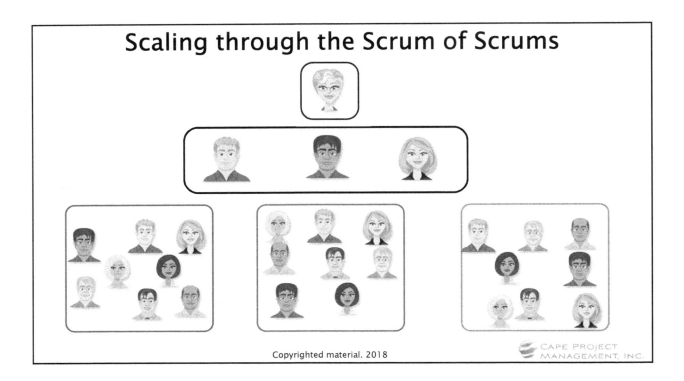

Scrum of Scrums Backlog

Priority	Issue	Owner
1	Team A needs write access to staging database	Team B
2	Team B QA wants info on API contract	Team C
3	OS on pre-production server needs to be updated	Team A
4	Patching downtime June 7, 5:00 – 6:00 am	All
5	………	

Integration Approaches

- Include all integration activities as part of each teams backlog
  - This is "true" Scrum: Produce a "potentially shippable product increment" at the end of each sprint.
- Hardening Sprints, Release Sprints, Stabilization Sprints
  - The team stops focusing on delivering new features or architecture, and instead spends their time on stabilizing the system and getting it ready to be released.
  - Can be performed by existing teams or different "integration" team.

Benefits of Hardening Sprints

- Very difficult to integrate across a large number of teams during the Sprint.
- Often frequent releases are not consumable by customer, so no reason to ensure "shippable" every Sprint.
- Automated and manual regression testing across the product may not fit in the Sprint.
- Deployment readiness and training with operations is needed once the product is integrated.
- Organizational requirements for go-live outside the scope of development. E.g. security audits, regulatory gates, etc.

Anti-patterns of Hardening Sprints

☐ We don't have enough time to test that component properly, so we'll do it in hardening.

☐ We don't have time to fix all of the cosmetic bugs we produced in this sprint, so we'll do it in hardening.

☐ Let's defer customer support training entirely to hardening.

☐ The design is still too volatile to document. We'll wait until it stabilizes and document it in hardening.

Copyrighted material. 2018

Additional Best Practices

Common Sprint Reviews

1. Instead of multiple Sprint Review meetings, hold a common Sprint Review especially if you are following the single product release model.

Common Sprint Retrospectives

1. Each team holds an individual Sprint Retrospective meeting followed by a common Sprint Retrospective where results are discussed that concern multiple teams.

Synchronous or Asynchronous Sprints

1. Synchronous Sprints work well when releases are aligned with Sprints and when there are common Sprint Reviews and Sprint Retrospectives.

2. Asynchronous works well there are common Product Owner and stakeholders yet different Sprint Reviews.

Copyrighted material. 2018

Summary

- ☐ Have Single Product Backlog
- ☐ Have Single Product Owner
- ☐ Hold Scrum of Scrums
- ☐ Determine an Integration Approach
- ☐ Consider common Sprint Review and Retrospectives
- ☐ Have a plan for synchronizing Sprints

ONLINE ACTIVITY

Module 2–5 Knowledge Check

Take a 18 question practice exam to test your understanding Lean and other Agile Methods.

Module 2-5 Knowledge Check

Questions

1. Put the following phases of the Agile Unified Process in order:

Correct Order
Inception
Elaboration
Construction
Transition

2. What are the following:

> **Focus on the business need**
> **Deliver on time**
> **Collaborate**
> **Never compromise quality**
> **Build incrementally from firm foundations**
> **Develop iteratively**
> **Communicate continuously and clearly**
> **Demonstrate control**

Correct	Choice
	None of the Above
	The principles of DSDM
	The practices of LeSS
	The principles of Agile UP
	The PM Declaration of Interdependence

3. **Put the following Crystal properties in order by impact on success:**

Correct Order
Easy Access to Expert Users
Focus
Frequent Delivery
Osmotic Communication
Personal Safety
Reflective Improvement
Technical Environment with CI and Automation

4. **Which of the following is NOT considered an enterprise Agile method?**

Correct	Choice
	DAD
	SAFe
	LeSS
	XP

5. **Alistair Cockburn created the Crystal Family of Agile Methods, all of whose names contain colors of quartz crystals taken from geology. What two characteristics of an Agile project are used to determine the color of the Crystal method?**

Correct	Choice
	Size and duration
	Duration and complexity
	Size and criticality
	Duration and criticality

6. The technique used to analyze the flow of information and materials through a system to eliminate waste is:

Correct	Choice
	Fishbone diagramming
	Flow charting
	Value stream mapping
	Pareto analysis

7. What of the following is not a step in the Value Stream Mapping process?

Correct	Choice
	Define the current state
	Collect data
	Amplify Learning
	Depict the future state
	Develop an implementation plan

8. This Agile methodology's properties includes Focus, Osmotic Communication and Project Safety:

Correct	Choice
	Scrum
	Kanban
	Extreme Programming
	Crystal

9. **Which one is not a value of Lean Development?**

Correct	Choice
	Pursue perfection
	Ensure collective code ownership
	Balance long-term improvement and short-term improvement
	After a project flows, keep improving it

10. **What Agile concept expresses delivering value in slices rather than in layers/stages?**

Correct	Choice
	Definition of Done
	Value Mapping
	Sashimi
	Lean Value

11. **Which is NOT a principle of Lean?**

Correct	Choice
	Eliminate waste
	Time-boxed events
	Deliver fast
	Delay commitment

12. Which Agile method goes through the following stages:

Feasibility Study
Business Study
Functional Model
Design and Build
Implement

Correct	Choice
	Dynamic Systems Development Method (DSDM)
	Rational Unified Process (RUP)
	Feature Driven Development (FDD)
	Lean Software Development
	Scrum

13. Which of the following is not an Agile approach?

Correct	Choice
	Feature Driven Development (FDD)
	Extreme Programming (XP)
	Dynamic Systems Development Method (DSDM)
	Crystal Clear
	Program Evaluation Review Technique (PERT)

14. Match a definition (on the right) to a Lean principle (on the left).

Correct	Choice
Eliminate Waste	Refactor - eliminate code duplication to zero
Create Knowledge	Schedule irreversible decisions at the last responsible moment
Build Quality In	Maintain a culture of constant improvement
Defer Commitment	Focus on the entire value stream
Optimize the Whole	Create nothing but value

15. When there are multiple Scrum Teams working on one project, what is the approach for integrating the project work?

Correct	Choice
	Maintain a single product backlog
	Manage dependencies via Scrum of Scrums
	Consider a Chief Product Owner role
	Align project teams by technology, feature or location
	All of the above

16. Pick three items which are considered wastes of Software Development.

Correct	Choice
	Partially Done Work
	Continuous Integration
	Task Switching
	Refactoring
	Defects

17. One of the major tools and techniques used in Lean Software Development is Value Stream Mapping. What is the primary purpose of value stream mapping?

Correct	Choice
	To improve business processes
	To identify and eliminate waste
	To ensure product quality
	To Limit WIP

18. The purpose of the Scrum of Scrums is to perform what function?

Correct	Choice
	To increase knowledge of Agile within the organization
	To manage cross-team dependencies working on the same project
	To ensure team building and staff development occurs
	To provide dashboard reporting to executives

Value Driven Delivery

All About Agile: Module 3

Version 4.0

"We **increase return on investment** by making continuous flow of value our focus."
        ~From the PM Declaration of Interdependence

http://pmdoi.org/

Agile Triangle

Value
- ☐ Meets or exceeds customer value expectations
- ☐ Value "chunks" are delivered in time-boxed releases

Quality
- ☐ Today's quality: Is the product reliable?
- ☐ Tomorrow's quality: Is the product adaptable to change?

Constraints
- ☐ Scope: all planned major value-generating capabilities are delivered.
- ☐ Cost: actual costs are within agreed to limits
- ☐ Schedule: actual schedule is within agreed to limits

Copyrighted material. 2018

Focus on Value

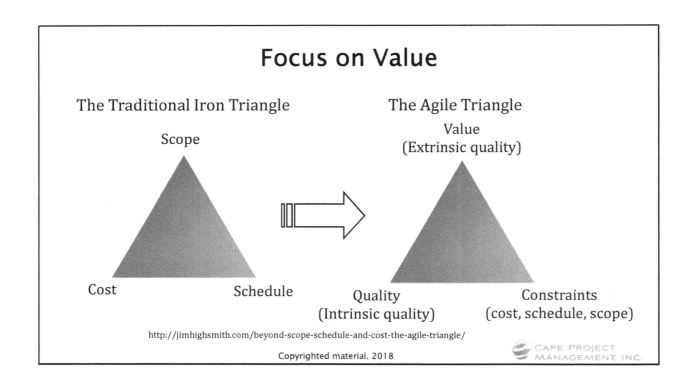

The Traditional Iron Triangle

Scope

Cost   Schedule

The Agile Triangle

Value
(Extrinsic quality)

Quality
(Intrinsic quality)

Constraints
(cost, schedule, scope)

http://jimhighsmith.com/beyond-scope-schedule-and-cost-the-agile-triangle/

Copyrighted material. 2018

Quality Defined

- Intrinsic Quality
  - All of the qualities that were built into the product: suitability, durability, reliability, uniformity, maintainability.
- Extrinsic Quality
  - Perceived quality
  - Value to the customer

Kelada, Joseph, *Integrating Reengineering with Total Quality*

Copyrighted material. 2018

Adding Value

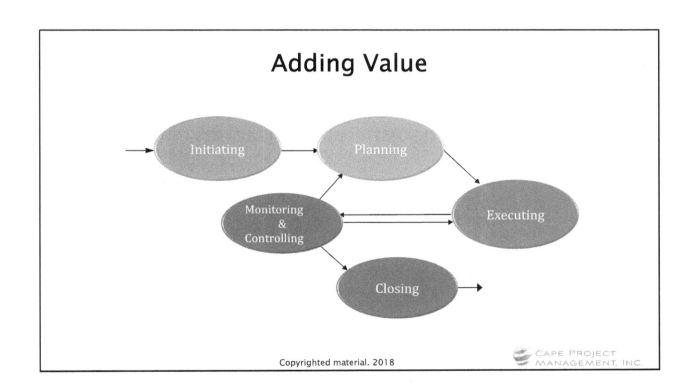

Copyrighted material. 2018

Value during Initiating

Determine the expected value of projects when initiating a project using:

□ Return on Investment (ROI)

□ Net Present Value (NPV)

□ Internal Rate of Return (IRR)

□ Payback Period

□ Opportunity Cost

Return on Investment

□ A performance measure used to evaluate or compare the efficiency of an investment

$$\text{ROI (\%)} = \frac{\text{Net Program Benefits}}{\text{Program Costs}} \times 100$$

□ The higher the ROI, the better the outlook

Net Present Value

- □ NPV is used in capital budgeting to analyze the profitability of an investment or project
- □ NPV compares the value of a dollar today to the value of that same dollar in the future
- □ If the NPV of a prospective project is:
  - ◘ Positive, the project should be accepted
  - ◘ Negative, the project should be deferred or rejected

CAPE PROJECT
MANAGEMENT, INC.

Internal Rate of Return (IRR)

- □ The higher a project's IRR, the more desirable it is to undertake the project

Internal Rate of Return

n = number of cash flows

CF_i = cash flow at period i.

IRR = Internal Rate of Return

$$0 = \sum_{i=1}^{k} CF_i \cdot \left[\frac{1 - (1 + IRR)^{-n_i}}{IRR} \right] \cdot \left[(1 + IRR)^{-\sum_{q < i} nq} \right] + CF_0$$

CAPE PROJECT
MANAGEMENT, INC.

Payback Period

- Period of time required to recoup the funds expended in an investment
- Also called the break-even point
- Often used because it is easy to apply and easy to understand
- Has serious limitations because it does not account for the time value of money. The approach to take this into account is called the Discounted Payback Period.

Opportunity Cost

- Opportunity cost is the loss of potential future return from the best alternative project when a choice is required for several mutually exclusive projects.

For example:

- Project A has a potential return of $25,000
- Project B has a potential return of $20,000
- Project C has a potential return of $10,000
- The opportunity cost for selecting Project A for completion over Project B and C will be $20,000 (the "potential loss" of not completing the second best project).

Value during Planning

Plan for the project to deliver value using:

☐ Agile chartering

☐ Value stream mapping

☐ Customer-valued prioritization

Agile Chartering

Section	Purpose
Vision	The vision defines the "Why" of the project. This is the higher purpose, or the reason for the project's existence.
Mission	This is the "What" of the project and it states what will be done in the project to achieve its higher purpose.
Goals and Success Criteria	The success criteria are management tests that describe effects outside of the solution itself.

A simplistic approach to chartering

Define Value

For software built for internal use:
- Save money
- Increase efficiency
- Solve problems that are costing money or decreasing efficiency
- Improve customer satisfaction
- Generate revenue by supporting or improving service offerings

For software built for commercial sale:
- Generate revenue through sale
- Improve/expand market share
- Open new markets

The IRACIS* mnemonic helps us remember to look for business benefit that will:
- **I**ncrease **R**evenue
- **A**void **C**ost
- **I**ncrease **S**ervice

* Gane & Sarson's IRACIS model, 1977

Customer-Valued Prioritization

- User Story mapping
- MoSCoW prioritization
- Minimally Marketable Features (MMF)
- Minimum Viable Product (MVP)
- Cumulative voting
- Kano analysis
- Pareto analysis
- Relative prioritization
- Risk-based prioritization
- Kitchen prioritization

User Story Mapping

- User Story Mapping is Jeff Patton's approach to organize and prioritize user stories
- Unlike typical user story backlogs, Story Maps:
  - Make the workflow or value chain visible
  - Show the relationships of larger stories to their child stories
  - Help confirm the completeness of your backlog
  - Provide a useful context for prioritization
  - Plan releases in complete and valuable slices of functionality

Steps to User Story Mapping

1. Product Roadmap Definition
2. User Story Definition
3. User Story Decomposition
4. Release Planning

Step 1–Product Roadmap Definition

☐ Spatial arrangement:

   ☐ Lay out your product roadmap by major user stories, themes or epics

   ☐ Arrange them left to right in the order you want to make these stories available

CAPE PROJECT MANAGEMENT, INC.

Step 2– User Story Definition

Create and arrange the user stories that will be performed within each epic or theme.

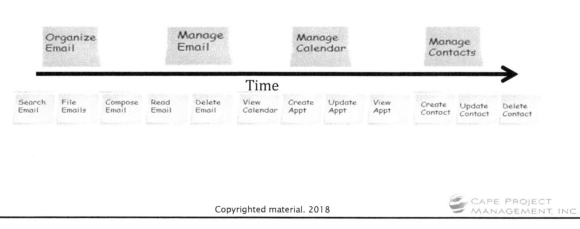

CAPE PROJECT MANAGEMENT, INC.

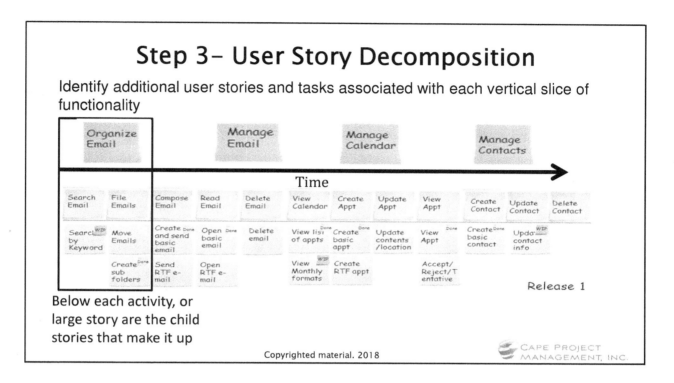

Step 3– User Story Decomposition

Identify additional user stories and tasks associated with each vertical slice of functionality

Below each activity, or large story are the child stories that make it up

Copyrighted material. 2018

Step 4 – Release Planning

- Prioritize user stories based on product roadmap and product goal
  - Product goals describe what outcome or benefit is received by the organization after the product is put into use
  - Use product goals to identify incremental releases, where each release delivers some benefit
- Create horizontal swim-lanes to group features into releases
- Arrange features vertically by priority from the user's perspective
- Split user stories into pieces that can be deferred until later releases

Copyrighted material. 2018

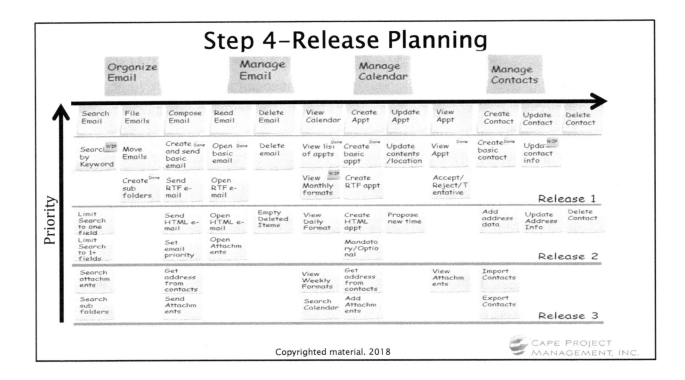

MoSCoW Prioritization

Acronym	Description
M - MUST	Describes a requirement that must be satisfied in the final solution for the solution to be considered a success.
S - SHOULD	Represents a high-priority item that should be included in the solution if it is possible. This is often a critical requirement but one which can be satisfied in other ways if strictly necessary.
C - COULD	Describes a requirement which is considered desirable but not necessary. This will be included if time and resources permit.
W - WON'T	Represents a requirement that stakeholders have agreed will not be implemented in a given release, but may be considered for the future.

CAPE PROJECT
MANAGEMENT, INC.

Minimally Marketable Features (MMF)

- ☐ Identify the product's most desirable features
- ☐ Prioritize their value
- ☐ Plan your releases around the features
- ☐ Release the highest–value features first
- ☐ Collaborate on one feature at a time
- ☐ Perform releases as often as possible
- ☐ Can be related to user story approach via epics or themes
- ☐ Common to Feature Driven Development (FDD)

Minimum Viable Product (MVP)

- ☐ The product with the highest return on investment versus risk.
- ☐ Just those core features that allow the product to be deployed, and no more.
- ☐ It allows you to test an idea by exposing an early version of your product to the target users and customers, to collect the relevant data, and to learn from it.

Source: Agile Product Management with Scrum: Creating Products that Customers Love, Roman Pichler

Cumulative Voting

- Hundred dollar method
- Give each stakeholder $100 in play money and they can "spend" it the requirements they want the most
- Can use points, stickers, etc.

Copyrighted material. 2018

Kano Analysis

Need	Definition
Exciters/Delighters	Exceeds customer needs, and a "nice to have." Contributes 100% to positive customer satisfaction.
Performance/Linear	Competitive requirements that the customer "wants", typically an improvement over current system.
Basic/Baseline	Meets minimum requirements and is a "must have." If these features don't exist, the customer is dissatisfied.
Indifferent	Least important to the customer. They will likely return little or no business value.

Copyrighted material. 2018

Kano Analysis, Graphical

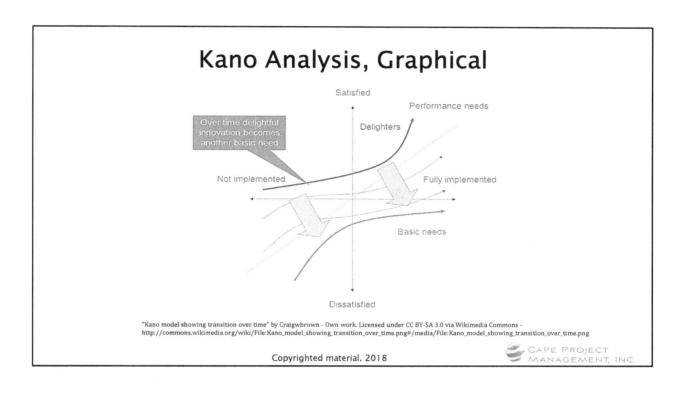

"Kano model showing transition over time" by Craigwbrown - Own work. Licensed under CC BY-SA 3.0 via Wikimedia Commons -
http://commons.wikimedia.org/wiki/File:Kano_model_showing_transition_over_time.png#/media/File:Kano_model_showing_transition_over_time.png

Copyrighted material. 2018

Risk Adjusted Backlog

- Similar to typical Risk Management
- Assign probability(P): 0-100%
- Determine impact (I): Days
- Risk exposure: Probability x Impact
  - Use risk exposure to reprioritize your backlog and re-estimate story points at every Sprint

Copyrighted material. 2018

Risk-based Prioritization

Complete:

□ High-value, high-risk stories first

□ High-value, low-risk stories next

□ Low-value, low-risk stories next

□ Avoid low-value, high-risk stories

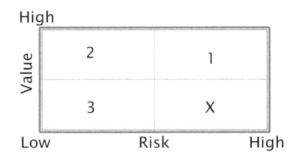

CAPE PROJECT
MANAGEMENT, INC.

Pareto Analysis

□ The 80/20 rule

□ Which 20% of items will yield 80% of the business value?

□ Used in backlog planning, prioritization, design considerations, etc.

CAPE PROJECT
MANAGEMENT, INC.

Pareto Analysis, Graphical

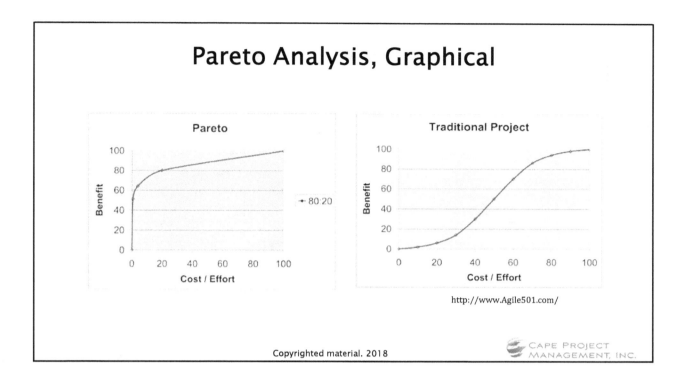

http://www.Agile501.com/

Copyrighted material. 2018

Relative Prioritization/Ranking

1. List all of the requirements or features
2. Estimate the relative benefit
3. Estimate the relative penalty
4. Determine the total value
5. Estimate the relative cost
6. Estimate the relative risk
7. Calculate priority number
8. Sort the list of features by priority

Relative Prioritization is ultimately determined by the needs of the customer.

Copyrighted material. 2018

Relative Prioritization/Table

Feature	Relative Benefit	Relative Penalty	Total Value	Value %	Relative Cost	Cost %	Relative Risk	Risk %	Priority
1. Query status of a vendor order									
2. Generate a Chemical Stockroom inventory report									
3. See history of a specific chemical container									
4. Print a chemical safety datasheet									
5. Maintain a list of hazardous chemicals									
6. Modify a pending chemical request									
7. Generate an individual laboratory inventory report									
8. Search vendor catalogs for a specific chemical									
9. Check training database for hazardous chemical training record									
10. Import chemical structures from structure drawing tools									
Totals									

Copyrighted material. 2018

Kitchen Prioritization

- ☐ Front Burner: Stories that the Team has agreed to do in the current Sprint
- ☐ Back Burner: High priority, well-defined Stories that are being made actionable so that they will be ready for the next Sprint Planning – created during backlog grooming
- ☐ Fridge: Items (Stories or Epics) that are in scope for the Release, but are not yet ready to be taken to Sprint Planning either due to prioritization or readiness
- ☐ Freezer: Items that are out of the scope of the Release
- ☐ Inbox: Items that have not yet been prioritized into a bucket (or, in this case, an appliance)
- ☐ Done: Stories that have been completed

https://uploads.strikinglycdn.com/files/56888/5b9f15b3-7010-4f9a-b591-58e5b69c6463/Scrum-101-A-Pocket-Guide.pdf

Copyrighted material. 2018

Value during Executing

Ensure you deliver value through:

□ Incremental delivery

□ Work in Progress (WIP) limits

□ Prototypes/Simulations/Spikes

Value through Incremental Delivery

Principle	Why Do This?
Work in order of business priority	Building incrementally by feature gives you a better chance to complete the features most important to the business and deliver value first.
Mitigate risks	Project failure is defined by not meeting the stakeholder requirements. Deliver in chunks and expect feedback. "Fail Sooner"
Deliver early	Anything that can earn value should be put into production as soon as possible
Be flexible	Allow the business to change its priorities

Work-in-Progress (WIP) Limits

☐ Limit work-in-progress to meet the capacity of the team

☐ Goal is to complete high-value features before beginning new features

☐ Prevents poor quality decisions that are made in time-boxed iterations

☐ Promotes a cross functional team

Prototypes and Simulations

Throwaway or rapid prototyping

☐ Create a model that will eventually be discarded rather than becoming part of the final delivered software

☐ Also called Spike solutions in XP

Evolutionary prototyping

☐ Build a very robust prototype in a structured manner and constantly refine it until it is production-ready

Incremental prototyping

☐ The final product is built as separate prototypes

☐ At the end the separate prototypes are merged in an overall design

Spikes

Spikes, an invention of XP, are a special type of User Story used to drive out risk and uncertainty. They are time-boxed to prevent excess analysis.

- Spikes may be used for estimating upcoming features
- Spikes may be used to perform feasibility analysis
- Spikes may be used for basic research to familiarize the team with a new technology or domain.
- Some features and stories contain significant technical or functional risk, spikes can be used to gain confidence in an approach
- When a Feature or story is be too big to be estimated confidently, spikes can be used to analyze the implied behavior so they can split the story into estimable pieces

Value during Monitoring & Controlling

- Monitor that you are delivering customer value through:
- Earned Value Management (EVM)
- Agile Approaches

Earned Value Management (EVM)

- Simplified for Agile
- Planned Value (PV) is a straight line due to iterative development
- Left Y axis represents points as scope, left X axis represents project spend
- Schedule performance index (SPI) using points and cost performance index (CPI) using feature value over actual cost can be used:
  - Planned/Actual 30/25 pts is an SPI of .83
  - Features completed value/costs $2.2m/2.8m = CPI of .79

Earned Value Management (EVM)

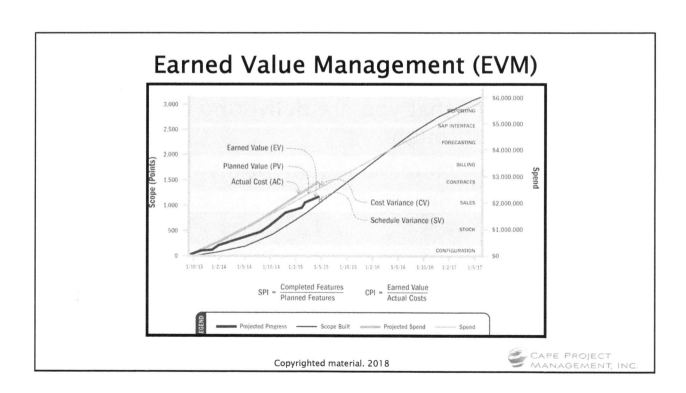

Monitoring and Controlling Value

Sprint Goals

□ The Team commits to work that aligns with the Sprint Goal

Sprint Reviews

□ Validating value to stakeholders

Approved Iterations

□ Accepting only value-added work

Approved Iterations

□ Meet the definition of Done

□ Is communicated to all Team members and stakeholders

□ Are posted in Agile tools and on walls

□ The Product Owner updates Roadmaps and Release Plans

Sashimi

- ☐ An Agile concept whereby you deliver value in slices rather than in layers
- ☐ You build the minimum amount of code that is necessary to connect all of the parts of the software and start building the actual functionality.
- ☐ This approach provides early delivery of the software and enables the development team and customers to experience the software very early in the development process.

CAPE PROJECT
MANAGEMENT, INC.

Sashimi Development

☐ Iteration 1
☐ Iteration 2
☐ Iteration 3

- Verify functional slices
- Verify user stories satisfy acceptance test case
- Adhere to definition of done
- Verify incremental integration
- "Unofficial" testing for feedback
- Exploratory testing

CAPE PROJECT
MANAGEMENT, INC.

Measuring Success in Agile

Business Outcomes (Value)	Time to Market (Lead Time)	Ability to Innovate (Quality)
• Revenue per Employee • Employee Satisfaction • Customer Satisfaction	• Release Frequency • Release Stabilization • Cycle Time	• Product Cost Ratio • Installed Version Index • Usage Index • Innovation Rate • Defects

Closing

http://www.ebmgt.org/portals/agilitypath/Documents/EBMgt_Guide_v1_CWT.pdf

CAPE PROJECT MANAGEMENT, INC.

Current Value Metrics

Revenue per Employee	Gross Revenue / #employees
Product Cost Ratio	All expenses in the organization that develops, sustains, provides services, markets, sells, and administers the product or system.
Employee Satisfaction	Engaged employees that know how to maintain, sustain and enhance the software systems and products are one of the most significant assets of an organization.
Customer Satisfaction	Sound management, solid software, and creative, fulfilled employees.

CAPE PROJECT MANAGEMENT, INC.

Time to Market Metrics

Release Frequency	The time needed to satisfy the customer with new, competitive products.
Release Stabilization	The impact of poor development practices and underlying design and code base. Stabilization is a drag on competition that grows with time.
Cycle Time	The time (including stabilization) to satisfy a key set of customers or to respond to a market opportunity competitively.

Copyrighted material. 2018

Ability to Innovate Metrics

Installed Version Index	The difficulty customers face installing a new release. The relatively low value of new releases, or even the # of customers that are evaluating alternatives.
Usage Index	Determines a product that is burdensome and difficult to use and excess software that must be sustained even though it is rarely used.
Innovation Rate	Growth of technical debt caused by poorly designed and developed software. Budget is progressively consumed keeping the old software alive.
Defects	Measures increasingly poor quality software, leading to greater resource and budget to maintain it and potential loss of customers.

Copyrighted material. 2018

ONLINE ACTIVITY

Module 3 Knowledge Check

Take a 22 question practice exam to test your understanding
of Value Driven Delivery

Module 3 Knowledge Check

Questions

1. 80% of the value comes from 20% of the work. Which law is this referring to?

Correct	Choice
	Parkinson's Law
	Moore's Law
	Pareto's Law
	Jevon's Paradox

2. When performing earned value analysis on an Agile project, it is not possible to use story points to calculate the schedule performance index (SPI).

Correct	Choice
	True
	False

3. The following formula can be used to calculate the cost performance index (CPI) on an Agile project.

Correct	Choice
	True
	False

4. What is a Japanese term used in Lean software development is an activity that is wasteful, unproductive, and doesn't add value?

Correct	Choice
	Sashimi
	Kanban
	Muda
	Kairoshi

5. The backlog is ordered by:

Correct	Choice
	The needs of the Product Owner
	Risk
	Complexity
	Size

6. DSDM uses MoSCoW technique to create the prioritized requirements list. In MoSCoW technique, 'M' stands for:

Correct	Choice
	Most useful
	Must have
	Must not have
	Minimum marketable feature

7. In the Kano Model of customer satisfaction, this type of feature makes a product unique from its competitors and contributes 100% to positive customer satisfaction:

Correct	Choice
	Exciter
	Performance
	Must-have
	Threshold

8. Identify the three components of the Agile Triangle.

Correct	Choice
	Quality
	Value
	Cost
	Constraints
	Scope
	Leadership

9. In what order do you select requirements to work on in a risk adjusted backlog?

Correct Order
High Risk Low Value
Low Risk High Value
Low Risk Low Value
High Risk High Value

10. The length of time to recover the cost of a project investment is the:

Correct	Choice
	Net Present Value
	Payback Period
	Earned Value
	ROI

11. Net present value (NPV) is a ratio that compares the value of a dollar today to the value of that same dollar in the future. An NPV that is negative suggests what?

Correct	Choice
	The project should be rejected
	I don't have enough information
	The project should be deferred
	The project should be put on hold until the value is 0

12. Which one is NOT a level of need in the Kano Model?

Correct	Choice
	Basic Needs
	Performance Needs
	Enabling Needs
	Excitement Needs

13. Assuming all projects require the same amount of up-front investment, the project with the highest _____ would be considered the best and undertaken first.

Correct	Choice
	Earned Value Management (EVM)
	Internal Rate of Return (IRR)
	Payback Period
	Budget at Completion (BAC)

14. The way that we calculate the number of years it takes to break even from undertaking a project which also takes into account the time value of money is the:

Correct	Choice
	Pay-back period
	Discounted pay-back period
	NPV
	Cumulative cash flow

15. Match each component of the Agile Triangle (on the left) to its associated description (on the right).

Correct	Choice
Value	Releasable Product
Quality	Reliable, Adaptable Product
Constraints	Cost, Schedule, Scope

16. A time-boxed period to research a concept and/or create a simple prototype is called a(n):

Correct	Choice
	Sprint
	Iteration
	Spike
	Retrospective

17. The acronym MoSCoW stands for a form of:

Correct	Choice
	Estimation
	Risk identification
	Prioritization
	Reporting

18. Project has an IRR of 12%, and Project Y has an IRR of 10%. Which project should be chosen as a better investment for the organization?

Correct	Choice
	It depends on the payback period
	Project Y
	Project
	Project or Y, depending on the NPV

19. Which of the following is NOT a prioritization technique?

Correct	Choice
	User Story Mapping
	Planning Poker
	Minimally Marketable Features (MMF)
	Kano analysis
	Kitchen Prioritization

20. Sequence the steps to User Story Mapping. (drag and drop)

Correct Order
Product Roadmap Definition
User Story Definition
User Story Decomposition
Release Planning

21. Choose which three statements are true about Approved Iterations:

Correct	Choice
	Meets the definition of Done
	There is no technical debt
	The Architect has approved it
	It is communicated to all Team members and stakeholders
	As a result, the Product Owner updates Roadmaps and Release Plans

22. **"Fail Sooner" is a benefit of Incremental Development.**

Correct	Choice
	True
	False

Stakeholder Engagement

All About Agile: Module 4-1
Agile Requirements

Version 4.0

Best Practices Engaging Stakeholders

- Understand why stakeholder involvement is important.
- You need to understand why active stakeholder involvement is important and what the impact to your project will be if you don't have it.
- Get support from the stakeholders themselves.
- Educate senior management. In many organizations senior management will need to determine, and then support, the level of involvement of stakeholders.
- Be flexible. Although you would like to be co-located with your stakeholders and have instant access to them, it doesn't always happen that way.

Best Practices Engaging Stakeholders

□ More access is generally better, but there are several reasons why it can be difficult to gain access to them on a continual basis.

□ Be prepared to work with stakeholder representatives.

□ Active stakeholder participation is crucial to the success of your project because without it you won't know what your stakeholders actually need.

□ Throughout the project there will be pressure to divert stakeholders away from the project so that they can focus on their normal "day jobs".

Copyrighted material. 2018

Strategies for Working Together

□ **Timely decisions.** Stakeholders must to be prepared to share business knowledge with the team and to make both pertinent and timely decisions regarding project scope and requirement priorities.

□ **Inclusive requirements.** Adopt inclusive requirements techniques and participatory design principles, which stakeholders can easily learn and adopt.

□ **Increased IT knowledge.** For stakeholders to effectively support your project , they need to invest the necessary time to learn about the things that they manage, they need to actively participate in the development of your system.

□ **Take an enterprise view.** You need to work with other project teams if your system needs to integrate with other systems.

□ **Knowledge transfer to the maintenance team.** Maintenance developers need to work with you to learn your system.

Copyrighted material. 2018

Stakeholder Engagement

Requirements Techniques
User Stories
Personas
Wireframes
Backlogs

Key Principles for Agile Requirements

- Active user involvement is imperative
- Agile teams must be empowered to make decisions
- Requirement are emergent and evolve as software is developed
- Agile requirements are 'barely sufficient'
- Requirements are developed in small pieces
- Enough's enough – Pareto's Law
- Cooperation, collaboration and communication between all team members is essential

Requirements Considerations

Written requirements:

- Can be well thought through, reviewed and edited
- Provide a permanent record
- Are easily shared with groups of people
- Time consuming to produce
- May be less relevant or superseded over time
- Can be easily misinterpreted

Verbal requirements:

- Instantaneous feedback and clarification
- Information-packed exchange
- Easier to clarify and gain common understanding
- Easily adapted to any new information known at the time
- Can spark ideas about problems and opportunities
- Can be vague if they are not validated

Copyrighted material. 2018

Interpreting Requirements

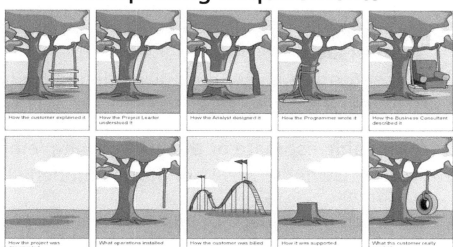

Copyrighted material. 2018

User Stories

seek to combine the strengths of written and verbal communication, where possible supported by a picture.

* Kent Beck coined the term user stories in Extreme Programming Explained 1st Edition, 1999

Agile Requirements – User Stories

☐ Agreement between customer and developer to have a conversation.

☐ A User Story is a very high-level definition of a requirement.

☐ Contains just enough information to produce a reasonable estimate of the effort to implement it.

☐ Product Owner writes User Stories on behalf of customer

   ◘ Written in language of business to allow prioritization

   ◘ Customer is primary product visionary

Product Backlog Creation: Writing User Stories

As a (role), I want (goal/desire)

or

As a (role), I want (goal/desire) so that (benefit)

- As a user, I want to search for employees by their first and last names.

- As an administrator, I want to be able to reset passwords for any user so that I can help them if they lose their password.

Copyrighted material. 2018

User Stories have 3 parts

Card *What is the goal of a user*	As a (user role), I want to (goal) so I can (reason) *Example:* *As a registered student, I want to view course details so I can create my schedule*
Conversation *How to achieve the goal using the system?*	Discuss the card with a stakeholder. Just in time analysis (JIT) through conversations. *Example:* *What information is needed to search for a course?* *What information is displayed?*
Confirmation *How to verify if the story is done and complete, and the goal is achieved*	Record what you learn in an acceptance test. *Example:* *Student can access course catalog 24 x 7* *Student cannot choose more than three courses*

http://ronjeffries.com/xprog/articles/expcardconversationconfirmation/

Copyrighted material. 2018

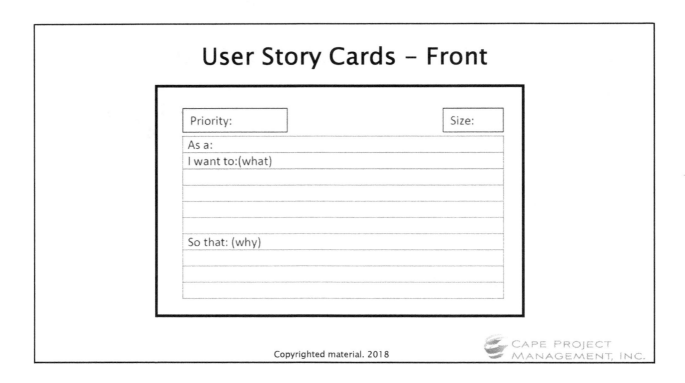

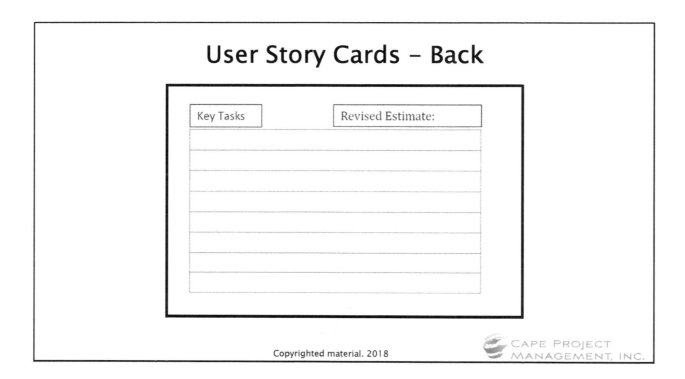

How detailed should a User Story be?

Detailed enough...

- ☐ User stories should only provide enough detail to make a reasonably low risk estimate of how long the story will take to implement. When the time comes to implement the story developers will go to the customer and receive a detailed description of the requirements face to face.

http://www.extremeprogramming.org/rules/userstories.html

Why use User Stories?

- ☐ Emphasizes verbal communication
- ☐ Understood by everyone
- ☐ Works for iterative development
- ☐ Encourages deferring detail
- ☐ Encourages participatory design

Agile Requirements Hierarchy

- **Themes**: Groups of related User Stories. Often the User Stories all contribute to a common goal or are related in some obvious way, such as all focusing on a single function.
- **Epics**: They resemble themes in the sense that they are made up of multiple User Stories. As opposed to themes, however, these types of User Stories often comprise a complete workflow for a user.
- **User Stories**: A self-contained unit of work agreed upon by the developers and the stakeholders. User Stories are the building blocks of your sprint. Note: Often technical requirements or other "non-user" requirements are called "Stories."
- **Tasks**: A fundamental unit of work that must be completed to make a progress on a User Story.

Copyrighted material. 2018

Agile Requirements Hierarchy

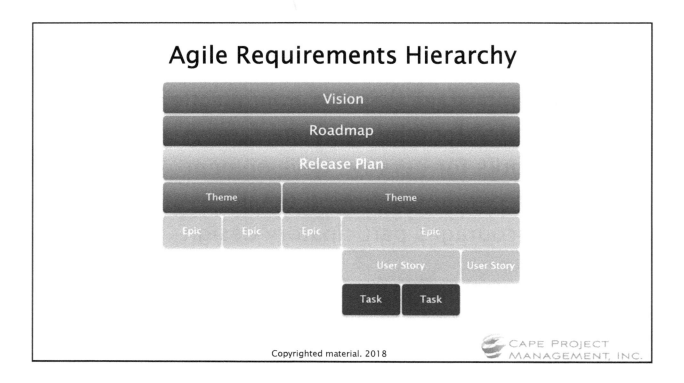

Copyrighted material. 2018

What is an Epic – CURB

Complex: The item might be too complex to be understood well enough to be committed to.

Unknown: Maybe nobody on the team knows enough about the story to even make a guess whether it can be committed to.

Risky: There are too many unknowns; it is too risky to commit to the story without further investigation or a mitigation strategy.

Big: It could just be too big to do in one Sprint, even though it is well understood.

CAPE PROJECT
MANAGEMENT, INC.

Writing Stories

- ☐ Good stories are:
  - ◘ Independent
  - ◘ Negotiable
  - ◘ Valuable to users or customers
  - ◘ Estimable
  - ◘ Small
  - ◘ Testable   (INVEST)

CAPE PROJECT
MANAGEMENT, INC.

Independent

- ☐ Stories that depend on other stories are difficult to prioritize and estimate
- ☐ Dependent Story:
  - ◘ As a student, I want to be able to log in and update my profile
- ☐ Independent Stories
  - ◘ As a student, I want to be able to log in
  - ◘ As a student, I want the ability to update my profile

Negotiable

- ☐ User Stories serve as reminders not contracts
- ☐ The story should convey the problem, not the solution. This way the solution is negotiable.
- ☐ Details need to be fleshed out in conversation

Valuable

- Both to people using the software and paying for the software
- Avoid stories valued only by developers (make the benefits to customers/users apparent for these stories)
- Usually this means that people should understand the 'why' behind the User Story.
- Example
  - "All connections to the database are through a connection pool" could be rewritten as "Up to 50 users should be able to use the application with a 5-user database license"

Examples of specifying value to users

Good:

- "A user can search for jobs"
- "A company can post new jobs"

Bad:

- "The software will be written in C++"
- "The data elements should be added to sysdb"

Estimable

- □ 3 common reasons why a story might not be estimable
- □ Not enough information or team lacks domain knowledge
    - ◘ Get details from customer
- □ New technology or not enough knowledge in the team
    - ◘ Perform spike to explore technology
- □ Story is too big
    - ◘ Split the story into smaller ones

Spikes

- □ Spikes, an invention of XP, are a special type of User Story used to drive out risk and uncertainty.
- □ Spikes may be used for basic research to familiarize the team with a new technology or domain.
- □ They are time-boxed to prevent excess analysis.
- □ Spikes may be used for estimating features in the next Sprint

Small

- Small enough to use in planning
- Split Compound or Complex Stories
  - Conversations may reveal multiple stories
  - Split along Create/Replace/Update/Delete (CRUD)
  - Split along data boundaries
  - Use spikes to analyze complexity
- Combine too small stories
  - If a story is too small, it will take more time to define and test than to develop

 CAPE PROJECT
MANAGEMENT, INC.

Activity

How would you split these stories?

- As an admin, I want to search for a user.
- As a customer, I want to pay online.

 CAPE PROJECT
MANAGEMENT, INC.

Testable

- ☐ Can't tell if story is "done" without tests
- ☐ Include Acceptance Criteria as part of the User Story
- ☐ Be aware of words like intuitive, fast or modern in your Agile requirements.
- ☐ Aim for most tests to be automated

Acceptance Criteria

- ☐ Acceptance criteria define the boundaries of a User Story, and are used to confirm when a story is completed and working as intended.
- ☐ The tests are written before development
- ☐ They are ideally created by the Product Owner
- ☐ Does not replace unit tests
- ☐ Often written on the back of the User Story card

Writing Acceptance Tests

User Story: As a student, I want shopping cart functionality to easily pay tuition online.

Acceptance Criteria:

- Student information is retained in a database
- Payment can be made via credit card
- An acknowledgment email is sent to the student after completing the transaction

CAPE PROJECT
MANAGEMENT, INC.

Why use Acceptance Tests?

- They get the team to think through how a feature or piece of functionality will work from the user's perspective
- They remove ambiguity from requirements
- They form the tests that will confirm that a feature or piece of functionality is working and complete.

CAPE PROJECT
MANAGEMENT, INC.

Define Roles

- ☐ Brainstorm an initial set of user roles
- ☐ Organize the initial set
- ☐ Consolidate roles
- ☐ Refine the roles
- ☐ Prioritize by role

Attributes worth considering when defining roles

- ☐ Frequency with which user will use software
- ☐ User's level of expertise with domain
- ☐ User's general level of proficiency with computers and software
- ☐ User's level of proficiency with this software
- ☐ User's general goal for using software

Additional User Modeling

Identify personas

- Fictitious users
- Should be described sufficiently so everyone on team feels like they know this "person"
- Choose personas that truly represent user population

Extreme personas

- Define users who are going to stress the system

Copyrighted material. 2018

Personas

- Archetypal users of an application
- Fictitious but based upon knowledge of real users
- Help guide the functionality and design
- More accurate user stories can be written using personas

Copyrighted material. 2018

Persona Components

- ☐ Personal profile
- ☐ Experience
- ☐ Personal goals
- ☐ Professional goals

Persona Example

- ☐ Jim is 50 years old and works as a mechanic with a company offering road service to customers when their car breaks down. He has worked in the job for the past 10 years and knows it well. Many of the younger mechanics ask Bob for advice. He always knows the answer to tricky mechanical problems.
- ☐ He is getting a new computer installed in his van. He doesn't own a computer, and he is a little intimidated by this type of technology.
- ☐ He is very nervous that he is going to look stupid if he can't figure it out.

What should you consider when building this system?

Activity: Create an Extreme Persona

Directions:

1. Pick one of the following applications or an internal application and create an Extreme Persona for supporting the requirements process.
   - Exam tool for taking the Scrum Master Certification exam
   - Self-service application for ordering dentures online
   - A simulation software to teach first-time drivers
2. Create a profile below.
3. Be prepared to share your answers with the class.

Personal profile	

ACTIVITY

Create an extreme persona

Copyrighted material. 2018

Other Story Types

- **Spike stories** are an XP term that describes Stories that figure out answers to tough technical or design problems. Most Spikes get thrown away, which differentiates them from Architecturally Significant Stories

- **Architecturally Significant Stories** are functional Stories that cause the Team to make architectural decisions.

- **Analysis Stories** exist because they find other stories.

- **Infrastructure Stories** add to or improve the infrastructure the team is using.

Copyrighted material. 2018

DevOps

- Acknowledges that Infrastructure, Operations and Maintenance are not just external stakeholders.
- Incorporates Operations and Maintenance staff into Agile Teams.
- Formalizes the practice of operations and system engineers participating together in the entire service lifecycle, from design through the development process to production support.
- DevOps is also characterized by operations staff making use many of the same techniques as developers for their systems work.

Copyrighted material. 2018

DevOps

Responsible for creating the technical or Non-Functional Requirements

- Performance requirements
- Tech requirements related to deployment and support
- Requirements to develop the guidelines for rapid rollback and roll forward
- Security/firewall requirements

Copyrighted material. 2018

Non-Functional Requirements

☐ Written by development team, architect, tech lead, system engineers

☐ Don't have to be written as User Stories

☐ Often part of the Definition of Done

☐ Non-Functional Requirements (NFRs) should be part of the Acceptance Criteria

☐ Written to prevent technical debt and improve overall value and quality

Copyrighted material. 2018

Examples of NFRs in Definition of Done

☐ All code must be peer reviewed within 4 hours of check-in.

☐ If a change is made to the web services interface, the change must be documented on the official web services api wiki page<link to api on wiki>.

☐ All code must have automated testing that is consistent with the "Automated Testing Guidelines"<link to guidelines on wiki>.

Copyrighted material. 2018

Examples of NFR in Acceptance Criteria

☐ Test that the system responds to all non search requests within 1 second of receiving the request.

☐ Test that the system responds to all search requests within 10 seconds of receiving the request.

☐ Test that the system logs a user out after 10 seconds of inactivity and redirects their browser to the home page.

☐ Test that any time a person's credit card number is shown in the application, that only the last 4 digits display.

Copyrighted material. 2018

Prioritizing Non-Functional Requirements

Projects have to balance delivering features along with doing all the important behind-the-scenes work. Leaving non-functional development until very late in the project has two major problems:

1. It costs more. If it was performed earlier it would have been easier, taken less time and left more capacity, time and budget for business value adding features.

2. It creates project risks that can lead to project problems. By avoiding risk reduction work such as proving some architectural component in an early iteration because it did not have a high business priority, the project is exposed to risks that could delay or jeopardize it.

Copyrighted material. 2018

Wireframes

- □ Low-fidelity (prototype)
- □ Black and white
- □ Combined to create a story board – sequence of screens
- □ Iteratively improved
- □ Validates design and understanding of user stories

CAPE PROJECT
MANAGEMENT, INC.

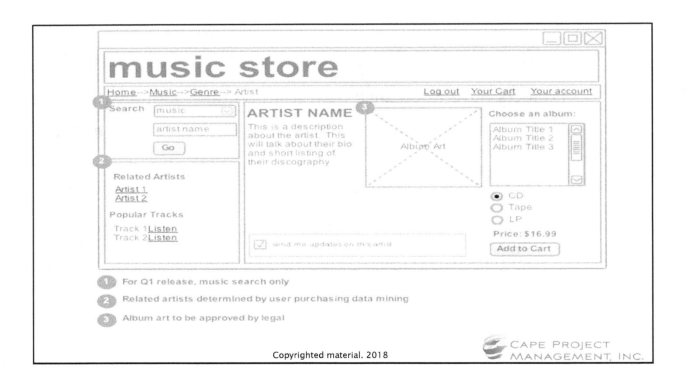

CAPE PROJECT
MANAGEMENT, INC.

Gathering Stories: Tools and Techniques

- User Interviews
- Prototyping
- Questionnaires
- Observation
- Story Writing Workshops

Story Writing Workshops

- The best technique for identifying and formulating user stories.
- The purpose of the workshop to identify as many User Stories as possible at a very high level.
- Similar to brainstorming, brings together the users, who then discuss and identify as many User Stories as possible.
- In Scrum this is performed by the Product Owner, in XP the development team participates.
- This workshop does not prioritize and estimate the User Stories but solely identifies requirements.

Guidelines for Good Stories

- ☐ Start with themes or epics
- ☐ Create user stories that meet the criteria of INVEST
- ☐ Include user roles in stories rather than saying "user"
- ☐ Don't rely solely on stories if they can be better expressed in other ways
- ☐ Size your story appropriately for the time frame it may be implemented in

Copyrighted material. 2018

CAPE PROJECT MANAGEMENT, INC.

Definition of "Ready"

- ☐ Story defined and written
- ☐ Story traceable to source document (where appropriate)
- ☐ Acceptance criteria defined
- ☐ Dependencies identified
- ☐ Size estimated by delivery team
- ☐ User experience included (where appropriate)
- ☐ Performance criteria identified (where appropriate)
- ☐ Person who will accept the User Story is identified
- ☐ Team has a good idea about how to demo the User Story

Copyrighted material. 2018

CAPE PROJECT MANAGEMENT, INC.

ONLINE ACTIVITY

Module 4–1 Knowledge Check
Take a 18 question practice exam.

Module 4-1 Knowledge Check

Questions

1. Which of the following is the hierarchy of User Story creation.

Correct	Choice
	Task, User Story, Feature, Theme
	Goal, Epic, Activity, User Story
	User Story, Epic, Theme, Feature
	Theme, Epic, User Story, Task

2. Non-functional requirements should be written as user stories whenever possible.

Correct	Choice
	True
	False

3. Operations and Maintenance staff should not be part of the Agile team.

Correct	Choice
	True
	False

4. Match the story types on the left to their definition on the right (drag and drop):

Correct	Choice
Spike	Stories that are created to find other stories
Architecturally Significant	Stories to improve the infrastructure the team is using
Analysis	Stories that figure out answers to tough technical or design problems
Infrastructure	Stories are functional Stories that cause the Team to make architectural decisions

5. A common reason a story may not be estimable is the:

Correct	Choice
	Team lacks domain knowledge.
	The story did not include a role.
	Developers do not understand the tasks related to the story.
	Team has no experience in estimating.

6. At completion of iteration planning, the team has finished identifying the tasks they will commit to for the next iteration. Which of the following tools best provides transparency into the progress throughout the iteration?

Correct	Choice
	Hours expended chart
	Management baseline chart
	Burndown chart
	Gantt chart

7. Well-written User Stories that follow the INVEST model include which attributes?

Correct	Choice
	Negotiable, Estimable, Small
	Independent, Valuable, Timely
	Independent, Negotiable, Smart
	Valuable, Easy-to-use, Timely

8. Wireframe models help Agile teams:

Correct	Choice
	Test designs
	Confirm designs
	Configure reports
	Track velocity

9. A reminder for the developer and Product Owner to have a conversation is:

Correct	Choice
	The Sprint planning meeting
	Backlog grooming
	A User Story
	An Agile reminder

10. Match the definitions (on the right) to each of the characteristics of a good User Story (on the left).

Correct	Choice
Negotiable	If a story does not have discernable value it should not be done
Valuable	A story is not a contract
Small	A story has to be able to be sized so it can be properly prioritized
Testable	User Stories average 3-4 days of work
Independent	Each story needs to be proven that it is "done"
Estimable	Stories can be worked on in any order

11. Match each Agile requirement type (on the left) to its definition (on the right).

Correct	Choice
Feature	Describes the interaction of the users with the system
User Story	Any requirement that is NOT a User Story (e.g. technical enabling, analysis, reminder to have conversation)
Story	Fundamental unit of work that must be completed to make a progress on a Story
Task	Business solution, capability or enhancement that ultimately provides value to the business.

12. Suppose your team is working to create a commercial website and is in the process of developing User Stories by role. One team member suggests rather than only thinking about the target user, we should also think of some exceptional users who use the system very differently. What type of user is this team member referring to?

Correct	Choice
	Performance Tester
	Extreme Persona
	High Risk User
	Admin Role

13. CRUD is an acronym that defines a way to split stories. What does CRUD stand for:

Correct	Choice
	Create/Replace/Update/Define
	Capture/Replace/Update/Define
	Create/Read/Update/Delete
	Create/Review/Update/Done

14. The definition of an Epic can be written using the acronym CURB. What does CURB stand for.

Correct	Choice
	Create/Update/Replace/Big
	Complex/Unknown/Risky/Big
	Compound/Unknown/Risky/Basic
	Complicated/Unusual/Really Big

15. While developing a story during the iteration, team discovered new tasks that were not identified earlier. A new complicated task is discovered such that the User Story cannot be completed during the Sprint. What should the Team do?

Correct	Choice
	Discuss the situation with the Scrum Master and see if there is still a way to meet the iteration goals.
	Let the Product Owner decide if there is still a way to meet the iteration goals.
	Modify the scope of other User Stories to allow completion of the Sprint backlog.
	Drop the User Story and inform the Product Owner that it will be delivered in the next iteration.

16. What can be described as "one or two written sentences; a series of conversations about the desired functionality."

Correct	Choice
	Epic
	Product roadmap
	User Story
	Story point

17. User Stories are:

Correct	Choice
	Negotiable
	Created by the Agile Project Manager
	The foundation of the roadmap
	Baselined and not allowed to change

18. What is the reason to develop personas as part of User Story creation?

Correct	Choice
	When the conversation is centered on the high-level flow of a process
	When trying to capture the high-level objective of a specific requirement
	When communicating what features will be included in the next release
	When trying to better understand stakeholder demographics and general needs

Stakeholder Engagement

All About Agile: Module 4-2
Information Radiators

Version 4.0

Information Radiators

- ☐ Publically posted information
- ☐ Easy to read
- ☐ Can be understood at a glance
- ☐ Can change frequently
- ☐ Easy to manage

Information Radiators Types

☐ Backlogs

☐ User Story Maps

☐ Burndown Charts

☐ Burnup Charts

☐ Cumulative Flow Diagrams

Types of Backlogs

Type	Definition
Product	Set of prioritized requirements aligning with product vision
Release	The minimum requirements that would support a release. • Smallest possible release contains one Sprint • "Done-Done"
Sprint	A subset of requirements selected according to the velocity (capacity) of the team

Product Backlog

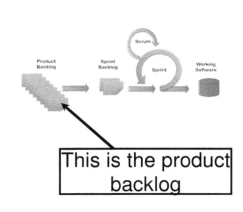

This is the product backlog

- The requirements
- A list of all desired work on the project
- Ideally expressed such that each item has value to the users or customers of the product
- Prioritized by the product owner

Copyrighted material. 2018

CAPE PROJECT MANAGEMENT, INC.

Risks in Product Backlog

The Product Backlog can contain anything:
- Bugs
- Enhancements
- Whole projects
- Issues
- Risks
- Threats
- Opportunities

Copyrighted material. 2018

CAPE PROJECT MANAGEMENT, INC.

Make the Product Backlog DEEP

- **Detailed Appropriately:** User stories on the product backlog that will be done soon need to be sufficiently well understood that they can be completed in the coming sprint. Stories to be developed later should be described with less detail.

- **Estimated:** The product backlog is more than a list of all work to be done; it is also a useful planning tool. Because items further down the backlog are not as well understood (yet), the estimates associated with them will be less precise than estimates given items at the top.

- **Emergent:** A product backlog is not static. It will change over time. As more is learned, user stories on the product backlog will be added, removed, or reprioritized.

- **Prioritized:** The product backlog should be sorted with the most valuable items at the top and the least valuable at the bottom. By always working in priority order, the team is able to maximize the value of the product or system being developed.

Roman Pichler, author of *"Agile Product Management with Scrum: Creating Products That Customers Love"*

Copyrighted material. 2018

Work Remaining – Product Backlog

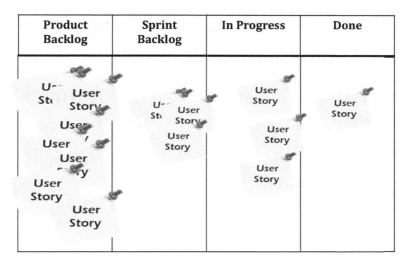

Product Backlog	Sprint Backlog	In Progress	Done

Copyrighted material. 2018

261

Product Backlog Examples

Sprint Backlog

- Created at Sprint Planning Meeting
- Based upon story size, priority and velocity
- User Stories have meet the definition of Ready
- The team has committed to this Sprint backlog as their forecast.

Sprint Backlog

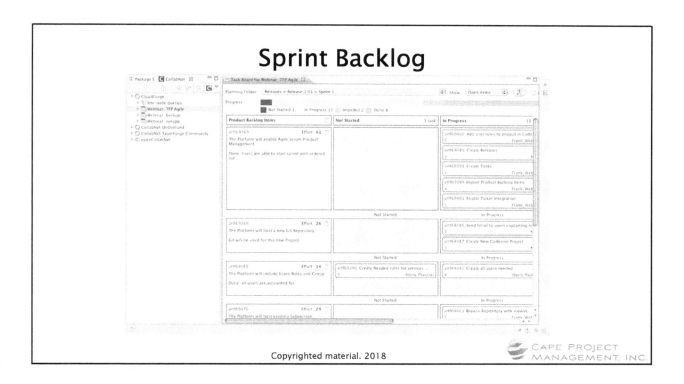

Selecting the Sprint Backlog

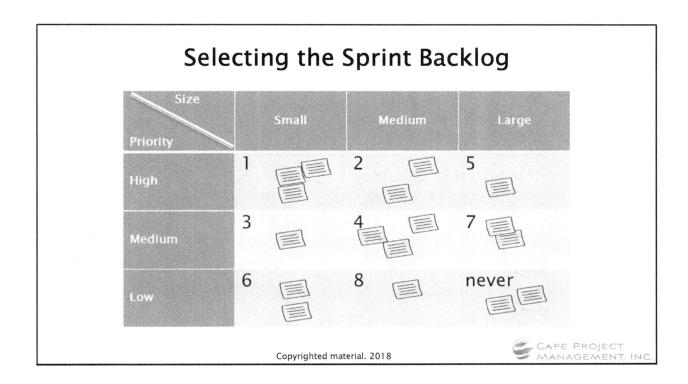

Burndown Charts

- Tracks work remaining
- At-a-glance information
  - Number of user stories committed
  - Duration of Sprint
  - Target velocity
  - Performance against plan
    - Above the line – behind schedule
    - Below the line – ahead of schedule
- Sprint burndown
- Release burndown
- Burndown bar chart

CAPE PROJECT MANAGEMENT, INC.

Velocity

- Velocity = Capacity
- Number of story points to be completed in Sprint
- First Sprint is a guess
- Estimate improves over time
- Account for work done and disruptions on the project
- Based upon team synergy

CAPE PROJECT MANAGEMENT, INC.

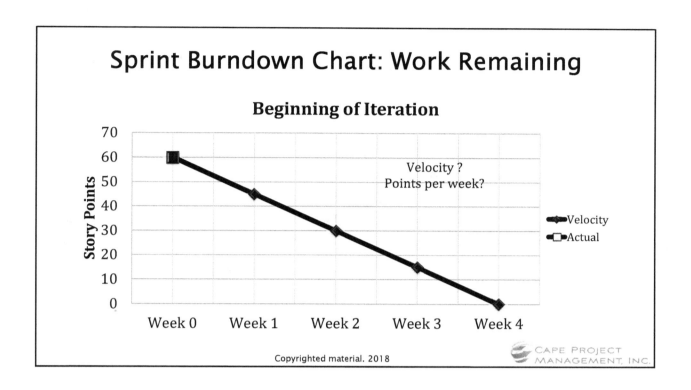

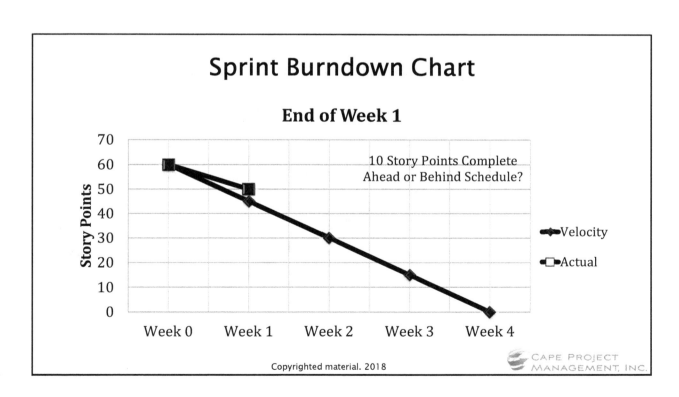

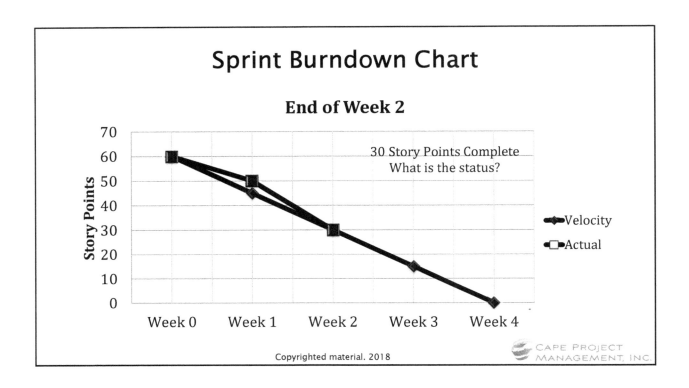

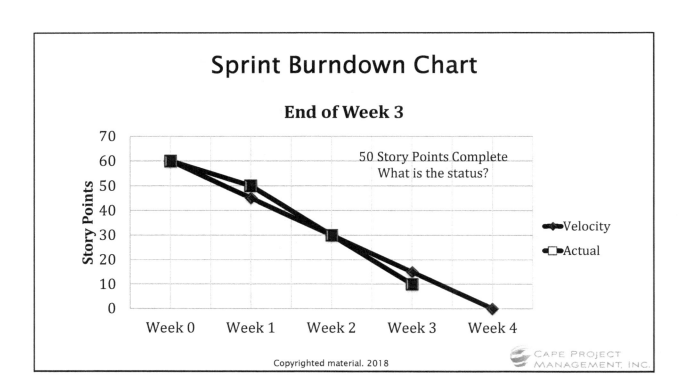

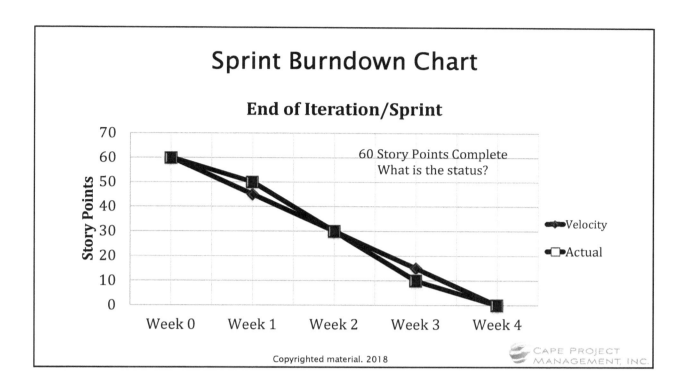

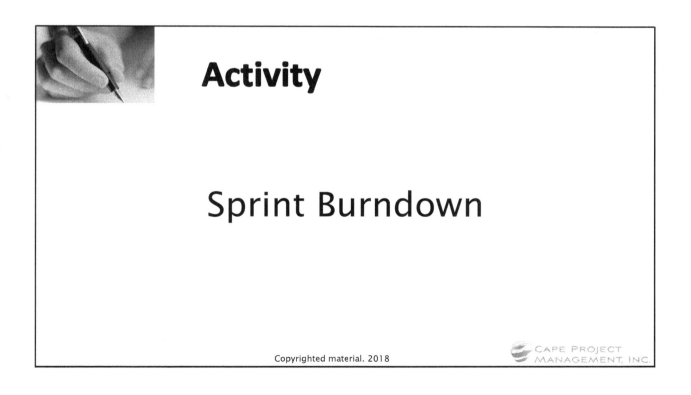

Story Points

Days

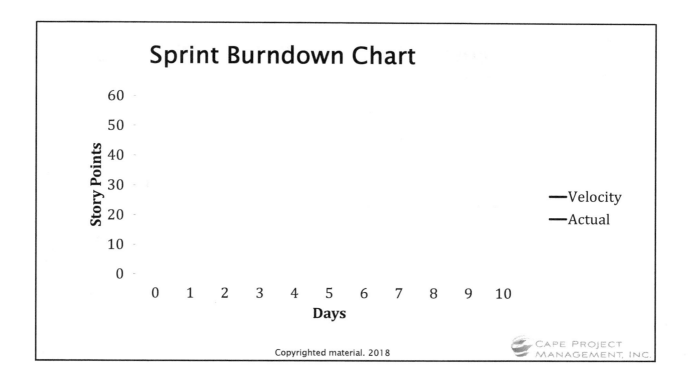

Forecasting Velocity for Release Planning

- ☐ Rolling Average
  - ◘ Used for new teams
  - ◘ 3-Sprint rolling average is most common

    Sprint 1=30 points, Sprint 2= 26 points, Sprint 3= 40 points, Forecast Sprint 4 = 32 points
- ☐ Yesterday's Weather
  - ◘ The last Sprint's velocity is the only "truth"
  - ◘ Typically used in more mature teams

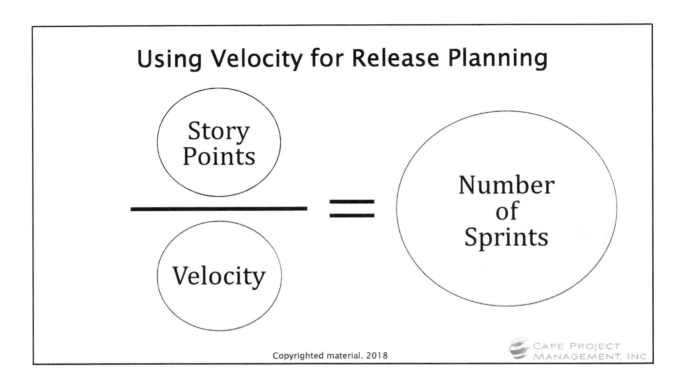

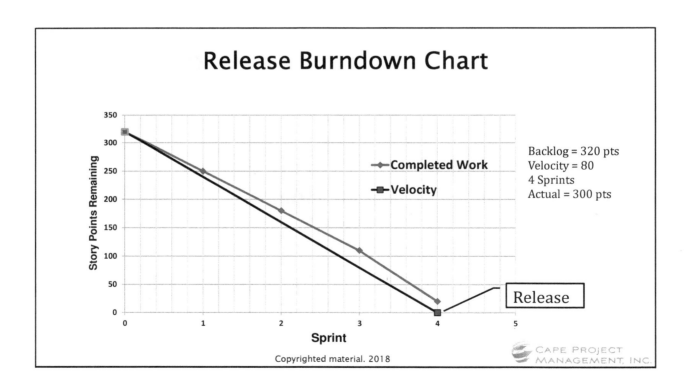

Burndown Bar Charts

- Shows net change in work remaining
- As stories are completed, the top of the bar is lowered
- When stories are added to the original set, the bottom of the bar is lowered
- When stories are removed from the original set, the bottom of the bar is raised
- When the estimate for a story changes, the top of the bar moves up or down

CAPE PROJECT
MANAGEMENT, INC.

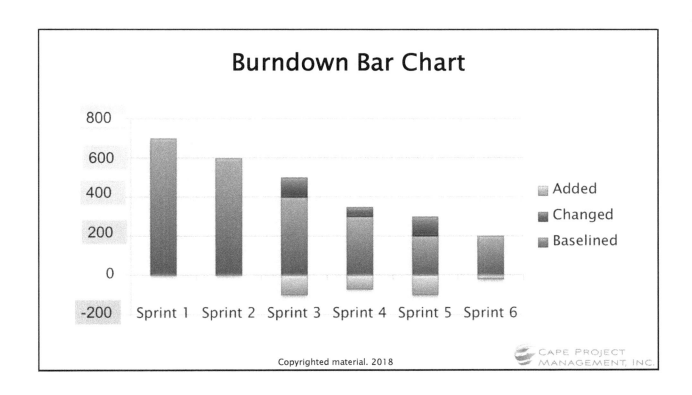

CAPE PROJECT
MANAGEMENT, INC.

Burnup Charts

- Shows accepted work
- Starts at 0 and grows to 100%

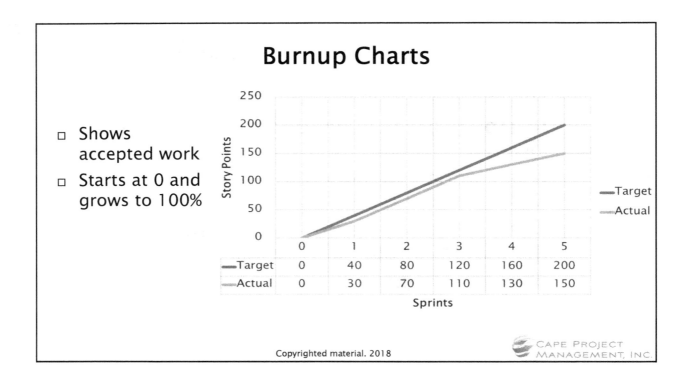

Sprints	0	1	2	3	4	5
Target	0	40	80	120	160	200
Actual	0	30	70	110	130	150

Copyrighted material. 2018

CAPE PROJECT MANAGEMENT, INC.

Cumulative Flow Diagrams

- Shows WIP in a graphical format
- Shows the different states of user stories
- Can track Kanban states or Scrum states
- Is an information radiator

Copyrighted material. 2018

CAPE PROJECT MANAGEMENT, INC.

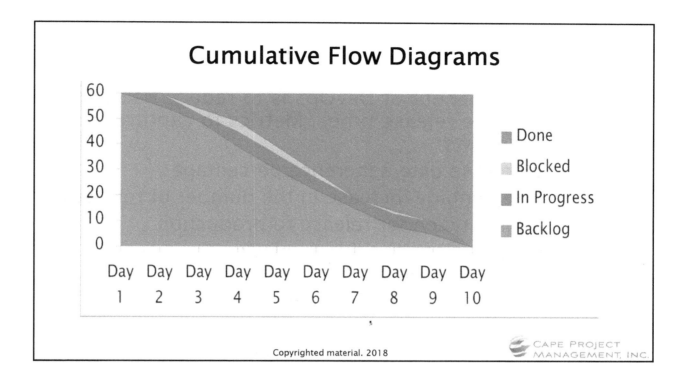

Cumulative Flow Diagrams

(Legend: Done, Blocked, In Progress, Backlog)

The KPIs (Key Performance Indicators) of Agile

- **Actual Stories Completed vs. Committed Stories** – the team's ability to understand and predict its capabilities. To measure, compare the number of stories committed to in iteration planning with those stories identified as completed in the iteration review.
- **Technical Debt Management** – the known problems and issues delivered at the end of the Sprint. It is usually measured by the number of defects.
- **Team Velocity** – the consistency of the team's estimates from iteration to iteration. Calculate by comparing story points completed in the current iteration with points completed in the previous iteration; aim for +/– 10 percent.
- **Quality Delivered to Customers** – Are we building the product the customer needs? Does every release provide value to customers? This can best be measured by surveying the customers and stakeholders.
- **Team Enthusiasm** – Often called the "Happiness Metric," it is a major component for a successful Agile team. If teammates aren't enthusiastic, no process or methodology will help. Measuring enthusiasm can be done by observation or, the most straightforward approach, simply asking team members "Do you feel happy?" and "How motivated do you feel?"
- **Retrospective Process Improvement** – the Team's ability to revise its development process to make itself more effective and enjoyable for the next iteration. This can be measured using the count of retrospective items identified, the retrospective items the team committed to addressing and the items resolved by the end of the iteration.

http://pragmaticmarketing.com/resources/9-Scrum-metrics-to-keep-your-team-on-track

DevOps Metrics

◻ A key benefit of DevOps is to reduce risk and improve release times. Metrics to capture this are as follows:

- ◘ Release date adherence percentage
- ◘ Percentage increase in the number of releases
- ◘ Time taken for release to production
- ◘ Defects attributable to platform/support requirements
- ◘ Percentage of NFRs met

ONLINE ACTIVITY

Module 4–2 Knowledge Check
Take a 20 question practice exam to test your understanding.

Module 4-2 Knowledge Check

Questions

1. Suppose your team velocity is 8 story points, and the product backlog items are ordered by priority as shown below. If you are in a Sprint Planning meeting and need to commit to the User Stories for the next iteration, which ones will you select?

   Story 1 = 3 Story Points
   Story 2 = 4 Story Points
   Story 3 = 3 Story Points
   Story 4 = 1 Story Points

Correct	Choice
	Story 1 and 2
	Story 2, 3, & 4
	Story 1, 2, & 3
	Story 1, 2, & 4

2. Which following statement is the least accurate regarding the Burndown chart?

Correct	Choice
	It is calculated using hours or points
	It is updated by the development team daily
	It provides insight into the quality of the product
	It reflects work remaining

3. Based on the following information, determine the number weeks until the next release:

Length of a Sprint = 2 weeks

Velocity of team = 35 points

Number of story points assigned to the minimum marketable features (MMF) = 280 points

Correct	Choice
	16 weeks
	9 weeks
	8 weeks
	12 weeks

4. At completion of iteration planning, the team has finished identifying the tasks they will commit to for the next iteration. Which of the following tools best provides transparency into the progress throughout the iteration?

Correct	Choice
	Hours expended chart
	Management baseline chart
	Burndown chart
	Gantt chart

5. Based upon this Burndown chart, is this project ahead of schedule or behind schedule?

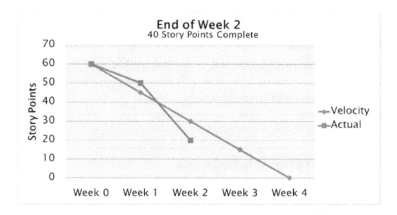

Correct	Choice
	Behind schedule
	Ahead of schedule

6. How do you read a burndown bar chart? Match the phrases below to create instructions.

Correct	Choice
As tasks are completed	the bottom of the bar is raised.
When tasks are added to the original set	the top of the bar moves up or down.
When tasks are removed from the original set	the top of the bar is lowered.
When the amount of work involved in a task changes	the bottom of the bar is lowered.

7. Which of the following is an example of an information radiator?

Correct	Choice
	An email of a status report
	A whiteboard showing the state of work
	A face-to-face conversation
	A text of a quick question to the Product Owner

8. Which of the following is NOT a KPI (key performance indicator) of Agile?

Correct	Choice
	Actual Stories Completed vs. Committed Stories
	Technical Debt Management
	Team Velocity
	Quality Delivered to Customers
	Team Enthusiasm
	Team Attendance

9. Which of the following is NOT a metric that measures the performance of DevOps in Agile.

Correct	Choice
	Release date adherence percentage
	Percentage increase in the number of releases
	Business value realized per release
	Defects attributable to platform/support requirements
	Percentage of NFRs met

10. When reading a burn-down chart, what does each status measurement say about project performance? Match the items below.

Correct	Choice
Actual Work Line is below the Ideal Work Line	Behind Schedule
Actual Work Line is on the Ideal Work Line	On Schedule
Actual Work Line is above the Ideal Work Line	Ahead of Schedule

11. The trend of work remaining across time in a Sprint, a release, or a product, with work remaining tracked on the vertical axis and the time periods tracked on the horizontal axis is called a _____.

Correct	Choice
	Progress Chart
	Parking Lot Chart
	Burndown Chart
	Burnup Chart

12. At the end of first iteration, the team finishes User Stories A, B and 50% of C. What is the team velocity?

The story sizes were:
Story A = 8 Points
Story B = 1 Points
Story C = 5 Points
Story D = 3 Points

Correct	Choice
	11.5
	16
	14
	9

13. Typically calculated in story points, this is the rate at which the team converts "Done" items in a single Sprint (drag and drop):

Correct	Choice
	Burndown rate
	Burn-up rate
	Velocity
	Capacity

14. The best description of a Sprint backlog is:

Correct	Choice
	Daily progress for a Sprint over the Sprint's length
	A prioritized list of tasks to be completed during the project
	A prioritized list of requirements to be completed during the Sprint
	A prioritized list of requirements to be completed for a release

15. Based upon this Burndown chart, is this project trending ahead of schedule or behind schedule?

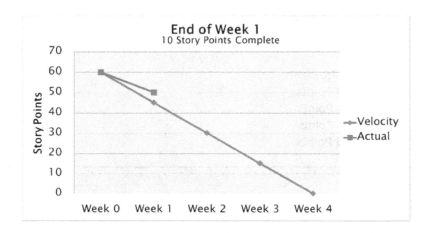

Correct	Choice
	Ahead of schedule
	Behind schedule

16. Which is a report of all the work that is "done?"

Correct	Choice
	Burndown chart
	Sashimi
	Kanban chart
	Completion chart

17. Product Backlog Items (PBI) described as emergent, are expected to:

Correct	Choice
	Become new technology requirements
	Become the highest priority items
	Be the most recent stories added to the backlog
	Grow and change over time as software is developed

18. Which of the following sets of tools is least likely to be utilized by an Agile team?

Correct	Choice
	Digital camera, task board
	Smart board, card wall
	WBS, PERT charts
	Wiki, planning poker cards

19. Highly visible project displays are called (drag and drop):

Correct	Choice
	Project radiators
	Information refrigerators
	Information radiators
	Project distributors

20. Which of the following statements is true for measuring team velocity?

Correct	Choice
	Velocity is not accurate when there are meetings that cut into development time.
	Velocity tracking does not allow for scope changes during the project.
	Velocity measurements account for work done and disruptions on the project.
	Velocity measurements are disrupted when some project resources are part-time.

Team Performance

All About Agile: Module 5

Version 4.0

Team Performance Topics

Communication
- Face-to-face
- Osmotic communication
- Active listening
- Distributed teams

Leadership
- Conflict resolution
- Decision making
- Coaching
- Facilitation
- Servant leadership

Face-to-Face Communication

"The most efficient and effective method of conveying information to and within a development team is face-to-face conversation." – the Agile Manifesto

□ Co-located teams benefits from this type of communication

□ User story creation with team members present is highly desirable

□ Providing feedback during the Sprint would be desirable face-to face

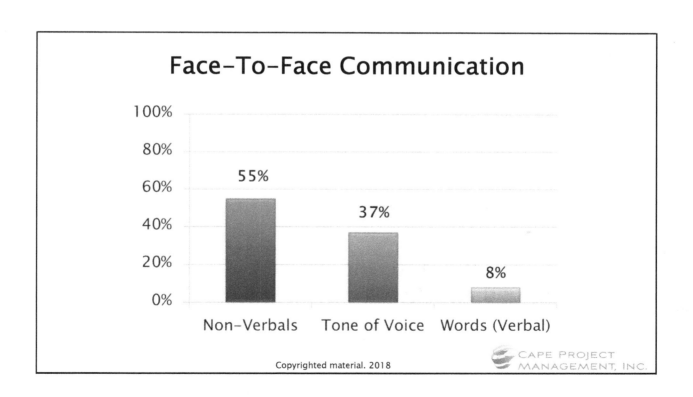

Osmotic Communication

- The basis of the open workspace model of XP
- Information flows into the background hearing of team members
- Pick up relevant information as though by osmosis
- Supports fewer meetings
- Studies show double the productivity and decreased time to market

Open Workspace

- Have the complete team sit together, e.g. co-located
- Sit close enough to the people you collaborate without having to get up
- Leave room for individuality in your workspace

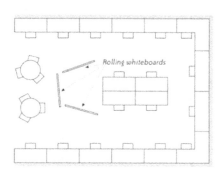

http://jamesshore.com/Agile-Book/sit_together.html

Virtual Team Workspaces

Create a fishbowl

- ☐ Connect with remote team member with an open video all day

Remote Pairing

- ☐ Set up a shared screen environment to perform peer programming or pair testing

---

3 Levels of Listening

Level I – Internal Listening

- ☐ Listening to our own thoughts and judgements
- ☐ Although we hear what a person is saying we focus on what it means to us.

Level II – Focused Listening

- ☐ Focus on what the person is saying
- ☐ In this level, we hear each individual word and how the person expresses them. The words and the story they tell is heard in their context. The core skills of summarizing, clarifying, paraphrasing and restating are essentially used in this stage to deepen understanding and to build trust.

Level III – Global Listening

- ☐ Listening focus is on more than just the words.
- ☐ At this level of listening the listener I taking in the emotions behind the words, the body language, the gestures and the tones being used. This level of listening gives the listener a heightened sense of awareness and access to their intuition.

http://www.reiningleadership.com/whitepaper2.html

Active Listening Skills

☐ **Clarify**: Ask for clarification if an element of a discussion is vague. Examples of clarifying questions include: I am not sure I quite understand; or do you mean that...?

☐ **Paraphrase**: Use paraphrasing to confirm that you really do understand what they just told you. Repeat back, in your own words, what you have just heard. "So I think you are saying...","It sounds to me like...", "I think I understand, but I want to make sure."

☐ **Summarize**: After a long discussion, it can be useful to try to summarize what you think the speaker's main points were. The summary is similar to paraphrasing, with the exception that you are trying to cover just the main points, not everything the speaker said.

Distributed Teams

☐ Team members are geographically dispersed

☐ Effective communication requires leveraging technology:
- ☐ Email
- ☐ SMS/instant messaging
- ☐ Video conferencing
- ☐ Interactive white boards
- ☐ Collaboration tools

☐ Commit to more informal communications

Social Media Communication

- More Agile, open-source development has created an environment where developers cooperate more by using social media tools and collaborative environments.
- Open source development communities make the "Team" part of a larger collaborative team.
- Developer-centric sites: GitHub, Stack Overflow and Reddit.
- "Tools like Bugzilla, Git and Gerrit are little more than social activity streams that organize conversations around code and builds, rather than selfies and cat videos."

http://www.eweek.com/developer/how-software-developers-use-social-collaboration-in-the-Agile-age.html

Copyrighted material. 2018

CAPE PROJECT
MANAGEMENT, INC.

Leadership In Agile

- Leading Agile projects
- Conflict resolution
- Negotiation
- Decision making
- Servant leadership and facilitation

Copyrighted material. 2018

CAPE PROJECT
MANAGEMENT, INC.

Negotiation

- Negotiation is communication with two or more parties to reach an agreement / resolve conflicts
- Focus is on "collaboration over contract negotiation"
- Negotiation strategies
  - **Distributive negotiation**: adopt extreme positions initially and work to reach a deal through tactics on the assumption that value is limited
  - **Integrative negotiation**: work together to achieve something by creating more values for a win–win solution

Copyrighted material. 2018

4 Key Elements of Negotiation

1. Separate people from the problem
2. Focus on interests, not positions
3. Invent options for mutual gain
4. Use objective criteria

Focuses on a "win–win" solution

Fisher, Roger and William Ury. Getting to Yes: Negotiating Agreement
Without Giving In. New York, NY: Penguin Books, 1983.

Copyrighted material. 2018

Collaboration

- Collaboration = Working together through effective communication, making sure all members agree, resolve conflicts, create a win-win situation and move forward with a group consensus
- Customer collaboration and team collaboration are important for Agile projects

CAPE PROJECT MANAGEMENT, INC.

Conflict Types

1. Lack of role clarity
2. Difference in prioritizing tasks
3. Working in silos
4. Lack of communication
5. Waiting on completion of task

Conflict is a necessary part of team development.

http://www.brighthub.com/office/project-management/articles/95971.aspx

CAPE PROJECT MANAGEMENT, INC.

Five Levels of Conflict

1. Problem to Solve
2. Disagreement
3. Contest
4. Crusade
5. World War

http://Agile.dzone.com/articles/Agile-managing-conflict

CAPE PROJECT
MANAGEMENT, INC.

Level 1: Problem to Solve

- Involves everyday frustrations and aggravations
- Team members likely feel anxious
- The team remains focused on determining how to fix the problem
- Information flows freely, and collaboration occurs
- Team members use words that are clear, specific, and factual
- The language abides in the here and now, not in talking about the past
- Level 1 is constructive disagreement that characterizes high-performing teams

CAPE PROJECT
MANAGEMENT, INC.

Level 2: Disagreement

- □ Simmering conflict between team members.
- □ Self-protection becomes as important as solving the problem.
- □ Team members distance themselves from one another to ensure they come out OK in the end or to establish a position for compromise they assume will come.
- □ They may talk offline with other team members to test strategies or seek advice and support.
- □ People aren't hostile, just wary.
- □ Facts play second fiddle to interpretations and create confusion about what's really happening.

CAPE PROJECT MANAGEMENT, INC.

Level 3: Contest

- □ Often, multiple issues cluster into larger issues or create a "cause"
- □ The aim is to win
- □ A compounding effect occurs as prior conflicts and problems remain unresolved. Factions emerge in this fertile ground from which misunderstandings and power politics arise
- □ People begin to align themselves with one side or the other
- □ Blaming flourishes
- □ In this combative environment, talk of peace may meet resistance
- □ People may not be ready to move beyond blaming

CAPE PROJECT MANAGEMENT, INC.

Level 4: Crusade

- Resolving the situation isn't good enough.
- Team members believe the people on the "other side" of the issues will not change.
- Factions become entrenched and can even solidify into a pseudo-organizational structure within the team.
- People and positions are seen as one, opening up people to attack for their affiliations rather than their ideas.
- The overall attitude is righteous and punitive.

Level 5: World War

- It's not enough that one wins; others must lose.
- Only one option at level 5 exists: to separate the combatants (aka team members) so that they don't hurt one another.
- No constructive outcome can be had.

Adaptive Leadership / Situational Leadership

☐ The leader adapts how he/she leads based on the specific environment or situation in order to be most effectively, e.g. the maturity stage of the team: forming, storming, norming, performing

☐ Focusing on value-added activities instead of blindly following processes

☐ Openness and transparency are highly valued to facilitate communication amidst changes

Copyrighted material. 2018

CAPE PROJECT
MANAGEMENT, INC.

Adaptive Leadership / Situational Leadership

"While the activities of an adaptive leader seem endless, there are four critical actions that should be embraced: improving speed-to-value, having a passion for quality, doing less, engaging and inspiring staff."

~ Jim Highsmith

Copyrighted material. 2018

CAPE PROJECT
MANAGEMENT, INC.

Emergent Leadership

As teams work together, it is natural for a leader to emerge from the group during their interactions. Emergent leadership occurs in the following way:

1. Orientation: During the orientation stage, potential leaders are believed to announce their "candidacies" for the emergent-leadership position.

2. Conflict: During the conflict stage, two or more leaders pass the "candidacy threshold" causing leadership conflict.

3. Emergence: Finally, in the emergence stage, group members willingly subordinate themselves to the leader who has passed the "emergence threshold."

CAPE PROJECT
MANAGEMENT, INC.

Participatory Decision Making

- The fundamental principle is viewing decision making as a win-win process and treating all participants with respect.

- All collaborative practices are based on trust and respect, or perhaps more precisely, on building trust and respect.

- Everyone has a different perspective or a different experience, which brings needed diversity to the decision process.

- A little extra time taken on decision making in the early stages of a project will significantly reduce time as the project continues.

- A benefit to a participatory process is that as understanding of the process, including the decision criteria, increases, the time required to make similar decisions in the future decreases rapidly.

Jim Highsmith, *Agile Project Management: Creating Innovative Products*

CAPE PROJECT
MANAGEMENT, INC.

Diversity in Agile Teams

- Diversity is critical for highly-effective teams.
- The more complex the problem, the more personality and experience diversity you want on your team.
- Different approaches to solving problems and backgrounds help the team see what their options are.
  - For example, new college graduates often have an advantage over those with experience. They don't know the problem you need solved can't be solved. They've been trained through 4 years of college that all problems can be solved before the end of the semester. They will bring that optimism to work.
- If you only look for people with similar backgrounds and experience then you will most likely get similar ideas and problem-solving.
- Most leaders are not aware of the influences that cultural differences can have on team dynamics.
  - Underestimating the impacts of cultural diversity on your team can be disastrous, creating barriers and even team breakdown.
- These impacts can be even more pronounced on Agile self-organizing teams.

Copyrighted material. 2018

CAPE PROJECT
MANAGEMENT, INC.

Team Values (Scrum)

Original:

- **Openness**: There should be no secrets between/amongst Team Members about things relevant to the project.
- **Focus**: Everything that the Team does must have a focus; and the Team Members must focus on what is important in everything they do.
- **Commitment**: The Team makes and keeps its commitments; and the Team Members must have commitment to the Team and the Product itself.
- **Respect**: Team Members should always do the best they can do at any given moment; they should respect all points of view, including those of their Stakeholders.
- **Courage**: The Team must have the courage to make reality visible, the courage to say No; and Team Members must have the courage to be open with each other.

New:

- **Visibility**: The Team must make the current state of the Product visible; that is, the details of production belong to the Team, but the state of the Product is available to all.
- **Humor**: Since everyone is always doing the best they can, everyone needs a sense of humor; if we can't laugh at the things we do, we'd have to cry.

http://blog.3back.com/infographic/team-values/

Copyrighted material. 2018

CAPE PROJECT
MANAGEMENT, INC.

How to create cross-functional teams

Cross functional teams are critical when you need people with different expertise to solve a problem. Steps for setting up a successful team include:

1. Begin by setting a goal for your team. What are its objectives, and why has it been set up?
2. Identify the roles that you need to fill, and the types of people you want in those roles.
3. Use the best people available, even if they don't necessarily agree with your views or your ways of working.
4. Establish ways of working together including creating a team charter or working agreement.
5. Ensure there is a servant leader to lead the team to collaborative decision making.

Creating a self-organizing team

☐ Getting the right people
☐ Articulating the product vision, boundaries, and team roles
☐ Encouraging interaction and information flow between teams
☐ Facilitating participatory decision making
☐ Insisting on accountability
☐ Steering, not controlling

How to Develop New Skills on a Cross-Functional Team

☐ **Limit the number of focus areas for each team.** Initially have cross-functional teams focus on a limited number skills areas, for example development and QA. The team members then work together to accomplish tasks.

☐ **Try Pair Programming.** Pair programming can be a powerful technique when used in Agile teams. Encourage team members to pair up with those who have different technical backgrounds and work together on areas that are new to at least half of the pair.

☐ **Emphasize that their performance will not be judged.** Sometimes team members feel self-conscious if they are taking the time to learn a new skill. Their velocity will likely decrease, bringing down the team velocity. As more tasks can be handled by more members of the team, the velocity will increase.

CAPE PROJECT
MANAGEMENT, INC.

How to Motivate Teams

☐ Link the individual's success to the cross-functional team's success.

☐ Establish clear performance standards and expectations related to the team. Individuals need to know how well they're performing as a member of the cross-functional team, and that evaluation should be separate from a functional department evaluation.

☐ It's also often a good idea to reward the team as a whole. This contributes to team unity and cohesiveness.

☐ All of these rewards should include formal and informal recognition. It's just as important to hear people say "thank you" on a regular basis as it is to receive something tangible.

☐ Recognition events can also communicate team success, and demonstrate this to the wider organization.

CAPE PROJECT
MANAGEMENT, INC.

Development Mastery Models

☐ Tuckman's

☐ Dreyfus

☐ Shu Ha Ri

How Teams Develop – Tuckman's Model

Forming

Storming

Norming

Performing

Forming

- In this stage, most team members are positive and polite. Some are anxious, as they haven't fully understood what work the team will do. Others are simply excited about the task ahead.

- The leader will play a dominant role at this stage, because team members' roles and responsibilities aren't clear.

- This stage can last for some time, as people start to work together, and as they make an effort to get to know their new colleagues.

Storming

- This is the stage where many teams fail.
- Storming often starts where there is a conflict between team members' natural working styles.
- If it has not been clearly defined how the team will work, people may feel overwhelmed by their workload.
- Some people may question the worth of the team's goal, and they may resist taking on tasks.
- Team members who stick with the task at hand may experience stress, particularly as they don't have the support of established processes, or strong relationships with their colleagues.

Norming

- ☐ This is when people start to resolve their differences, appreciate colleagues' strengths, and respect the leader.
- ☐ Now that the team members know one another better, they may socialize together, and they are able to ask each other for help and provide constructive feedback.
- ☐ People develop a stronger commitment to the team goal, and start to see good progress towards it.
- ☐ There is often a prolonged overlap between storming and norming, because, as new tasks come up, the team may lapse back into behavior from the storming stage.

Copyrighted material. 2018

Performing

- ☐ The team reaches the performing stage when hard work and minimal friction leads to the achievement of the team's goal.
- ☐ The structures and processes set up support this well.
- ☐ The leader can concentrate on developing individual team members.
- ☐ It feels easy to be part of the team at this stage, and people who join or leave won't disrupt performance.

Copyrighted material. 2018

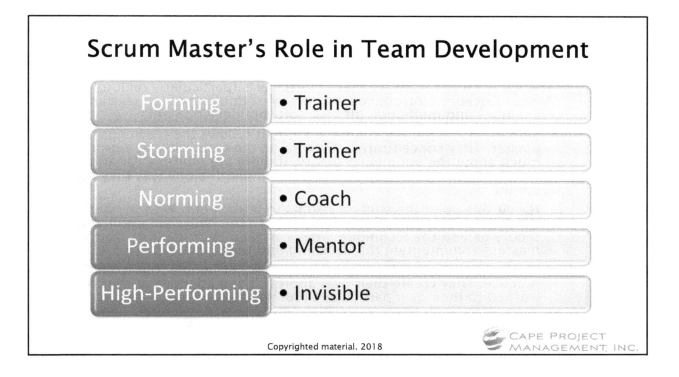

Scrum Master's Role in Team Development

Forming	• Trainer
Storming	• Trainer
Norming	• Coach
Performing	• Mentor
High-Performing	• Invisible

Copyrighted material. 2018

Dreyfus Model of Skills Acquisition

The concept of skill acquisition lies in helping the teacher understand how to assist the learner in advancing to the next level:

- **Novice**: Needs to be told exactly what to do. Very little context to base decisions off of.
- **Advanced beginner**: Has more context for decisions, but still needs rigid guidelines to follow.
- **Competent**: Begins to question the reasoning behind the tasks, and can see longer term consequences.
- **Proficient**: Still relies on rules, but able to separate what is most important.
- **Expert**: Works mainly on intuition, except in circumstances where problems occur

Copyrighted material. 2018

Shu-Ha-Ri

The name comes from Japanese martial arts (particularly Aikido), and Alistair Cockburn introduced it as a way of thinking about learning techniques and methodologies for software development.

☐ **Shu**: In this beginning stage the student follows the teachings of one master. They concentrate on how to do the task, without worrying too much about the underlying theory. If there are multiple variations on how to do the task, they concentrate on just the one way they are being taught.

☐ **Ha**: At this point the student begins to branch out. With the basic practices working they now start to learn the underlying principles and theory behind the technique. They can then start learning from other masters and integrate that learning into their practice.

☐ **Ri**: Now the student isn't learning from other people, but from their own practice. They create their own approach and adapt what they have learned to their own particular circumstances.

http://martinfowler.com/bliki/ShuHaRi.html

An Agile Leadership Model

☐ Process Knowledge

☐ Technical Skillset

☐ Business Experience

☐ Facilitation Skills

☐ Training Skills

☐ Coaching Skills

☐ Servant Leadership Skills

Process Knowledge

- ☐ Refer often to the Agile Manifesto
- ☐ Read the latest books, blogs, podcasts and webinars by industry leaders; Mike Cohn, Ken Schwaber, Jeff Sutherland, Martin Fowler, Alistair Cockburn, Esther Derby, Lyssa Adkins, Roman Pichler
- ☐ Attend Agile conferences and Meetups
- ☐ Join societies: Agile Alliance, Scrum Alliance, Lean Systems Society, PMI
- ☐ Pursue certifications: CSM, PSM I, PSM II, PMI-ACP, CSP

Technical Skillset

- ☐ Software Developer: Craftsmanship, Code Katas, Open Source Contribution
- ☐ Business Analyst: IIBA, BPMN
- ☐ Test / QA: ISTQB, Exploratory testing, Automation skills, Specification By Example, Testing communities
- ☐ Project Manager: PMI, Servant leadership, Team dynamics
- ☐ System Engineer: Technical Certifications, ITIL, DevOps

  ...or whatever skills will make you better at your key role

Business Experience

- ☐ Develop Business Domain knowledge: Market awareness, future trends and directions
- ☐ Financial management skills
- ☐ Marketing skills
- ☐ Human Resources skills
- ☐ Learn Agile Business Processes: Agile in the Business, Lean Startup, Agile Business Process Management

Copyrighted material. 2018

Facilitation Skills

- ☐ Techniques: Brainstorming, Icebreakers, Affinity Mapping, Open Space
- ☐ Achieving session goals and objectives
- ☐ Being neutral and impartial
- ☐ Keeping focus
- ☐ Achieving consensus with conflicting priorities and opinions
- ☐ Keeping decisions and actions visible

Copyrighted material. 2018

Affinity Mapping

- Use affinity mapping in a workshop environment when you want participants to work together identifying, grouping and discussing issues.
- The affinity diagram organizes ideas with following steps:
  - Record each idea on cards or notes.
  - Look for ideas that seem to be related.
  - Sort cards into groups until all cards have been used.

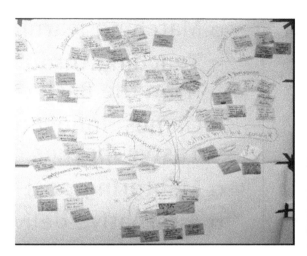

CAPE PROJECT
MANAGEMENT, INC.

Open Space Facilitation

- Participants gather together with only a stated "Theme" and a minimal framework. Individuals propose sessions they'd like to lead, or sessions they'd like to see someone else step up and lead. Through the alchemy of self-organization, a schedule emerges, composed of sessions people feel passionate about pursuing.
- All participants attend and sit in a large circle or concentric circles. The facilitator begins by introducing Open Space and explaining the 4 Principles:
  - Whoever comes are the right people.
  - Whatever happens is the only thing that could.
  - It starts when it starts.
  - It's over when it's over.
- Open Space is known for its apparent lack of structure and welcoming of surprises, it turns out that the Open Space is actually very structured but that structure is perfectly fit to the people and the work at hand.

http://www.openspaceworld.org/cgi/wiki.cgi?AboutOpenSpace

CAPE PROJECT
MANAGEMENT, INC.

Training Skills

- ☐ Matching learning to content and audience
- ☐ Teaching through demonstration: "Training from the Back of the Room"
- ☐ Games: Innovation Games, Gamestorming, Tastycupcakes.org
- ☐ Mentoring post-training
- ☐ Alternative delivery methods

CAPE PROJECT
MANAGEMENT, INC.

Agile Collaboration Games

- ☐ Games improve retention of principles learnt, they can be played in a team environment and they bring playfulness to learning and collaborative decision-making required for estimation or prioritization such as planning poker.
- ☐ Devise one by systematically following a well-defined process:
  1. Define the problem around improving process / practice or value.
  2. Identify the objectives that you would like to drive home.
  3. Decide on the type for the game you are about to devise.
  4. Brainstorm and invent the game by being inspired, demonstrate courage while choosing options and "keep it simple."
  5. Debrief and learn to course correct and improve.

http://tastycupcakes.org/

CAPE PROJECT
MANAGEMENT, INC.

Coaching Skills

- Ask Coaching Questions:
  - They are truly open ended
  - They are not asked with a "correct" answer in mind
  - They invite introspection
- Actively monitor and assess team performance
- Acknowledge desired teamwork behaviors and skills through feedback
- Embrace conflict as a sign of growth and development
- Coach by example

CAPE PROJECT MANAGEMENT, INC.

Coaching Don'ts

- Coach from a distance
- Coach only to problem solve
- Lecture instead of coach
- Try to change too much
- Lose objectivity
- Be too theoretical
- Be inflexible
- Avoid tough conversations

CAPE PROJECT MANAGEMENT, INC.

Servant Leadership Skills

- ☐ Traditional leadership is "command-and-control"
  - ☐ "Workers need to be monitored closely"
- ☐ Servant leadership is based upon trust
  - ☐ "Team members are self-motivated"
- ☐ An Agile servant leader needs to:
  - ☐ Protect the team from outside distractions
  - ☐ Remove impediments to the team's performance
  - ☐ Communicate and re-communicate project vision
  - ☐ "Move boulders and carry water"—in other words, remove obstacles that prevent the team from providing business value

Servant Leadership

- ☐ Critical to building self-organizing teams
- ☐ More difficult, but more rewarding
- ☐ Facilitates the team to address the tasks
- ☐ Fosters an environment that is trusting and respectful; supports collaboration

Characteristics of a Servant Leader

- Promoting self-awareness
- Listening
- Serving those on the team
- Helping people grow
- Coaching vs. controlling
- Promoting safety, respect and trust
- Promoting the energy and intelligence of others

Implementing Servant Leadership

- Make sure you have the right people on the team
  - Passion
  - Skills
  - Capacity
- Trust first
- Let the team members propose the approach to make the project a success
- Provide support, remove obstacles and stay out of the way
- Ensure leaders develop their Emotional Intelligence

Emotional Intelligence

- The ability or skill to identify, assess, monitor and control or influence the emotions and feelings of oneself and others.
- Don't let emotions take over but let emotions work for you.

5 Factors of Emotional Intelligence

1. **Perceiving**: The ability to recognize, acknowledge and attend to the emotions of one's own self and other team members.
2. **Managing**: The ability to express emotions in a controlled manner.
3. **Decision making**: The ability to apply emotions effectively in decision making.
4. **Achieving**: The ability to generate the emotions that will motivate oneself towards pursuit of a desired goal.
5. **Influencing**: The ability to motivate others in the pursuit of a goal, by evoking similar emotions in others as well.

Self-Assessment

- Periodically assess yourself and your team
- Identify strengths and weaknesses adopting processes and using tools
- Determine level of competence of skills needed to perform the role
- Identify obstacles and willingness to embrace the self-organizing team
- Focus on continuous improvement

Activity

Scrum Master
Self-Assessment

Activity: Agile Self-Assessment

Directions:
1. Review and identify your level for each component of the matrix.
2. What is your highest competency?
3. What competency do you need to work on most?
4. What competency are you strong at but don't really enjoy?
5. Pair-up and review

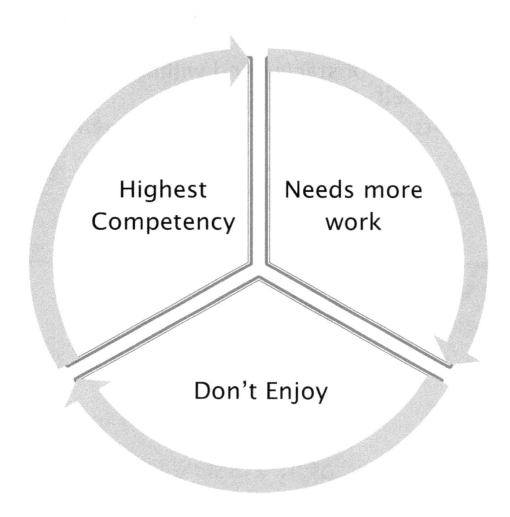

	Beginner	Practitioner	Master	Coach	Expert
Process Knowledge	Aware of principles and practices. Participated in an Agile project	Understand the principles and practices. Actively working in and improving an Agile project	Can setup and lead an Agile project. Experience as an Iteration Manager/ Scrum Master	Significant Agile project experience in varied environments. Can adapt to suit project environments	Well recognized with the industry and maintain public presence.
Technical Skillset	Work in a team using core skills (BA, Dev, Tester, PM)	Lead of a discipline within a team. Established standard of practice and quality within a team	Remains current with best-practice and industry trends in relevant discipline.	Recognized by peers as a technical expert in relevant discipline.	Creating and publishing new techniques.
Business Experience	Clear understanding of the business, the operating environment and the market	Comfortable discussing business process. Understand factors influencing business success.	Understand market trends and strategy. Sought after for business advice and analysis of impacts.	Understand risk, finance and strategic elements that impact business. Experience running a business unit.	Have run a successful business in your industry. Sought after to advise on running business.
Facilitation Skills	Comfortable working with and leading a group. Ad-hoc facilitation of Agile team ceremonies.	Experienced in facilitating group discussion of complex issues. Leads the facilitation of Agile team ceremonies.	Leads multi-day workshops and planning events for large or newly formed teams.	Facilitates sessions involving complex people issues. Facilitates sessions involving multiple stakeholders and conflicting priorities.	Facilitates senior executive sessions and/or large groups of people.
Training Skills	Enjoy helping other learn. Supports learning initiatives within the team environment.	Have some experience delivering training to small teams.	Comfortable delivering training to larger groups. Participate in developing and updating training content.	Significant training experience across multiple courses. Comfortable writing and piloting new course content.	Recognized and sought after as a trainer. Have trained a number of other trainers.
Coaching Skills	Understand the role and difference between coach, mentor and advisor.	Can provide ad-hoc coaching within current team.	Recognized as a leader and am able to follow a simple coaching model for helping people to resolve their own problems.	Adapt coaching style to suit situation, team and staff level. Comfortable coaching peers and executive staff.	Recognized and sought after as a coach not only in Agile but in other areas of work. Capable of coaching C-level executives

Leading Agile Projects

- Learn the team members' needs.
- Learn the project's requirements.
- Act for the simultaneous welfare of the team and the project.
- Create an environment of functional accountability.
- Have a vision of the completed project.
- Use the project vision to drive behavior.
- Serve as the central figure in successful project team development.
- Recognize team conflict as a positive step.
- Manage with an eye toward ethics.
- Remember that ethics is not an afterthought, but an integral part of our thinking.

Jeffrey Pinto, Project Leadership from Theory to Practice

Copyrighted material. 2018

PMI Code of Ethics

- Ethics is about making the best possible decisions concerning people, resources and the environment. Ethical choices diminish risk, advance positive results, increase trust, determine long term success and build reputations. Leadership is absolutely dependent on ethical choices. The values that the global project management community defined as most important were: responsibility, respect, fairness, and honesty.

https://www.pmi.org/about/ethics/code

Copyrighted material. 2018

The Role of the Project Manager in Agile Projects

- □ The project manager is the person assigned by the performing organization to lead the team that is responsible for achieving the project objectives. ~ The PMBOK® Guide – 6th ed.

- □ Shift from being the center of the team to serving the team.

- □ As a servant leader, project managers encourage the distribution of responsibility to the Team.

Copyrighted material. 2018

ONLINE ACTIVITY

Module 5 Knowledge Check

Take a 22 question practice exam to test your understanding.

Copyrighted material. 2018

Module 5 Knowledge Check

Questions

1. What does the term "fishbowl" refer to in terms of communication on Agile teams?

Correct	Choice
	An all-day live video connection with a remote team member
	All team members sharing a common workspace
	All stakeholders in an all-day program review
	A test lab where you watch actual customers test an application
	None of the above

2. Match the response options to each level of conflict.

Correct	Choice
Level 1: Problem to Solve	Accommodate, negotiate, get factual
Level 2: Disagreement	Establish safe structures again
Level 3: Contest	Do whatever is necessary
Level 4 : Crusade	Collaboration or consensus
Level 5 : World War	Support and safety

3. There are no project managers on Agile projects.

Correct	Choice
	True
	False

4. Which of the following is NOT an approach to prevent mini-waterfall occurring within an iteration.

Correct	Choice
	Pair Programming
	Mob Programming
	Swarming
	Limit WIP
	None of the above

5. When we practice active listening, what are the levels through which our listening skills progress?

Correct	Choice
	Self-centered listening, Focused listening, Intuitive listening
	Internal listening, Focused listening, Global listening
	Global listening, Focused listening, Intuitive listening
	Interested listening, Focused listening, Global listening

6. The Japanese terms for an Agile developmental mastery model is:

Correct	Choice
	Kaizen
	Shu-Ha-Ri
	Sashimi
	Muda

7. Which development mastery model of skill acquisition lies in helping the teacher understand how to assist the learner in advancing to the next level?

Correct	Choice
	Tuckman
	Dreyfus
	Shu-Ha-Ri
	Kaizen

8. Which of the following is NOT one of the 5 common conflict types?

Correct	Choice
	Compensation anxiety
	Working in silos
	Difference in prioritizing tasks
	Waiting on completion of task dependencies

9. The Project Leader's primary responsibilities are to "move boulders and carry water." What is this an example of?

Correct	Choice
	Command and control leadership
	The leadership metaphor
	Servant leadership
	Leadership by example

10. Osmotic communication is when team members obtain information from overheard conversations.

Correct	Choice
	True
	False

11. What is the Open Space concept?

Correct	Choice
	When cubicles walls are removed for an Agile team.
	It is a meeting designed to allow Agile practitioners to meet in self-organizing groups where they can share their latest ideas and challenges.
	It is a core principle of DSDM
	The choice to collocate all team members for the beginning of a project.

12. Emotional intelligence includes all of the following except:

Correct	Choice
	Perceiving
	Managing
	Influencing
	Achieving
	Committing
	Decision making

13. Suppose you are a Scrum Master on a new Agile team. Which of the following strategies is best way to resolve conflict on the team?

Correct	Choice
	Smooth over
	Ignore
	Use your authority
	Dictate
	Collaborate

Feedback when incorrect: Collaborate is a formal term for resolving conflict on a team.

14. On Agile teams, conflict is to be avoided at all cost.

Correct	Choice
	False
	True

15. Teams of members working in different physical locations are called:

Correct	Choice
	Co-located Teams
	Global Teams
	Outsourced Teams
	Distributed Teams

16. What is the sequence of Tuckman's stages of team formation and development progress?

Correct Order
Forming
Norming
Performing
Storming

17. Match each activity on the left to its definition on the right (drag and drop).

Correct	Choice
Coordination	The developer submits code for testing. The U designer checks that the developer implemented it correctly.
Cooperation	The Product Owner adjusts some story priority to meet the dependency of another team.
Collaboration	Pair programming
Communication	A slide presentation by the Product Owner to stakeholders

18. There are four critical actions that should be embraced by an adaptive leader: improving speed-to-value, having a passion for quality, doing less, and _____.

Correct	Choice
	Facilitating meetings
	Ensuring effective communication
	Engaging and Inspiring staff
	Managing conflict

19. On an Agile team, the project leader works to remove impediments from blocking the team's progress. This is known as what type of leadership?

Correct	Choice
	Consensus-driven
	Functional management
	Servant
	Command and control

20. When the Agile team works in the same location, the team is said to be_____.

Correct	Choice
	Co-located
	Functional
	Outsourced
	Distributed

21. All of the following are TRUE about communicating on distributed teams ECEPT:

Correct	Choice
	Should consider instant messaging tools
	Have a higher need for videoconferencing
	Need to spend more effort communicating
	Should have an easier Storming phase

22. A servant leadership role includes:

Correct	Choice
	Shielding team members from interruptions
	Making commitments to stakeholders
	Determining which features to include in an iteration
	Assigning tasks to save time

23. High-performing teams feature which of the following sets of characteristics?

Correct	Choice
	Consensus-driven, empowered, low trust
	Consensus-driven, empowered, plan-driven
	Constructive disagreement, empowered, self-organizing
	Self-organizing, plan-driven, empowered

24. Self-organizing teams are characterized by their ability to:

Correct	Choice
	Do their own filing
	Sit where they like
	Make local decisions
	Make project-based decisions

25. When comparing communication styles, which of the following are true?

Correct	Choice
	Paper-based communication has the lowest efficiency and the highest richness.
	Paper-based communication has the highest efficiency and the lowest richness.
	Face-to-face communication has the highest efficiency and the highest richness.
	Face-to-face communication has the highest efficiency and the lowest richness.

Adaptive Planning

All About Agile: Module 6

Version 4.0

Adaptive Planning Topics

Planning Techniques
- Progressive Elaboration
- Product Vision
- Product Roadmap
- Release Planning
- Agile Discovery

Sizing and Estimating
- Story Points
- Wideband Delphi
- Affinity Estimating
- Monte Carlo Method
- Agile Analysis and Design

Agile Contracts

CAPE PROJECT
MANAGEMENT, INC.

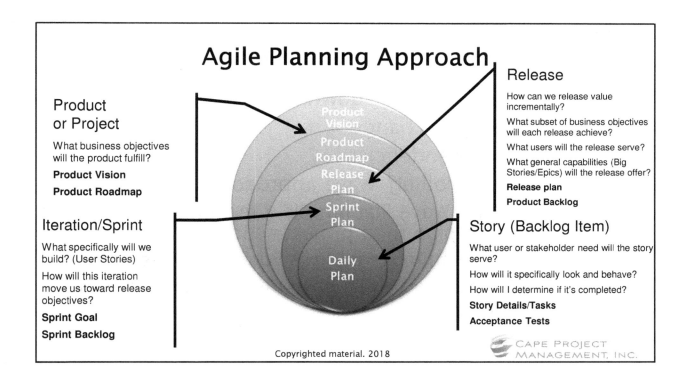

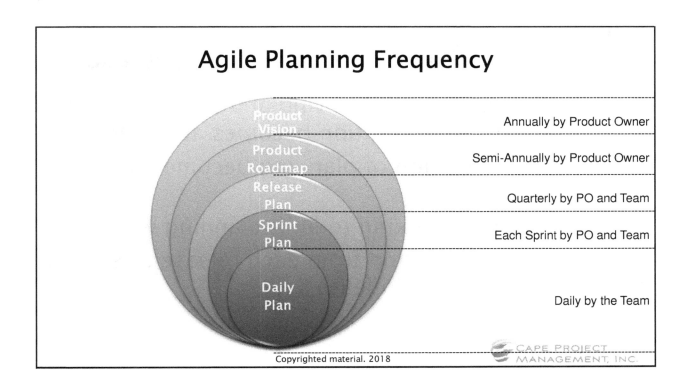

Agile Plans

- ☐ Typically are top-down
- ☐ Are easy to change
- ☐ Limit dependencies
- ☐ Follow a rolling-wave approach
  - ◘ Rolling Wave Planning is a technique that enables you to plan for a project as it unfolds.
  - ◘ This technique requires you to plan iteratively.
  - ◘ You plan until you have more visibility and then re-plan.

Copyrighted material. 2018

Agile Planning: Progressive Elaboration

- ☐ Continuously improving and detailing a plan as more information becomes available
- ☐ Each iteration of planning becomes more accurate
- ☐ Use time-boxing to limit planning window
- ☐ Use information from each release to support plan for next release

Copyrighted material. 2018

Agile Planning

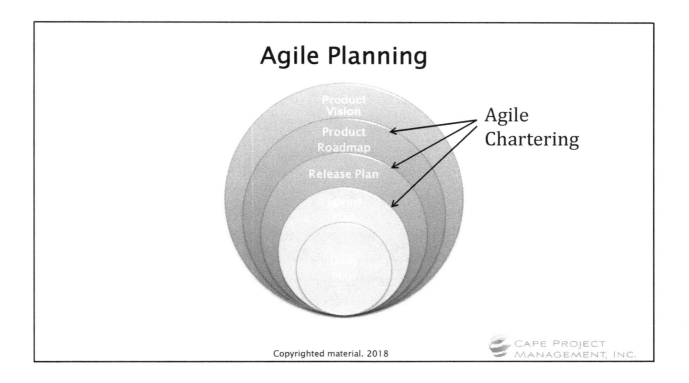

Agile Chartering

Copyrighted material. 2018

Developing a Vision

- ☐ The product vision is key to the success of the project.
- ☐ The product vision should align with the company vision.
- ☐ The vision should be revisited frequently.
- ☐ All releases of the product should related back to the vision.

Copyrighted material. 2018

Effective Vision Statements

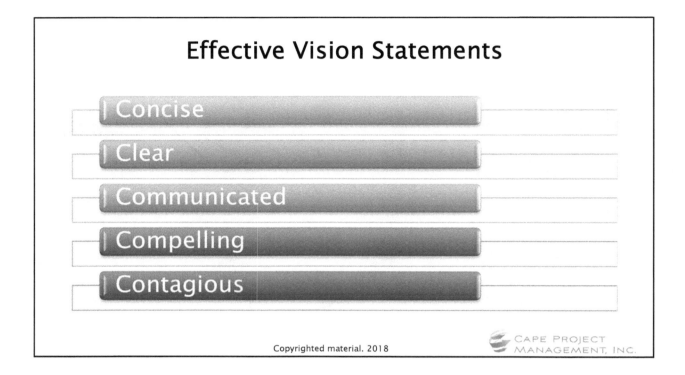

Concise

Clear

Communicated

Compelling

Contagious

CAPE PROJECT
MANAGEMENT, INC.

Effective Vision Statements

- **Concise:** An effective vision statement must be short and simple so it can be understood and articulated by everyone in the organization.
- **Clear:** Lack of clarity may be the single greatest failure of a healthy vision.
- **Communicated:** A vision statement can be concise and clear, but unless it is communicated well, it has little power.
- **Compelling:** You should be able to see clearly in the vision statement something that will naturally move people toward greater commitment and decisive actions.
- **Contagious:** The vision statement should be something that makes the organization proud.

CAPE PROJECT
MANAGEMENT, INC.

Effective Vision Statements

"To be the world's most customer-centric company."

"Making the best possible ice cream, in the nicest possible way"

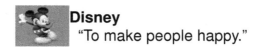

"Give customers the freshest, highest quality foods you can buy and provide them with friendly service in a sparkling clean environment."

Disney
"To make people happy."

Company Vision vs. Product Vision

Company Vision

□ Our goal is to make learning more desirable, accessible, and meaningful for learners. By doing this, we have a shared sense of purpose with teachers, administrators, and leaders at all levels that are working to improve outcomes for learners.

Product Vision

□ The Learning Management System (LMS) will enhance the educational experience by giving students and educators more ways to stay engaged online – both in and outside of the classroom. It will give students and faculty access to their courses, content, and grading and will allow them to participate in an online learning community on their desktop and variety of mobile devices.

Product Roadmap

- A roadmap is a planned future, laid out in broad strokes
  - Planned or proposed product releases, listing high level functionality or release themes, laid out in rough timeframes
  - Usually the target calendar or fiscal quarter
  - For a period usually extending for 2 or 3 significant feature releases into the future

Copyrighted material. 2018

 CAPE PROJECT MANAGEMENT, INC.

Product Roadmap Example

	June	July	August	September	October	November
Platform	Installation	Single User / Multi User			Mobile	
Courses	Public Listing		Course Selection	Course Add/Drop		
Grading			View Grades	Manage Grades		
Discussion Groups				Public Groups	Course Groups	
Student Profiles					Student Clubs	

Copyrighted material. 2018

CAPE PROJECT MANAGEMENT, INC.

A Product Roadmap

- High level themes for the next few releases
- Shows progress towards strategy
- Lots of "wiggle room"
- Example:
    1. Implement course listing functionality
    2. Implement grading functionality
    3. Implement discussion groups
    4. Implement student profiles

Agile Artifact Hierarchy

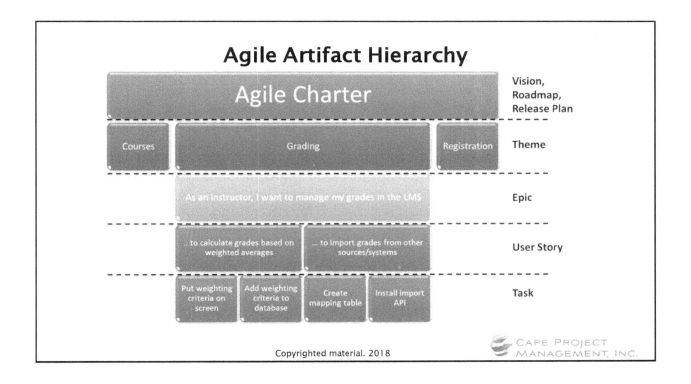

Backlog Management

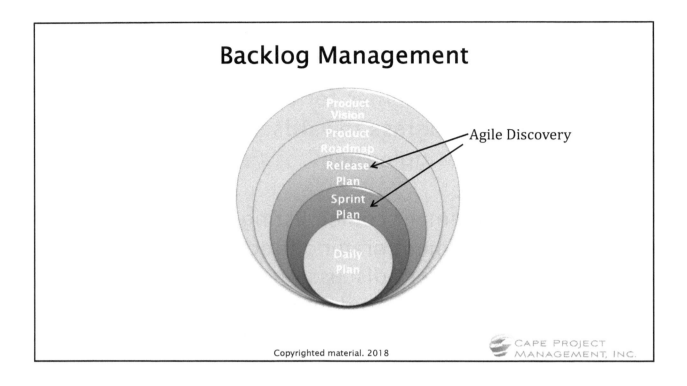

Agile Discovery

Agile Discovery

- **Desired Business Outcomes**: Document outcomes that are quantifiable and measurable.

- **High Level Architecture**: Outline a plan for the technical and business architecture/design of the solution.

- **High Level Delivery Plan**: Segment the solution into the smallest minimum viable products that realize the desired outcomes and sets out the order in which they are to be delivered.

- **Product Backlog**: Create an evolving prioritized list of all items of work which may be relevant to the solution.

- **Governance Approach**: Describe essential governance and organization aspects of the project and how the project will be managed.

- **High-Level Budget**: Create a project budget and release budget to support resource planning and scheduling.

Release Options

- Organized around business value
- Internal release versus external release
- Daily builds and continuous integration versus planned release schedule

Organize Backlog by Release

1. Identify features
2. Prioritize features
3. Split features using the MMF perspective
4. Estimate the value of the features
5. Estimate the cost of the features
6. Write stories for features
7. Create release plan by date or scope
8. Refine/groom backlog

http://www.netobjectives.com/files/Lean-AgileReleasePlanning.pdf

A Product Release Plan

- Goes into next level of detail
- Sets a common understanding
- A projection, not a commitment
- Example:
  - Release 1:
    - LMS Installed with pilot group logins validated
    - Pilot with 3 faculty and 60 students
    - Course listings available
  - Release 2:
    - Incorporate pilot feedback
    - Enable College of Engineering faculty and students
    - Implement course selection on-line
  - Release 3:
    - ...

CAPE PROJECT
MANAGEMENT, INC.

Agile Analysis and Design

What is Agile Analysis?
- Understand what will be built.
- Understand why it should be built.
- Determine how much it will likely cost to build (estimation).
- Determine in what order it should be built (prioritization).

What Agile Analysis isn't:
- It isn't a phase in the lifecycle of your project.
- It isn't a task on your project schedule.
- It isn't a means unto itself.

CAPE PROJECT
MANAGEMENT, INC.

Agile Analysis and Design

- **A highly evolutionary and collaborative process**: Developers and project stakeholders actively work together on a just-in-time (JIT) basis.
- **Communication rich**: Agile teams prefer communication techniques such as face-to-face discussion and video conferencing over documentation and email.
- **Highly iterative**: Analysis and design activities rely on each other: estimating is part of analysis and it relies on some design being performed.
- **Incremental**: The analysis work is broken done into small, achievable "chunks" of functionality.

http://agilemodeling.com/essays/agileAnalysis.htm

Copyrighted material. 2018

Agile Analysis and Design

Explores the problem statement:
- The goal is to identify and understand what your project stakeholders need of your system.

High level estimation and prioritization of requirements:
- It is during estimation and prioritization of requirements where software development becomes "real" for project stakeholders.

Artifacts are just "good enough":
- If any artifacts are created at all as the result of your agile analysis they should be lightweight.

http://agilemodeling.com/essays/agileAnalysis.htm

Copyrighted material. 2018

Backlog Refinement (Grooming)

The team and the Product Owner meet regularly to "groom the product backlog", in a formal or informal meeting which can lead to any of the following:

- Removing user stories that no longer appear relevant
- Creating new user stories in response to newly discovered needs
- Re-assessing the relative priority of stories
- Assigning estimates to stories which have yet to receive one
- Correcting estimates in light of newly discovered information
- Splitting user stories which are high priority but too coarse grained to fit in an upcoming iteration

Copyrighted material. 2018

Backlog Refinement

Refining stories in preparation for iteration planning

- Just in time refinement for flow-based Agile
- 1 hour per 2 week iteration – more than that could be considered overpreparing, meaning the team is spending too much time planning versus doing
- Multiple refinements until PO is satisfied

Copyrighted material. 2018

Types of Backlog Refinement

With Stakeholders:

☐ Prior to Sprint Planning meetings, the Product Owner collaborates with stakeholders to refine requirements for backlog items (usually focusing on ones that will be implemented soon, "just in time") and will adjust priorities according to business value.

With the Team:

☐ The Product Owner holds a standing meetings weekly to refine backlog items.

☐ 90% of this meeting is usually spent refining the items for the next sprint.

The "triad" Approach:

☐ A developer, tester and analyst get together and refine the backlog

Informally:

☐ The Product Owner will refine stories and their order in the backlog almost daily. This work may or may not include development team members.

CAPE PROJECT MANAGEMENT, INC.

Agile Estimation Goals

80% Accuracy with 20% Effort

Reduce Stress

Assist Planning

Allow for transparency

CAPE PROJECT MANAGEMENT, INC.

Agile Sizing and Estimating

□ Assumes all traditional estimates are inaccurate.

□ Focuses on rapid order of magnitude estimating.

□ There are two main components of Agile Estimating:

▪ **Estimation of Size**: A high-level estimate for each work item based upon the complexity is created using a neutral unit of measurement called "Story Points." Size is always estimated relative to other stories.

▪ **Estimation of Effort**: The amount of work that can be accomplished in a Sprint based upon the capacity and effort determines the Velocity of the team.

Copyrighted material. 2018

CAPE PROJECT
MANAGEMENT, INC.

Estimating and Sizing Techniques

□ Story points

□ Planning poker

□ T-Shirt Sizes

□ Fibonacci Sequence

□ Relative Estimating

□ Affinity Estimating

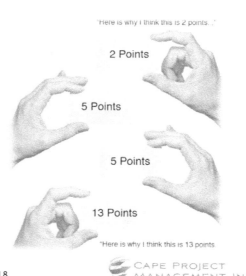

"Here is why I think this is 2 points..."

2 Points

5 Points

5 Points

13 Points

"Here is why I think this is 13 points..."

Copyrighted material. 2018

CAPE PROJECT
MANAGEMENT, INC.

Relative Estimating using Story Points

- Story Point Relative Estimation uses a "unit-less" number to estimate user stories by grouping requirements based on equivalent difficulty.

- In simple terms, it is a way of sizing user stories relative to each other. This technique, sometimes called Triangulation.

- A story point is an arbitrary measure of effort required to implement a user story.

- It's a number that tells the team how hard the story is. "Hard" can be related to complexity, unknowns, and/or effort.

Why use Story Points

- **Quick**: Rather, the goal is to quickly estimate a level of effort, and you can do it much faster than you can when using traditional estimating approaches.

- **Accurate**: By grooming the backlog, you resize and develop quick estimates of effort in an Agile manner. The rough classifications of story point relative estimation are a more accurate and flexible way to determine priorities and schedule.

- **Improves Over Time**: Over time, you can look at how many points your team typically completes within a sprint, and become better and better at relative estimating.

- **Project-Specific**: It's nearly impossible to predict an exact amount of hours for any given story, because hours are relative numbers. Creating a User Story benchmark for a project allows you to attain a more accurate picture of velocity.

Benchmarking

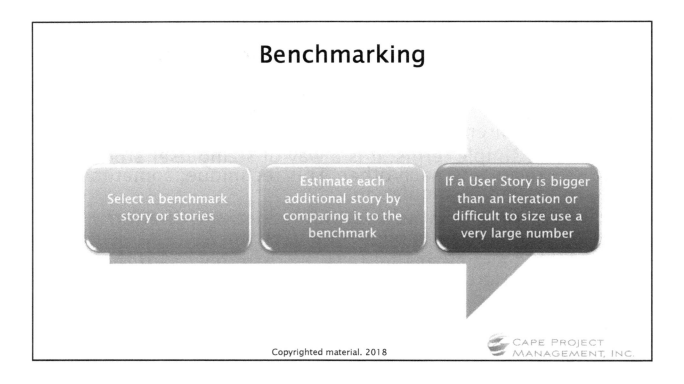

Select a benchmark story or stories

Estimate each additional story by comparing it to the benchmark

If a User Story is bigger than an iteration or difficult to size use a very large number

CAPE PROJECT
MANAGEMENT, INC.

Sizing Using Hours versus Points

- □ A Story point is a universal measurement across the team. It is not biased by the experience or skills or any individual on the team.
- □ After the 3rd or 4th sprint, the team reaches a rhythm and it becomes easier for the team to quickly estimate the product backlog.
- □ Mike Cohn* is big on breaking User Stories down into tasks, which are then estimated in hours.
- □ Mature teams can back into the hours once they have a stable velocity. This is key for budgeting release and contracting with customers.
- □ No "right" answer, just be consistent.

*Author of Use Stories Applied, 2004

CAPE PROJECT
MANAGEMENT, INC.

Agile Estimating

Ideal Time:
- "Perfect World" estimation approach for a user story to be completed
- Excludes non-programming time
- Assumes no interruptions

Elapsed Time:
- Actual time for user story to be completed
- Historical input into better estimates
- Key to Velocity calculation
- Same as calendar time

Copyrighted material. 2018

Part-Time Resources (Fractional Assignments)

- All of the team members should sit with the team full-time and give the project their complete attention.

- Difficult to estimate when team members aren't full-time.

- Fractional team members see an overall 15% reduction in productivity.

http://www.jamesshore.com/Agile-Book/the_xp_team.html

Copyrighted material. 2018

Planning Poker®

- ☐ Each card represents a size of User Story
- ☐ Everyone should agree on what an average size story is and give it a benchmark of 6
- ☐ Each story is given a card/size
- ☐ Play poker on each story until the variance is 1
- ☐ Choose the higher number for the Sprint plan
- ☐ If a User Story is bigger than an iteration or difficult to size use 15, 20, 25, 50 for Jack, Queen, King, Ace (Epic)

CAPE PROJECT MANAGEMENT, INC.

T-Shirt Sizes

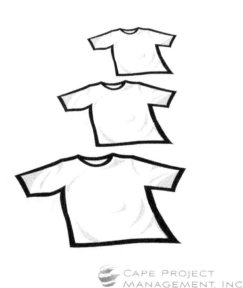

- ☐ Small, Medium, Large, X-Large, XX-Large
  - ☐ 1,2,4,8,16 Story Points
- ☐ Find your smallest story and give it a 1
- ☐ Use cards to estimate
  - ☐ Similar to planning poker

CAPE PROJECT MANAGEMENT, INC.

Fibonacci Sequence

- 0 1 1 2 3 5 8 13 21 34 55...
- Provides more flexibility for unknown larger stories
- Find your smallest story and give it a 1
- Limit the largest number
- Use index cards and estimate
  - similar to planning poker

Copyrighted material. 2018

CAPE PROJECT
MANAGEMENT, INC.

Relative Estimating

- Order each user story from easiest to hardest
- Estimate Stories relative to other User Stories
  - Use one of the Estimating Techniques to Size the Story
- Assign Story estimation units: 1,2,3,5,8,13...
  - Simplest Story = 1 effort unit
  - Hardest Story = 13 effort unit
  - Or impossible

Copyrighted material. 2018

CAPE PROJECT
MANAGEMENT, INC.

Affinity Estimating

☐ Facilitated process

☐ Each team member sequences a subset of the product backlog from smallest to largest user story

☐ The rest of the team validates and sequences as a group

☐ Bucket the user stories by a sizing method such as t-shirt size or Fibonacci sequence

Copyrighted material. 2018

Wideband Delphi Estimating

A consensus-based technique for estimating effort:

1. Review and clarify user stories among the team

2. Each team member creates an anonymous estimate

3. Summarize estimates and distribute

4. Focus on major variances and repeat #2

5. Repeat until variance is minimal

Copyrighted material. 2018

Monte Carlo Method

☐ Useful when not enough historical data

☐ One techniques is to assign best case and worst case effort based upon Fibonacci sequence

☐ A computer simulation generates random inputs up to 500 times to calculate probability

CAPE PROJECT MANAGEMENT, INC.

Sprint Planning

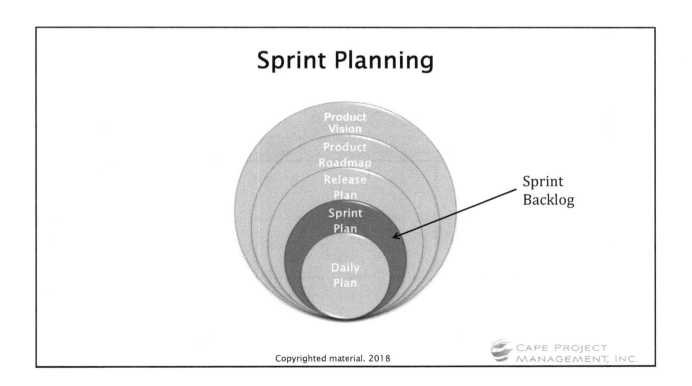

Sprint Backlog

CAPE PROJECT MANAGEMENT, INC.

Sprint Backlog

- Created at Sprint Planning Meeting
- Stories are selected based upon priority, size, and velocity
- Sprint Planning should proceed quickly if release planning and backlog refinement occur
- All User Stories must meet the definition of "Ready"
- Tasks are created for each User Story by the Development Team
- Tasks can be added throughout the Sprint

Copyrighted material. 2018

Sprint Backlog Planning

Priority \ Size	SMALL	MED	LARGE	X-Large
High				
Medium				
Low				

Copyrighted material. 2018

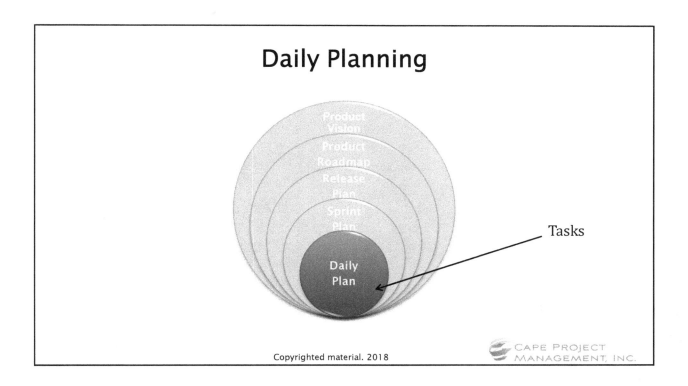

Daily Planning

Tasks

Create User Story Tasks

- In Sprint Planning, the team decomposes User Stories into tasks as a team
- Daily, team members update the tasks on the User Stories
- Best practices:
  - Attempt to size your tasks to take one team member between 4 hours to 2 days to complete
  - Create tasks that result in a deliverable unit of work when completed
  - Don't get caught deep diving into the details of each task
  - Ensure testing/automation tasks are included

Create User Story Tasks

User Story	Tasks
As a student, I want to be able to log in to the system	Code the...
	Design the...
	Meet with customer
	Design the UI
	Automate Tests
	Code the other...
As a faculty member, I want to update my contact information	Copy admin profile
	Design solution to...
	Write a test plan
	Automate tests
	Code the...

Copyrighted material. 2018

Sprint Zero Goals

□ The idea is simple: take an initial Sprint (called Sprint Zero, Iteration Zero, Inception Sprint, etc.) that has the following three goals:

1. Get some quality items on the Product Backlog,
2. Provide a minimal environment that enables the writing of quality code, and
3. Write a piece of real code, no matter how small.

Copyrighted material. 2018

Agile Contracting

"Customer collaboration over contract negotiation"

How to be Agile is an area that is typically not very Agile:

☐ Contract Models

☐ Pricing Models

☐ Delivery Approaches

CAPE PROJECT
MANAGEMENT, INC.

Comparison of Contract Model

Traditional Contract Model	Agile Contract Model
The requirements are contractual and specified upfront.	All items of work relevant to the solution are added to the product backlog which is not contractual and which evolves.
Changes 'controlled' by means of the change control mechanism.	Change is accommodated within the non-contractual product backlog.
Analysis, design, development and testing occur sequentially.	There is concurrent design and development.
An all-or-nothing solution.	The solution is broken down into solution increments.
Constituent 'modules' of software are worked on independently until integration takes place.	A continuous working and stable software system.
Testing is used as a contractual tool.	Testing performs many roles and is an integral part of the development process.
Success is measured by reference to conformance with the plans.	Success is measured by reference to the realization of the desired business outcomes and therefore deliver value.

CAPE PROJECT
MANAGEMENT, INC.

Comparison of Risk Profiles

Traditional Contract Model	Agile Contract Model
Customer is committed financially to entire project.	Financial commitment initially to Discovery only and then on a Release by Release basis.
No value delivered until the entire project (i.e. all of the requirements) has been completed.	Value delivered at the end of every Sprint.
No end-to-end system created until the end of the development project i.e. integration doesn't happen until just before testing.	End-to-end and fully working system delivered at end of first Sprint, and this continues to grow with each Sprint.
If the project is going awry the customer generally won't know until testing at the end of the project.	If the project is going awry, the customer should detect it during Discovery or at the end of every Sprint.
There is no attempt to control the order in which the requirements are tackled.	The highest risk and highest value items are tackled first.

Agile Contracting Pricing Models

□ Multi-tiered structure: Formal master contract with warranties, etc. but lightweight statement of work to address a dynamic scope, schedule and budge.

□ Value delivered: Payments made upon value-driven deliverables

□ Fixed Price Increments: Pay per epic, feature or group of user stories.

□ Not to Exceed T&M: Place a cap on cost

□ Graduated T&M: Rate increase if delivery is early.

□ Early Cancellation: Limit budget exposure

□ Dynamic Scope: Adjust features to capacity and timing, "Pay for Points" contracting

□ Team Augmentation: Highly collaborative T&M model

Agile Contracting Considerations

- **Time & materials** for duration of release
  - Risk: budget not fixed and little incentive for supplier to be efficient
  - Better solution: Capped Time and Materials that provides some protection for the customer
- **Fixed price** per agreed unit of effort or per release
  - Risk: less collaborative; reduces opportunity for continuous improvement
- **Incentive based** for mutually agreed upon units of work delivered before Completion Date or more than agreed units of work delivered by Completion Date
  - Risk: may increase technical debt

ONLINE ACTIVITY

Module 6 Knowledge Check

Take a 25 question practice exam to test your understanding of the Adaptive Planning.

Module 6 Knowledge Check

Questions

1. Match the contract types on the left to the terms on right:

Correct	Choice
Value delivered:	Rate increase if delivery is early
Fixed Price Increments:	Adjust features to capacity and timing, "Pay for Points" contracting
Not to Exceed T&M:	Highly collaborative T&M model
Graduated T&M:	Pay per epic, feature or group of user stories.
Dynamic Scope:	Place a cap on cost
Team Augmentation:	Payments made upon value-driven deliverables

2. What is a product roadmap?

Correct	Choice
	A list of reports and screens
	A view of release candidates
	Instructions for deployment
	A backlog prioritization scheme

3. In Backlog refinement, a "triad" is referring to:

Correct	Choice
	The Product Owner, tester and analyst
	A developer, tester and analyst
	The Scrum Master developer and tester
	A developer, analyst and Product Owner

4. Which of these statements is NOT correct about Ideal time and Elapsed time?

Correct	Choice
	Ideal time is the time that is actually required to complete the work without any interruptions
	Elapsed time is the amount of time that passes on clock (calendar days)
	Both of them convey the same meaning
	Normally elapsed days are not equal to ideal days

5. Which of the following is not part of Agile Discovery?

Correct	Choice
	Document business outcomes that are quantifiable and measurable
	Define the tasks that the team will perform during an iteration
	Outline a plan for the technical and business architecture/design of the solution
	Describe essential governance and organization aspects of the project and how the project will be managed

6. Agile Analysis is a phase in the lifecycle of an Agile project.

Correct	Choice
	True
	False

7. Pick the three statements that are true about Agile Analysis.

Correct	Choice
	It is a highly evolutionary and collaborative process
	It occurs at the beginning and end of a project
	It is communication rich
	It only includes the project team
	It explores the problem statement

8. It is not possible to have a fixed price contract in Agile.

Correct	Choice
	True
	False

9. Match the traditional contract model of the left with the Agile alternative on the right.

Correct	Choice
Changes 'controlled' by means of the change control mechanism.	Success is measured by reference to the realization of the desired business outcomes.
Analysis, design, development and testing occur sequentially.	Value delivered at the end of every Sprint.
Success is measured by reference to conformance with the plans.	The highest risk and highest value items are tackled first.
No value delivered until the entire project has been completed.	Change is accommodated within the non-contractual product backlog.
There is no attempt to control the order in which the requirements are tackled.	There is concurrent design and development.

10. What is the name of this facilitated process? One or more team members sequence the product backlog from smallest to largest User Story. The rest of the team validates the sequence. The whole team uses a sizing method such as T-shirt size or Fibonacci sequence to group the user stories.

Correct	Choice
	Relative estimation
	Pairwise comparison
	Planning Poker
	Affinity estimating

11. What Agile planning artifact is updated minimally once a year by the Product Owner?

Correct	Choice
	Product Vision
	Product Roadmap
	Release Plan
	Sprint Plan
	Daily Plan

12. What is the order the hierarchy of product definition?

Correct Order?
Epic
Product Roadmap
Product Vision
Task
Theme
User Story

13. Wideband Delphi is used by an Agile Project manager to support what activity?

Correct	Choice
	Prioritization
	Scheduling
	Estimation
	Risk Management

14. Which Agile estimation technique is based upon relative sizing?

Correct	Choice
	Ideal time
	Bottom up
	Story points
	Little's Law

15. What Agile planning artifact should be updated at minimum semi-annually?

Correct	Choice
	Product Vision
	Product Roadmap
	Release Plan
	Sprint Plan
	Daily Plan

16. Which is the process of continuously improving and detailing a plan as more detailed and specific information and more accurate estimates become available as the project progresses?

Correct	Choice
	Process Tailoring
	Pareto Analysis
	Progressive Elaboration
	Open Space Planning

17. Product roadmaps are more accurate the closer we get to an actual release.

Correct	Choice
	True
	False

18. What Agile planning artifact is created by the Product Owner and the development team?

Correct	Choice
	Product Vision
	Product Roadmap
	Release Plan
	Sprint Plan
	Daily Plan

19. When is Planning Poker used?

Correct	Choice
	During backlog prioritization
	As part of Pareto Analysis
	During User Story sizing and estimating
	As part of the Daily Stand-up

20. What is the correct sequence of activities in release planning?

Correct Order
Create release plan by date or scope
Estimate the cost of the features
Estimate the value of the features
Identify features
Prioritize features
Split features using the MMF perspective
Write stories for features

21. What type of time estimation excludes non-programming time?

Correct	Choice
	Ideal Time
	Elapsed time
	Duration
	Real Time

22. While managing the Agile Product Lifecycle, match the frequency with which you update the five Agile plans.

Correct	Choice
Product Vision	Quarterly by the Product Owner and teams
Product Roadmap	Each iteration by the team
Release Plan	Daily by the individual
Sprint Plan	Semi-Annually by The Product Owner
Daily Plan (Scrum)	Annually by Product Owner

23. Which of the following is NOT a characteristic of an Agile plan?

Correct	Choice
	Follows rolling wave planning approach
	Are top down
	Easy to change
	Shows dependencies of one task to others

24. _____ an estimate refers to estimating a story based on its relationship to one or more other stories.

Correct	Choice
	Triangulating
	Triaging
	Aggregating
	Disaggregating

25. Which of the following is NOT recognized as a "unit" that can be used for estimating the size of the requirements on your Agile project?

Correct	Choice
	Elapsed time
	Relative size
	Ideal time
	Ideal size

26. In what activity do the following steps occur:

Removing user stories that no longer appear relevant

Creating new user stories in response to newly discovered needs

Re-assessing the relative priority of stories

Correct	Choice
	Backlog Grooming
	Progressive Elaboration
	Sprint Planning
	User Story Mapping

27. Agile uses a number sequence for estimating. The series of numbers all begin with 0, 1, 1 and are calculated by adding the previous two numbers to get the next number. This number sequence is called:

Correct	Choice
	Sashimi
	Velocity
	Capacity
	Fibonacci

28. Team members who are part-time on your project will see at least a 15% reduction in their productivity per hour. The type of resource model in Agile is called:

Correct	Choice
	Collocated
	Fractional assignments
	Distributed resources
	Over-allocated resources

Problem Detection and Resolution

All About Agile: Module 7

Version 4.0

Problem Detection and Resolution

Risk Management

- Risk Identification

- Risk Analysis

- Risk Prioritization

- Risk Management Planning

- Risk Resolution

- Risk Monitoring

Quality Management

- Technical Debt

- Escaped Defects

- Hardening Iterations

- Definition of "Done"

- Continuous Integration

- Frequent Verification And Validation

- Acceptance Test Driven Development

- Test-driven Development/Test First Development

Risk Management in Agile

- Agile mitigates the most commons project risks:
    1. Intrinsic Schedule Flaw
    2. Specification Breakdown
    3. Scope Creep
    4. Personnel Loss
    5. Productivity Variance
- Risk management in Agile is "organic" since risk is addressed naturally as part of the project lifecycle.
- Qualitative risk analysis if preferred over traditional quantitative risk analysis to identify risk on Agile projects

Copyrighted material. 2018

Risk Management in Agile

- Risk identification – make a list of the risks that threaten the project
- Risk analysis – assess the likelihood and impact of each risk
- Risk prioritization – identify the significant risks based on likelihood and impact
- Risk-management planning – plan how to deal with each significant risk
- Risk resolution – execute the plan, i.e. deal with each significant risk
- Risk monitoring – monitor execution of the plans to deal with each significant risk and continue with risk identification

http://itsadeliverything.com/agile-risk-management

Copyrighted material. 2018

Risk Identification

- Risk identification is about making a list of the risks that threaten the project – the risk log.
- The daily meeting (whether Stand Up or Scrum) highlights impediments to the project – either risks or issues. Many of these can be dealt with by the team immediately.
- The collaborative nature of Agile estimating means there is more likelihood of identifying risky elements at the start.
- The empirical nature of Agile planning ensures capacity (i.e. velocity) is continuously recalibrated and so threats to the scheduled highlighted early.

Risk Analysis & Prioritization

- Identify the significant risks.
- Calculate the risk exposure by multiplying the likelihood (scale of 1–3) by the impact (also a scale of 1–3); this results in a value from 1–9.
- Any risk with a risk exposure of 6–9 is a significant risk that you need to manage.
- Risks with a risk exposure of 1–5 are not worth managing.
- You can also capture this approach in a Risk Heat Map.

Risk Heat Maps

- Post all risks on the heat map.
- The vertical axis represents the probability of a given risk occurring.
- Horizontal axis depicts the impact that the risk will have on the project or program should it materialize.
- If all the risks are clustered in the top right of the diagram then it is a very risky program or project.

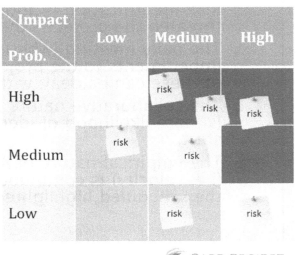

Risk Management Planning

Traditional Techniques

- **Accept**: Accepting the loss when it occurs. Only do this if the cost of addressing the risk is greater than the impact of the risk
- **Avoid**: Avoid the risk by not doing the activity that carries the risk
- **Mitigate**: Any method that reduces the impact or likelihood of the risk, hence the risk exposure
- **Transfer**: Get somebody else to accept the risk
- **Contingency**: Create a plan if the risk occurs

Risk Management Planning

Agile Techniques:

- The collaborative nature of an Agile team means that the team can share responsibility for resolving a particular risk.
- Agile often dictates bringing risky requirements forward in the schedule through the use of a Risk-Adjusted Backlog to provide more time to assess the risk of the item and to identify feasible solutions.
- Agile also promotes the idea of investigating risky requirements. Whether called a feasibility prototype (DSDM) or a Spike (XP).

Copyrighted material. 2018

Risk-Based Spike

- User Story created to address risk
- Purpose:
  - Familiarize the team with a new technology
  - Analyze the size of story
  - Create a prototype to validate assumptions
  - Test a technical risk

Copyrighted material. 2018

Risk Resolution

☐ Risk resolution means executing the risk-management plan, i.e. deal with each significant risk.

☐ If the Agile team has to do anything to resolve the risk then it has to be part of the "work".

☐ All work for Risk Resolution appears either on the product backlog as requirements and/or as tasks within User Stories.

Risk Monitoring

☐ The team must continue to monitor the risk-management plan dealing with each significant risk.

☐ Also monitor risk-management plan for risks that are being dealt with outside the Agile team.

☐ Techniques for monitoring risks include the Risk Burndown chart or graph.

Risk Burndown Chart

☐ Use the total risk exposure number and reduce it within the Sprint that each risk will be addressed.

☐ Plot the forecast and actual on a burndown chart as they are completed.

Risk Burndown Chart

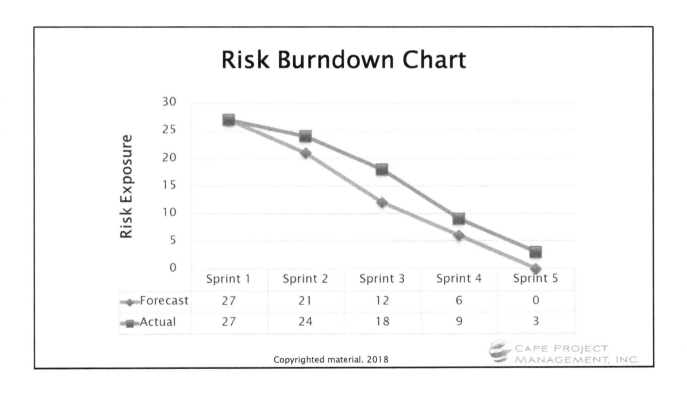

	Sprint 1	Sprint 2	Sprint 3	Sprint 4	Sprint 5
Forecast	27	21	12	6	0
Actual	27	24	18	9	3

Risk Burndown Graph

☐ Identify risks at the beginning of project

☐ Determine Probability and Impact

☐ Total score for all risks

☐ Update every Sprint

☐ At-a-glance view of reduction in risk

Risk Burndown Graph

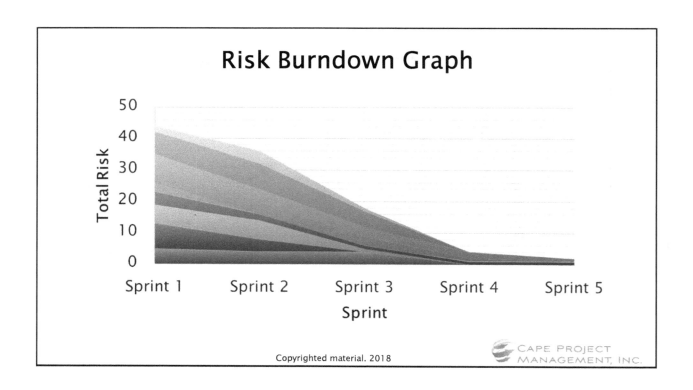

Quality Control in Agile

- □ Technical debt is more prevalent
- □ Continuous improvement is needed, similar to Six Sigma approach
- □ Inspect and adapt is critical
- □ Quality Assurance is not necessarily a separate role
- □ Product Owner is the single owner of quality decisions
- □ Focus is on business value

Technical Debt

- □ Development decisions made in the short term which cause more work in the long-term
- □ Not necessarily apparent to the user
- □ Difficult to measure because the code meets test cases and is not a defect
- □ Major challenge of Agile
- □ The higher the technical debt means the lower the intrinsic quality of the product

Intrinsic versus Extrinsic Quality

Intrinsic Quality:

☐ All of the qualities that were built into the product: suitability, durability, reliability, uniformity, maintainability.

Extrinsic Quality:

☐ Perceived quality

☐ Value to the customer

Technical Debt

Reckless	Prudent
"We don't have time for design"	*"We will have to ship and deal with consequences"*
Deliberate	
Inadvertent	
"I thought this was just a Proof of Concept"	*"Now we know how we should have built it"*

Escaped Defects

- Metric identifying defects that made it into production
- Add to product backlog and prioritize in the next two Sprints
- Treat as typical backlog items in Sprint
- Indicates:
  - Inaccurate velocity: team is taking on too much work
  - The team is operating as a "mini-waterfall" project
- Reduce velocity until the escaping defects metric is reduced

Hardening Iterations

- Final exploratory and field testing
- Checklist validation against release, QA and standards governance
- Release signoffs if you need them
- Create operations and support documentation
- Create a deployment package
- Communicate release to everyone
- Show traceability for regulatory compliance

Also called a "Tail". A long tail reflects broken Agile processes and an incomplete definition of done.

The Definition of Done?

- "The Definition of Done (DoD) as a tool for bringing transparency to the work a Scrum Team is performing. It is related more to the quality of a product, rather than its functionality." ~Scrum Guide
- Defined by Product Owner and Team and updated every Sprint
- Considerations
  - Quality Metrics
  - Coding standards
  - Test coverage
  - Integration testing
  - Documented (just *enough)*
- Risks of unclear definition
  - Inaccurate Velocity
  - Technical debt
- 0/100% Rule

https://www.scrum.org/Resources/Scrum-Glossary/Definition-of-Done

CAPE PROJECT
MANAGEMENT, INC.

Continuous Integration

- Fully automated build and test process
- Allows the team to build and test software many times a day
- XP rule – minimum daily builds
- Eliminates siloed approach to development
- Raises defects immediately
- Creates high-quality code

CAPE PROJECT
MANAGEMENT, INC.

Continuous Integration

Dependencies:
- Maintain a single source code repository
- Automate the build process
- Automate the testing
- Commit as a team to frequent builds
- Develop accurate version control
- Ensure test environment is true mirror of production

Frequent Verification and Validation (V&V)

- V&V occurs minimally every iteration
- Requirements and design:
  - V&V is the result of peer reviews with team members and with the customer
- For coding:
  - V&V is done through code reviews, unit testing and functional testing

Validation

☐ Did I build the right product?

☐ Does it meet the needs of the user and the organization?

☐ Am I accessing the right data?

☐ Am I able to work in the right environment?

☐ Did I satisfy the requirements?

Verification

☐ Did I build the product right?

☐ Am I meeting quality and coding standards?

☐ Am I avoiding technical debt?

☐ Am I accessing the data right in the right place in the right way?

☐ Did I test throughout development and have I allowed for feedback?

☐ What quality was measured throughout the life cycle?

Test-driven Development (TDD)

- □ Test first development that includes continuous design
- □ Assumes a design as-you-go approach
- □ Write automated test
- □ Run the test
- □ Build the code
- □ Run the test
- □ Refactor
- □ Repeat

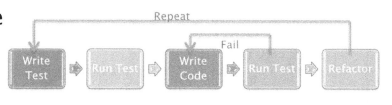

CAPE PROJECT
MANAGEMENT, INC.

Refactoring

Refactoring, as originally defined by Martin Fowler and Kent Beck, is: "A change made to the internal structure of software to make it easier to understand and cheaper to modify without changing its observable behavior."

Refactoring is performed:
- □ To fill in short-cuts
- □ To eliminate duplication and dead code
- □ To make the design and logic clear
- □ To make better and clearer use of the programming language
- □ To simplify the code and to make it easier to understand
- □ To make it easier and safer to change in the future

CAPE PROJECT
MANAGEMENT, INC.

Test-Driven Development

Benefits:

- Reduces the number of bugs by orders of magnitude
- Increases development speed, because less time is spent chasing bugs
- Improves code quality because of the increased modularity, and continuous and relentless refactoring
- Decreases maintenance costs because the code is easier to follow

Copyrighted material. 2018

CAPE PROJECT
MANAGEMENT, INC.

Acceptance Test Driven Development

- Discuss the Requirements: Solicit acceptance criteria from stakeholders
- Distill Tests: Modify the test plans to fit in automated testing framework
- Develop the Code: Connect the test to the code
- Implementing Code: Run the tests against the code
- Demo the tests: Use exploratory testing to try new scenarios

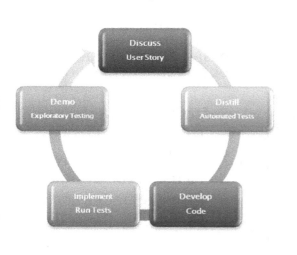

Copyrighted material. 2018

CAPE PROJECT
MANAGEMENT, INC.

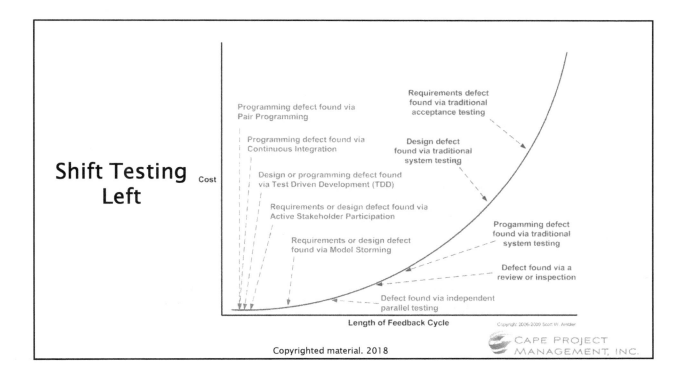

Exploratory Testing

- Unscripted testing where testers generally explore the application's functionality without restraint
- Encourage testers to plan as they test and to use information gathered during testing to affect the actual way testing is performed
- Often occurs after the iteration in the period between "done" and "done-done."
- Always performed in conjunction with traditional testing

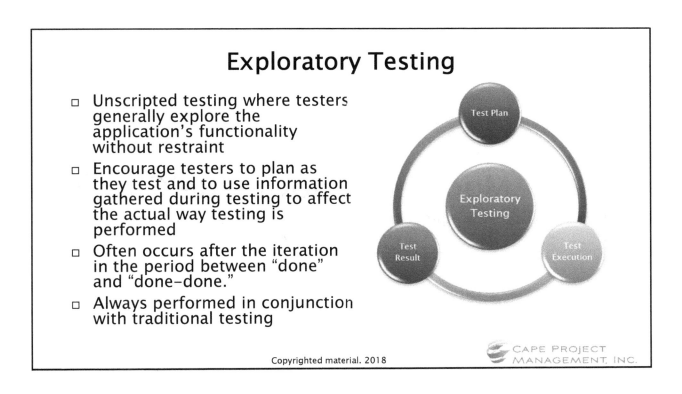

Benefits of Agile Testing

- On-going feedback to developers allows testers to ask the right questions at the right time.
- Early identification of dependencies, technical or testing challenges and roadblocks.
- Embraces change as a healthy and real part of software development.
- Team collaboration helps everyone work together toward a common goal.
- Quality comes first because final acceptance criteria are established prior to the work beginning.

Copyrighted material. 2018

ONLINE ACTIVITY

Module 7 Knowledge Check

Take a 20 question practice exam to test your understanding of Problem Detection and Resolution.

Copyrighted material. 2018

Module 7 Knowledge Check

Answers

1. When implementing Agile Project Management, risk management that occurs simply by following Agile best practices such as iterative planning and review activities is called:

Correct	Choice
	Adaptive risk management
	Intrinsic risk management
	Inherent risk management
	Organic risk management

2. Which statement is least accurate when providing a definition of "Done"?

Correct	Choice
	It is the exit criteria to determine whether a product backlog item is complete
	It may vary depending on the project
	It is defined by the Scrum Master
	It becomes more complete over time

3. An iteration prior to a release that includes final documentation, integration testing, training and some small tweaks is called:

Correct	Choice
	Hardening Iteration
	Buffer Iteration
	Release Iteration
	Integration Iteration

4. On a risk map or a risk heat map, the vertical and horizontal axes represent:

Correct	Choice
	Effort and Impact
	Probability and Impact
	Probability and Exposure
	Impact and Exposure

5. In Agile development, what is the term for the internal things that you choose not to do now, knowing they will impede future development if left undone?

Correct	Choice
	Escaped defects
	Verification and validation results
	Technical debt
	Intrinsic quality

6. All of the following are attributes of the definition of "Done", ECEPT:

Correct	Choice
	It is a static artifact
	Defined by the Product Owner and the Team
	Defines a complete, integrated product by the end of the Iteration
	Can lead to technical debt if not implemented properly

7. What is the purpose of running a test before you develop the code?

Correct	Choice
	To complete all test cases
	To ensure it fails
	To ensure it passes
	To be cross-functional

8. Agile development prevents technical debt.

Correct	Choice
	True
	False

9. Refactoring is a key way of preventing technical debt.

Correct	Choice
	True
	False

10. What is an Agile term for the time period when some or all of the following occur: beta testing, regression testing, product integration, integration testing, documentation, defect fixing.

Correct	Choice
	Spike
	Code Freeze
	Tail
	Lag

11. Which one is NOT a reason to perform a Spike?

Correct	Choice
	To perform basic research to familiarize the team with a new technology or domain
	To analyze the expected behavior of a large story so the team can split the story into estimable pieces.
	To defer a story until a later Sprint while still showing progress to the Product Owner
	To do some prototyping to gain confidence in a technological approach

12. What is a change made to the internal structure of software to make it easier to understand and cheaper to modify without changing its observable behavior?

Correct	Choice
	Pair Programming
	Continuous Improvement
	Test Driven Development
	Refactoring

13. Frequent verification and validation is key in Agile but each approach produces a very different result. Verification determines _____ whereas validation determines _____ .

Correct	Choice
	if the product is "done" | if the product is "done - done"
	if I am I building the product right | if I am I building the right product
	if I am I building the right product | if I am I building the product right
	if the product has passed unit testing | if the product has passed acceptance testing

14. Bugs reported by the customer that have slipped by all software quality processes are represented in this metric.

Correct	Choice
	Technical debt
	Escaped defects
	Risk burndown
	Code quality

15. Which of the following are 2 attributes of Exploratory testing?

Correct	Choice
	It involves minimum planning and maximum test execution
	It is typically automated
	It is unscripted testing
	It is often the sole testing technique

16. A technique in which a team collaboratively discusses acceptance criteria and then distills them into a set of concrete tests before development begins is called (drag and drop):

Correct	Choice
	Feature Driven Development (FDD)
	Acceptance Test Driven Development (ATDD)
	Test Driven Development (TDD)
	User Story workshops

17. The _____ the technical debt means the _____ the intrinsic quality?

Correct	Choice
	higher, higher
	higher, lower
	lower, lower

18. Technical debt is the total amount of less-than-perfect _____ in your project.

Correct	Choice
	Defects
	Design and implementation decisions
	Code commenting
	Code Sharing

19. Testing that often occurs between "Done" and "Done- Done" is:

Correct	Choice
	Acceptance testing
	Exploratory testing
	Unit Testing
	Test driven development

20. Which type of risk analysis does an Agile team use to identify risks on their project?

Correct	Choice
	Risk Burndown Chart
	Pareto Analysis
	Qualitative Risk Analysis
	Quantitative Analysis

Continuous Improvement

All About Agile: Module 8

Version 4.0

Continuous Improvement Topics

Retrospectives

- Sprint Retrospectives
- Advanced Retrospectives
- Intraspectives
- Futurespectives

Improvement Techniques

- Kaizen
- Knowledge Sharing
- Process Tailoring
- Principles of System Thinking
- Process Analysis
- 6 Sigma Approach – DMAIC
- Deming's Plan, Do, Check, Act
- Business Process Modeling
- Self-assessments

Retrospectives

- Takes place at the end of an iteration
- Examines the way work was performed
- Identifies ways to improve
- Basic questions
  - What went well?
  - What would you do differently next time?
- Use a neutral facilitator

Start / Stop / Continue

- Whole team gathers and discusses what they'd like to:

Start doing

Stop doing

Continue doing

This is just one of many ways to do a Sprint Retrospective.

Advanced Retrospectives Agenda

- **Set the Stage**: get the team ready to engage in the retrospective (5%)
- **Gather Data**: create a shared picture of what happened during the retrospective period (25–40%)
- **Generate Insights**: interpret and analyze the data to figure out what happened (25–40%)
- **Decide What to Do**: identify highest priority items to work on and put measurable goals on those items so they can be completed (10–20%)
- **Close the Retrospective**: reflect on the retrospective and how to improve it, and to appreciate accomplishments of the team and individual interactions (5–10%)

Esther Derby and Diana Larsen. 2006. *Agile Retrospectives: Making Good Teams Great.*

---

1. Set the Stage

"Getting the team ready to engage in the retrospective"

- Welcome everyone to the retrospective and express appreciation for hard work leading to retrospective and willingness to attend
- Provide a short amount of time for everyone to speak: to introduce themselves or to answer a simple question ("how did the sprint go?", "What are you looking for?")
- Describe the approach to the session: agenda, working agreements, time-boxes
- Activities:
    - Check-in: provide opportunity for everyone to talk and listen (as above)
    - ESVP: explorer / shopper / vacationer / prisoner – everyone thinks about why they are there

Working Agreements

- Develop a sense of shared responsibility.
- Increase members' awareness of their own behavior.
- Empower the facilitator(s) to lead the group according to the agreements.
- Enhance the quality of the group process.
- Strike a balance between task and process.
- The #1 Rule:
  - Each member of the team must agree to the guidelines. For example—if your team members want to add the guideline "everyone must be on time for meetings" and you know that you cannot uphold this commitment—do not say that you will. Instead, ask your team members if you can be flexible about meeting times.

Copyrighted material. 2018

2. Gather Data

"Create a shared picture of what happened during the retrospective period"
- Capture data about what occurred during the period
  - Events: new hire, important sale, decisions, milestones
  - Metrics: burndown charts, velocity, unit tests, build failures, features completed, cycle time
  - Stories and features completed
  - Emotions
- Activities:
  - Timeline: work in groups to remember what happened and place items on a timeline
  - Mad sad glad: find times or events when you were mad, sad, or glad
  - Triple nickels: 3 people take 5 minutes to write ideas, then pass to next person to elaborate
  - Locate strengths: pairwise interviews (not discussions!) About how the iteration or project went – be curious, ask follow questions
  - Color Code Dots: Team members use sticky dots to show events on the timeline where emotions ran high or low

Copyrighted material. 2018

3. Generate Insights

"Interpret and analyze the data to figure out what happened"

- Start asking why things happened
  - Look at conditions, interactions, patterns, breakdowns, deficiencies, risks surprises
  - Look both at bright spots of successes and dark spots of pain
  - Dig to get to root causes; first impressions are often correct but may not be deep enough to get to the problem
- Activities:
  - Brainstorming: free-form generation of ideas with minimal or no discussion; build on previous ideas to get new ones
  - Five whys: why did an event occur? Iterate on why and record the 4th or 5th iteration.
  - Identify themes: generated data contain common themes; try to group them to get to the common themes
  - Prioritize with dots: put from 1-4 dots on each idea to prioritize improvements
  - Force field analysis: identify forces for and against change

CAPE PROJECT MANAGEMENT, INC.

Force Field Analysis

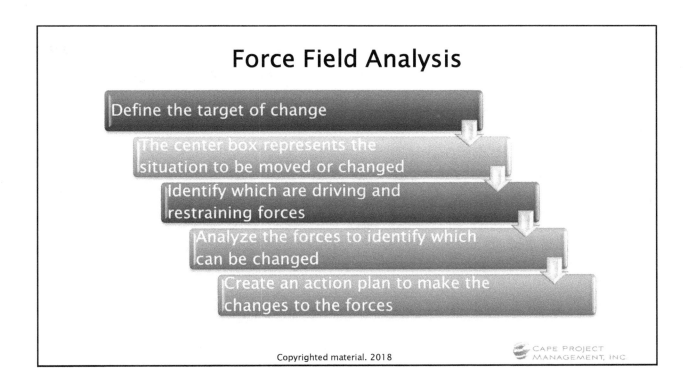

CAPE PROJECT MANAGEMENT, INC.

Force Field Analysis

Directions

1. Use the worksheet on the next page.

2. On the center box, write taking the PMI-ACP Exam

3. List all the forces FOR CHANGE in one column, and all the forces AGAINST CHANGE in another column.

4. Rate the strength of these forces and assign a numerical weight, 1 being the weakest, 5 being the strongest.

5. When you add the "strength points" of the forces, you'll see the viability of the proposed change.

The tool can be used to help ensure the success of the proposed change by identifying the strength of the forces against the change.

ACTIVITY SHEET: *Force Field Analysis*

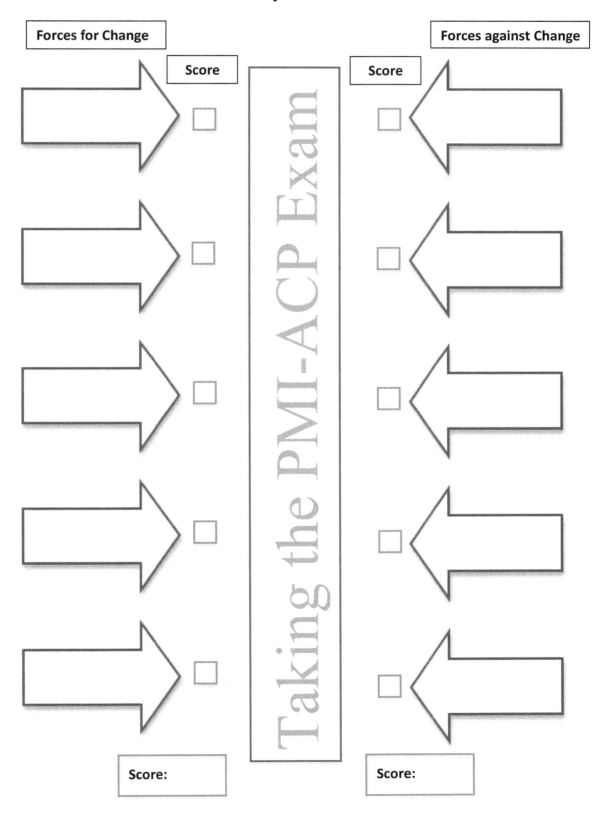

Activity

Force Field Analysis

4. Decide What to Do

"Identify highest priority items to work on and put measurable goals on those items so they can be completed"

- Generate potential experiments and improvements – what are the highest priority, the biggest impact, likely to succeed?
- Focus on a very small number of items first until you establish success
- Activities:
  - Dot voting: the team votes on what they think are the most important items
  - SMART goals: ideas that are specific, measurable, achievable, relevant, timely
  - Retrospective planning game: brainstorm tasks to implement improvement, then sequence, and team members volunteer

5. Close the Retrospective

"Reflect on the retrospective and how to improve it, and to appreciate accomplishments of the team and individual interactions"

- Important to reach closure on retrospective
  - Plan for documenting what occurred and for following up on improvements and experiments
  - Retrospect on the retrospective so the next one is even better
  - Take time for team to appreciate each other and celebrate successes
  - Appreciate the time and effort everyone has put into improving their team
- Activities:
  - +/− Delta: what to keep and build on, what to change
  - Appreciations: to allow team members to notice and appreciate each other. End the retrospective on a positive note.
  - Helped, hindered, hypothesis: Help the retrospective leader get feedback to improve skills and processes
  - Return on time invested (ROTI): Team members to give feedback on whether they spent their time well

Copyrighted material. 2018

Sailboat Retrospective

- Use a sailboat as a metaphor for your iteration. A successful iteration is the one that has completed its projected velocity. (The boat sailed to the island)
- Write on sticky notes and post them on a picture of a sailboat on the wall:
  - Write down things that you as a team did well during the iteration. Things that kept you moving. (The engine)
  - Write down what you as a team did NOT do well during the iteration. Things that held them back. (The anchors)
  - Write down what external influences impeded their progress or caused issues during the iteration. (The headwind)
  - Write down what external influences helped the iteration. (The tailwind)
- Pick up the extremely painful anchors and headwind and create plans to mitigate them.

Copyrighted material. 2018

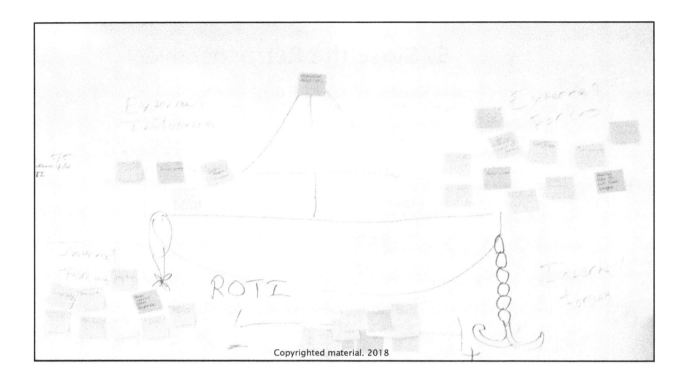

Things to Watch Out For

- People spend too much time emphasizing the negatives and don't take credit for the good things that happened.
- Nobody says anything and stares at the floor.
- One person dominates the discussion.
- People play the blame game.
- People don't let others finish what they're saying.
- The team identifies the same issues time after time and after a while they give up because nothing ever comes of it.

Effective Sprint Retrospectives

Rotate leadership:

☐ Rather than always have the same facilitator lead the retrospective, rotate leadership.

Vary the process:

☐ If you've been leading group discussions, try using structured activities to help the team think together.

Change the focus:

☐ If you've been concentrating on improving how the team works the Scrum process itself, switch the focus to engineering practices or teamwork.

Effective Sprint Retrospectives

Include different perspectives:

☐ For the retrospective after a release, include people who aren't part of the team.

Try appreciative inquiry:

☐ Instead of looking at where to improve, look at what's working well and how you can build on that.

Analyze recurrent themes:

☐ If your team is bringing up the same issues at each retrospective, examine the list of issues. If nothing changes as the result of your team's retrospectives, analyze the factors behind inaction.

Futurspectives

☐ In a futurespective you imagine that you are in the future, at the end of the project, and that you are performing a project retrospective to find out what contributed to the successful delivery of the project.

▸ Goal of a futurespective :
  ◦ What *will we do more of* in the future?
  ◦ What *will we do less of* in the future?
  ◦ What are the things we're not sure about and will monitor going forward?

CAPE PROJECT MANAGEMENT, INC.

Improvement Techniques

☐ Knowledge Sharing
☐ Process Tailoring
☐ Principles of System Thinking
☐ Process Analysis
☐ Deming's Plan, Do, Check, Act
☐ 6 Sigma approach – DMAIC
☐ Business process modeling
☐ Self-assessments

CAPE PROJECT MANAGEMENT, INC.

Agile Learning Cycles

□ Learning cycles assume that we are continually engaging in iterative cycles of learning.

□ In Agile, this can be represented as Build, Measure, Learn.

□ Reflected in Scrum as Inspect and Adapt.

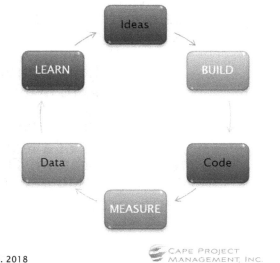

Copyrighted material. 2018

What is Kaizen?

□ Kai is an idea of change or the action to correct, Zen means "good"

□ Kaizen means "change for the better"

□ Kaizen is a Japanese business philosophy focused on making constant improvements. Its underlying concept stresses there will always be room for improvement.

□ Fundamentally, kaizen aims to improve all activities and processes and eliminate waste and excess.

Copyrighted material. 2018

Knowledge Sharing

- Knowledge sharing happens at many levels. Product demonstrations are an example of an obvious method:
  - Team to customer: Here is what we think you asked for and what we have been able to build. Please tell us if we are on the right track.
  - Customer to team: I like these bits, and this is okay, but you got this piece wrong. Oh, and that reminds me—we really need something over here to do X.
- An example of a less obvious way to share information is team co-location. This practice is not done to save space or ease management overhead.
- Retrospectives are also knowledge transfer vehicles.

CAPE PROJECT
MANAGEMENT, INC.

Process Tailoring

CMMI

Regulatory

Culture

Agile

CAPE PROJECT
MANAGEMENT, INC.

Process Tailoring

- Generic process tailoring is to tune the process to your project
- Agile process tailoring is to "right-size" the process to your organization
  - Just enough process to support the size and complexity of the project
- Agile projects should "tailor up"
  - Start with the bare minimum, and add process
- Process tailoring can be effective and productive, but there are risks involved. The following are the key ways to mitigate these risks:
  - Get used to normal, out-of-the-box agile before attempting to change it. The methods were created based on the collective wisdom of many experienced practitioners.
  - Carefully examine the motivation to drop, amend, or append a practice. Is the change to avoid a more fundamental problem, or will it be a add value to the organization?

Principles that Influence Tailoring

Factor	Tailoring Options
Steady or sporadic delivery	Deliver in a cadence like Scrum or in a flow like Kanban
Immature team	More frequent retrospectives
Frequent project interruptions	Make flow visible with Kanban board to determine impact
Poor quality	Introduce pair programming and other XP practices
Large team or multiple teams	Adopt a scaling framework
Inexperience with Agile	Retrain the team on an Agile framework

Process tailoring/Hybrid models

- There are many formal and informal Agile hybrid models.
- Hybrid scaled Agile approaches are very common:
  - SaFE, LeSS, DAD
- Approach:
  - Right size to your organization.
  - Start with the basics.
  - Change management and culture will dictate an evolutionary versus revolutionary approach.

CAPE PROJECT
MANAGEMENT, INC.

Principles of System Thinking

Software projects are characterized by:

- The level of complexity around requirements
- The complexity of the technology used on the projects.

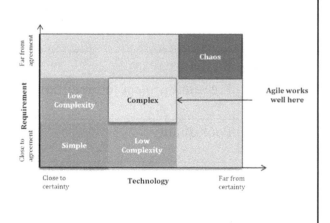

CAPE PROJECT
MANAGEMENT, INC.

Principles of System Thinking

- Agile methods can of course be used for simple projects, too, in which the organization and the team will get the benefits of increased collaboration, communication, and visibility.
- If there is no clear agreement on what we are supposed to be building or what approach and tools we are using to build it, then our project is in a state of chaos.
- We have to keep in mind this system-level understanding of the environment in which agile projects are operating when we think about modifying the methods.

Copyrighted material. 2018

 CAPE PROJECT MANAGEMENT, INC.

Process Analysis

- Process analysis is closely related to process tailoring and the principles of systems thinking. When we perform process analysis, we are reviewing and diagnosing issues. This analysis may then lead to a decision to tailor the process.
- Anti-Patterns:
  - One size fits all: it not possible to create the optimal methodology for all types of projects, al technologies, and all team sizes.
  - Too Heavy: There is a common but incorrect belief that the heavier a methodology is in artifacts and practices, the safer it is. However, adding weight to a methodology is not likely to improve the team's chance of delivering the project successfully. Instead, it diverts the team's time from the real goal of the project.
  - Embellished: We add in things that we think we "ought to" or "should" be doing, but we need to look out for these words as signals for potentially expensive, error-prone additions.
  - Untried: Many methodologies are untried. See what actually works on projects and use that, not something untried that we believe "should work."
  - Used once: Just because an approach worked under one set of circumstances does not guarantee it will work under another.
- Process Success Criteria:
  - The product got shipped.
  - The leadership didn't get fired for what they were doing (or not doing).
  - The people on the project found the approach to be effective and enjoyable.

Copyrighted material. 2018

 CAPE PROJECT MANAGEMENT, INC.

Deming's Plan, Do, Check, Act

Plan
- Establish the objectives and processes necessary to deliver results

Do
- Implement the plan, execute the change

Check
- Study the actual results

Act
- Perform corrective actions

Copyrighted material. 2018

Six Sigma Approach: DMAIC

Define
- Define the improvement opportunity.

Measure
- Measure the current performance to create a baseline.

Analyze
- Determine root cause of problem.

Improve
- Identify and implement creative solutions to fix and prevent process problems.

Control
- Monitor the improvements to ensure continued success.

Copyrighted material. 2018

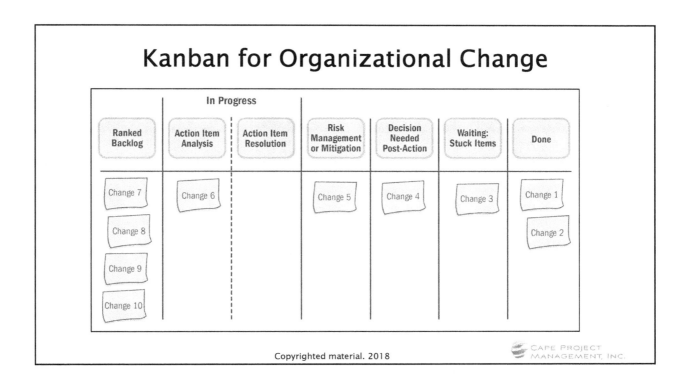

Agile Assessments

- Designed to enhance and improve Agile practices by assessing the current state of your organization
- A way to determine how closely you adhere to Agile principles
- A model which shows your organization on an Agile maturity continuum from an initial or ad-hoc level to a continuously improving, self-sustaining level

An Agile Maturity Model

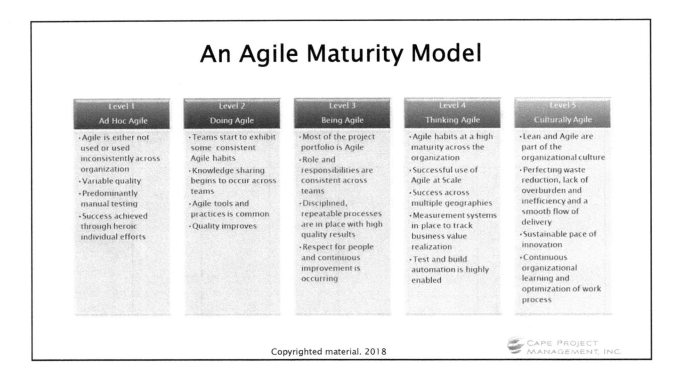

Level 1 Ad Hoc Agile	Level 2 Doing Agile	Level 3 Being Agile	Level 4 Thinking Agile	Level 5 Culturally Agile
• Agile is either not used or used inconsistently across organization • Variable quality • Predominantly manual testing • Success achieved through heroic individual efforts	• Teams start to exhibit some consistent Agile habits • Knowledge sharing begins to occur across teams • Agile tools and practices is common • Quality improves	• Most of the project portfolio is Agile • Role and responsibilities are consistent across teams • Disciplined, repeatable processes are in place with high quality results • Respect for people and continuous improvement is occurring	• Agile habits at a high maturity across the organization • Successful use of Agile at Scale • Success across multiple geographies • Measurement systems in place to track business value realization • Test and build automation is highly enabled	• Lean and Agile are part of the organizational culture • Perfecting waste reduction, lack of overburden and inefficiency and a smooth flow of delivery • Sustainable pace of innovation • Continuous organizational learning and optimization of work process

CAPE PROJECT MANAGEMENT, INC.

Activity

Agile Assessment

CAPE PROJECT MANAGEMENT, INC.

Self-Assessments

- Once all the questions have been asked and scored, the results are plotted on a radar (spider) diagram.
- The team is then involved in analyzing the chart to identify which areas could use improvement.

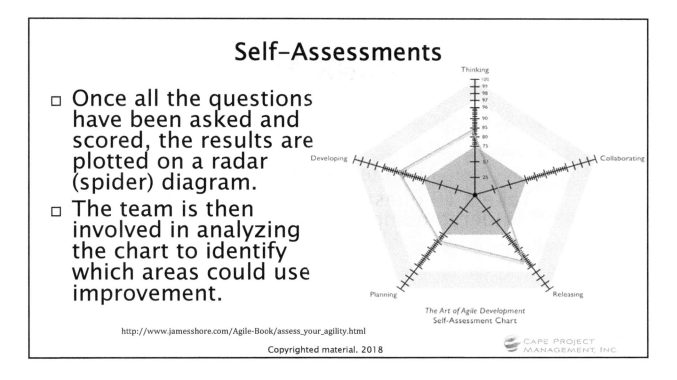

The Art of Agile Development
Self-Assessment Chart

http://www.jamesshore.com/Agile-Book/assess_your_agility.html

CAPE PROJECT
MANAGEMENT, INC.

Self-Assessment

Another model for assessing high-performing teams is offered by Jean Tabaka, this model investigate the following areas:

- **Self-organization**: Is the team self-organizing, rather than functioning in a command-and-control, top-down organization?

- **Empowered to make decisions**: Is the team empowered to discuss, evaluate, and make decisions, rather than being dictated to by an outside authority?

- **Belief in vision and success**: Do team members understand the project vision and goals, and do they truly believe that, as a team, they can solve any problem to achieve those goals?

- **Committed team**: Are team members committed to succeed as a team, rather than being committed to individual success at any cost?

- **Trust each other**: Does the team have the confidence to continually work on improving their ability to act without fear, anger, or bullying?

- **Participatory decision making**: Is the team engaged in participatory decision making, rather than bending to authoritarian decision making or succumbing to decisions from others?

- **Consensus-driven**: Are team decisions consensus-driven, rather than leader-driven? Do team members share their opinions freely and participate in the final decision?

- **Constructive disagreement**: Is the team able to negotiate through a variety of alternatives and impacts surrounding a decision, and craft the one that provides the best outcome?

CAPE PROJECT
MANAGEMENT, INC.

ONLINE ACTIVITY

Module 8 Knowledge Check
Take a 19 question practice exam to test your
understanding of Continuous Improvement.

Module 8 Knowledge Check

Questions

1. **Process tailoring is an iterative approach implementing and improving your SDLC process.**

Correct	Choice
	True
	False

2. **What is the Japanese business philosophy focused on making constant improvements?**

Correct	Choice
	Shu-Ha-Ri
	Kaizen
	Aikido
	Sashimi

3. **Match the project factor to the tailoring options:**

Correct	Choice
Steady or sporadic delivery	Introduce pair programming and other P practices
Immature team	Adopt a scaling framework
Frequent project interruptions	Retrain the team on an Agile framework
Poor quality	More frequent retrospectives
Large team or multiple teams	Make flow visible with Kanban board to determine impact
Inexperience with Agile	Deliver in a cadence like Scrum or in a flow like Kanban

4. Which of the following is an Agile improvement technique to address issues continuously, e.g. after daily stand-up?

Correct	Choice
	Retrospectives
	Futurespectives
	Intraspectives
	Verification Sessions

5. Similar to inspect and adapt in Scrum, this can be represented as Build, Measure, Learn.

Correct	Choice
	Six Sigma
	Agile Learning Cycle
	DMAIC
	Kaizen

6. When it the appropriate time to create working agreements?

Correct	Choice
	To set the stage in retrospectives.
	As part of project kick-offs
	Whenever a new team member joins
	All of the above

7. What is the purpose of practicing asking the "5 Why's"?

Correct	Choice
	To determine the scope of the Sprint
	To determine the root cause of an issue
	To determine the end result
	To determine the prioritized backlog

8. Your project management office (PMO) has suggested your project could benefit from some self-assessment work at the next retrospective. Which of the following benefits would they most likely be looking to achieve from a self-assessment?

Correct	Choice
	Gain insights for salary performance reviews
	Improve personal and team practices
	Identify personal traits for human resources counseling
	Assess compatibilities for pair programming assignments

9. Question: Which of the following BEST describes ROTI?

Correct	Choice
	Measure of product backlog items (PBI) remaining
	Measure of quality of features delivered in an iteration
	Measure of required effort to complete an iteration
	Measure of the effectiveness of the retrospective meeting

10. Sequence the activities that occur in a Retrospective meeting.

Correct Order
Set the Stage
Gather Data
Generate Insights
Decide What to Do
Close the Retrospective

11. You have been asked to review a different project team's recently enhanced methodology to assess its effectiveness and desirable characteristics. The types of characteristics that you should be looking for include evidence of:

Correct	Choice
	A preference for face-to-face communications, significant process weight, recommendations for larger teams to use lighter methods
	A preference for face-to-face communications, not too much process weight, recommendations for larger teams to use lighter methods
	A preference for face-to-face communications, significant process weight, recommendations for larger teams to use heavier methods
	A preference for face-to-face communications, not too much process weight, recommendations for larger teams to use heavier methods

2. The retrospective meeting:

Correct	Choice
	Is intended to promote continuous process improvements
	Is only held at the end of the project
	Is conducted to provide the sponsor with key information on team progress
	Is optional

13. Triple Nickels is a technique used to perform what activity in a retrospective meeting?

Correct	Choice
	Set the stage
	Generate Insights
	Gather Data
	All of the above

14. Which of the following are TRUE about the retrospective event in Scrum? (Choose 2)

Correct	Choice
	It is an opportunity to inspect the people, relationships, process, and tools in the last Sprint
	It is three hours for a one month Sprint
	It occurs before the Sprint Review
	It is the only time improvements are made during a Sprint

15. Your sponsor is asking about tailoring the company's newly adopted agile methodology. Your advice should be:

Correct	Choice
	Tailoring it will be a good way to learn the methodology
	Tailoring it will be a good way to ease into the initial adoption process
	We should tailor it first, then consider adopting it
	We should try it first, then consider tailoring it

16. The purpose of a retrospective is for the team to:

Correct	Choice
	Review stories planned for the next Sprint and provide estimates.
	Demonstrate completed User Stories to the Product Owner.
	Determine what to stop doing, start doing, and continue doing.
	Individually provide status updates on the User Stories in progress.

17. Which of the following is NOT a technique for continuous improvement?

Correct	Choice
	Self-Assessment
	Process Tailoring
	Sustainable Pace
	Retrospectives

18. What is the reason to perform a Force Field analysis with the team?

Correct	Choice
	Decide how to implement a change
	Generate insights
	Set the stage for the meeting
	Close out the retrospective

19. Process tailoring is best undertaken on agile projects when:

Correct	Choice
	Stakeholders want to try a new practice
	The team needs new processes to keep them engaged
	There are challenges in implementing agile practices
	A boost in team velocity is needed to meet the schedule

20. You are engaging in some process analysis and have been advised to watch out for the standard anti-patterns of poor methodology practice. The types of things you should be on the lookout for are processes that display signs of being:

Correct	Choice
	One-of-a-kind, disciplined, heavy, embellished
	One-size-fits-all, disciplined, heavy, embellished
	One-size-fits-all, intolerant, heavy, embellished
	One-of-a-kind, intolerant, embellished

Summary and Study Tips

All About Agile: Module 9

Version 4.0

Wrapping Up

□ Summary

□ Study Tips

□ What NOT To Worry About

□ Internet Observations

□ Have Fun!

Summary

- The knowledge contained in this course along with the practice exams will prepare you for the exam.
- Give yourself at least 12 weeks to prepare for the exam. Use one week Sprints with a Sprint goal for each iteration.
- Practice these techniques in real life while studying:
  - Create a Backlog
  - Burndown Chart
  - Kanban Task Boards
- Use free online tools and trials. Leankit is great for Kanban task management and is free.

Practice Exam Tips

- Take the exams attached to the modules until you get 100%
- Use our standalone practice exams from our 400 question test bank. Attempt to get 80% consistently on those. There are additional questions not covered here.
  - 25 questions with a one-hour countdown timer
  - 50 question with a two-hour countdown timer
  - 120 question practice with a three-hour countdown timer, just like the real exam
  - 300 questions with a 10 hour timer
- Also available in a paperback or on Kindle from Amazon: http://bit.ly/PMI-ACPonAmazon

What Not to Worry About

- You do not need to buy all 12 books
- There aren't any complicated formulas
- Do not need to study every Agile methodology; focus on Scrum, XP, Kanban and Lean

Agile Practice Guide Observations

- PMI's goal is to become framework neutral so there is an attempt to create some common terminology and practices.
- There are now 3 generic Agile roles, taken primarily from Scrum:
  - Team Facilitator
  - Cross Functional Team Members
  - Product Owner
- There was recognition that there is no PM role in Agile but the PM can play the role of Team Facilitator
- They have stated the need for PMOs in an Agile environment
- There are now 2 generic Agile approaches:
  - Iteration-based Agile
  - Flow-based Agile
- Transparency, Inspection and Adaptation (from Scrum) are now considered to be generally Agile

Agile Practice Guide Observations – Cont'd

- Stories now seem to be accepted terminology. I don't think they were even referred to in the initial version of the exam
- Hybrid and scaling were now acknowledged, though minimally
- I think they have embraced the following pure Agile concepts even though they are the very opposite of traditional PM:
  - Servant leadership
  - Generalizing specialists
  - Burndown charts and Kanban boards instead of Gantt charts
- Even though there was a lot alignment with Scrum, there were still some contradictions:
  - "The Product Owner sees the demonstration and accepts or declines the stories" – that is a big no no in formal Scrum. The Product Owner should be signing off throughout the iteration and showing the final product to stakeholders at the demonstration.
  - Iterations as usually 2 weeks – that is another false reality.
  - The Product Owner asks a "triad"; a developer, tester and analyst, to get together to write a story as a way to refine the backlog.

Observations from the Internet

- Minimal on Crystal, DSDM, or AgileUP
- Know the difference between product and project
- Know Scrum thoroughly
- Be familiar with Lean, Kanban, and XP
- Good summary blog:
  - http://wafimohtaseb.com/2012/02/27/pmi-acp-study-guide/

References and Recommended Reading

List of PMI's recommended books:

https://www.capeprojectmanagement.com/agile-exams/acp-exams/#reading

All of the references in the PMI-ACP Study Guide:

https://www.capeprojectmanagement.com/wp-content/uploads/2018/01/PMI-ACP_Study_Guide.pdf

Note: The password to open the document is "scrumdan". No quotes and no caps.

Thank-You!

Dan@CapeProjectManagement.com

Module 1 Knowledge Check

Answers

1. Which one is NOT one of the 5 common risk areas mitigated by Agile.

Correct	Choice
	Intrinsic schedule flaw
X	Stakeholder apathy
	Specification breakdown
	Personnel loss
	Productivity variation
	Scope creep

Feedback when incorrect: The book Waltzing with Bears lists the 5 common risk areas as: 1) Intrinsic Schedule Flaw 2) Specification Breakdown 3) Scope Creep 4) Personnel Loss 5) Productivity Variance

2. A key component of Agile software development is:

Correct	Choice
	Requirements should be complete before beginning development
	Change must be minimized
	Risk management is robust
X	Requirements are able to evolve during development

Feedback when incorrect: Requirements are able to evolve during development

3. Which is NOT a Scrum Role?

Correct	Choice
	Product Owner
X	Project Manager
	Scrum Master
	Team Member

Feedback when incorrect: Project Manager is not a Scrum Role

4. There must be a release every Sprint.

Correct	Choice
	True
X	False

Feedback when incorrect: Each Sprint should create a shippable piece of functionality, but is up to the Product Owner when to release.

5. No one, not even the Scrum Master, tells the development team how to build the product.

Correct	Choice
X	True
	False

Feedback when incorrect: They are self-organizing. No one (not even the Scrum Master) tells the Development Team how to turn Product Backlog into Increments of potentially releasable functionality.

6. Which one of the following is NOT a Scrum Event?

Correct	Choice
	Retrospectives
	Reviews or Demos
	Daily Stand-ups
X	Status Meetings

Feedback when incorrect: Status meetings are not a Scrum Event. Retrospectives, Reviews and Daily Stand-ups (or Scrums) are all part of the Scrum framework.

7. The ultimate goal of _____ is to deploy all but the last few hours of work at any time.

Correct	Choice
X	Continuous Integration
	Collective Code Ownership
	Asynchronous Builds
	Synchronous Builds

Feedback when incorrect: The ultimate goal of Continuous Integration is to deploy all but the last few hours of work at any time.

8. An artifact on an Agile project can best be described as:

Correct	Choice
X	A work output, typically a document, drawing, code, or model
	A document that describes how work the work needs to be done
	The Agile model of persona
	The deliverable from a Sprint retrospective

Feedback when incorrect: An artifact on an Agile project can best be described as a work output, typically a document, drawing, code, or model.

9. Which of the following sets of tools is least likely to be utilized by an Agile team?

Correct	Choice
	Digital camera, task board
	Wiki, planning poker cards
	Smart board, card wall
X	WBS, PERT charts

Feedback when incorrect: WBS and PERT charts are tools of traditional project management.

10. In Scrum, who is responsible for managing the team?

Correct	Choice
	Scrum Master
X	Development Team
	Product Owner
	Project Manager

Feedback when incorrect: The Development Team is responsible for self-management.

11. The Project Leader's primary responsibilities are to "move boulders and carry water." What is this an example of?

Correct	Choice
X	Servant leadership
	Leadership by example
	The leadership metaphor
	Command and control leadership

Feedback when incorrect: As a servant leader, the Scrum Master's primary responsibilities are to "move boulders and carry water"-in other words, remove obstacles that prevent the team from delivering business value, and to make sure the team has the environment they need to succeed.

12. On Agile teams, conflict is to be avoided at all cost.

Correct	Choice
	True
X	False

Feedback when incorrect: Innovation occurs only with the free interchange of conflicting ideas, a phenomenon that was studied and documented by Hirotaka Takeuchi and Ikujiro Nonaka, the godfathers of Scrum.

13. Incremental delivery means:

Correct	Choice
	Deliver nonfunctional increments in the iteration retrospectives.
	Release working software only after testing each increment.
X	Deploy functional increments over the course of the project.
	Improve and elaborate our Agile process with each increment delivered.

Feedback when incorrect: Incremental delivery is when you deploy functional increments over the course of the project.

14. Scrum is a software development methodology.

Correct	Choice
	True
X	False

Feedback when incorrect: Scrum is a process control methodology and is used for more than just software development projects.

15. What is a product roadmap?

Correct	Choice
	A list of reports and screens
	Instructions for deployment
	A backlog prioritization scheme
X	A view of release candidates

Feedback when incorrect: A product roadmap allows you to communicate where you want to take your product. You should be able to present at least three release candidates in your roadmap.

Module 2-1 Knowledge Check

Answers

1. Which of the following is does NOT relate a principle of the Agile Manifesto?

Correct	Choice
	Working software is delivered frequently
	Close, daily co-operation between business people and developers
	Projects built around motivated individuals, who should be trusted
X	Daily team meetings are necessary to review progress and address impediments

Feedback when incorrect: The Agile Manifesto does not dictate meeting lengths or frequencies.

2. Pick three attributes of an Agile PMO

Correct	Choice
X	Value Driven
X	Invitation Oriented
X	Multidisciplinary
	Functional
	Process Oriented

Feedback when incorrect: Agile PMOs are value driven, invitation oriented and multidisciplinary.

3. It is important to select a single project lifecycle for a project. "Hybrid" lifecycles can be confusing and counterproductive.

Correct	Choice
	True
X	False

Feedback when incorrect: False, it is common for different parts of projects to employ different lifecycles. The example in the Agile Practice guide is on a clinical trial that used a hybrid approach to be Agile for periodic reviews but successful delivery could only be at the end.

4. Match the project lifecycle to its characteristics:

Correct	Choice
Predictive	Fixed requirements, single delivery, cost control
Iterative	Dynamic requirements, single delivery, correctness
Incremental	Dynamic requirements, frequent smaller delivery, speed
Agile	Dynamic requirements, frequent smaller delivery, value driven

Feedback when incorrect: Predictive: Fixed requirements, single delivery, cost control

Iterative: Dynamic requirements, single delivery, correctness

Incremental: Dynamic requirements, frequent smaller delivery, speed

Agile: Dynamic requirements, frequent smaller delivery, value driven

5. Agile techniques have become critical for large organizations whose competitors are embracing disruptive technologies. Which of the following are example of a more recent disruptive technology?

Correct	Choice
X	Cloud computing
X	Google hangouts
X	On-demand printing
	Server farms
	Desktop computing

Feedback when incorrect: Organizations that embrace cloud computing, virtual offices like Google hangouts and on-demand printing are able to respond quickly and cheaply in the marketplace. Those same organizations embrace Agile techniques to get products to market.

6. Which of the following projects would typically require involve high-uncertainty work?

Correct	Choice
	Automated
	Construction
X	Product Design
	Electrical Appliances
X	Clinical Studies
X	Feasibility Studies

Feedback when incorrect: Product design, clinical studies and feasibility studies are all examples of high-uncertainty projects.

7. Match the Agile practice on the left to the high-level description on the right.

Correct	Choice
Lean	Strategic
Kanban	Evolutionary
XP	Engineering Practices
Scrum	Framework

Feedback when incorrect: Lean = Strategic

Kanban = Evolutionary

XP = Engineering practices

Scrum = Framework

8. The Agile Manifesto principle, "Our highest priority is to satisfy the customer through early and continuous delivery of valuable software," is achieved through which Scrum practice?

Correct	Choice
	Daily Scrum
	Release Planning
	Sprint Planning
X	Sprints

Feedback when incorrect: Sprints which are no longer than one month and often shorter promote continuous delivery to the customer

9. Which of the following is a weakness of an Adaptive PMLC Model?

Correct	Choice
	Does not waste time on non-value-added work
	Avoids all management issues processing scope change requests
	Does not waste time planning uncertainty
X	Cannot identify what will be delivered at the end of the project

Feedback when incorrect: Weaknesses of Adaptive PMLC Model include that you cannot identify what will be delivered at the end of the project.

10. Simplicity - the art of _____ - is essential

Correct	Choice
X	Maximizing the amount of work not done
	Maximizing the customer collaboration
	Minimizing contract negotiation
	Minimizing the amount of work done

Feedback when incorrect: Agile Manifesto Principle: Simplicity-the art of maximizing the amount of work not done-is essential.

11. This approach includes a visual process management system and an approach to incremental, evolutionary process changes for organizations.

Correct	Choice
X	Kanban
	Scrum
	Agile Unified Process
	Extreme programming

Feedback when incorrect: The Kanban approach includes a visual process management system and an approach to incremental, evolutionary process changes for organizations.

12. This management approach is based on knowing well defined goals but not the means for a solution.

Correct	Choice
	Traditional Project Management
X	Agile Project Management
	Extreme Project Management
	Emertxe Project Management

Feedback when incorrect: Agile Project Management (APM) - This management approach is based on knowing well defined goals but not the means for a solution

13. The best architectures, requirements, and designs emerge from:

Correct	Choice
	Hand-picked teams
	Co-located teams
X	Self-organizing teams
	Cross-functional teams

Feedback when incorrect: Agile Manifesto Principle: The best architectures, requirements, and designs emerge from self-organizing teams.

14. Continuous attention to _____ and good design enhances agility.

Correct	Choice
	Best architectures
	Robust plans
	Change control

Correct	Choice
X	Technical excellence

Feedback when incorrect: Agile Manifesto Principle: Continuous attention to technical excellence and good design enhances agility.

15. This Emertxe Project Management (xPM) approach is when neither a goal nor solution is clearly defined.

Correct	Choice
	True
X	False

Feedback when incorrect: Extreme Project Management (xPM) - This management approach is when neither a goal nor solution is clearly defined.

16. Which is NOT a principle of Lean?

Correct	Choice
	Eliminate waste
	Deliver fast
	Delay commitment
X	Time-box events

Feedback when incorrect: Time-boxed events are a practice of Scrum not Lean.

17. Simple Design, Pair Programming, Test-Driven Development, Design Improvement are all practices of which Agile methodology?

Correct	Choice
	Scrum
X	Extreme Programming (XP)
	Dynamic Systems Development Method (DSDM)
	Rational Unified Process (RUP)

Agile Unified Process (AgileUP)	
Crystal Clear	
Feature Driven Development (FDD)	

Feedback when incorrect: Simple Design, Pair Programming, Test-Driven Development, Design Improvement are all core practices of Extreme Programming (XP).

18. Pick the two PMLC models that are based upon the Agile Project Management (APM) approach:

Correct	Choice
	Linear
X	Iterative
	Incremental
X	Adaptive

Feedback when incorrect: Iterative and Adaptive PMLC models are based upon the Agile Project Management (APM) approach.

19. Which of the following is NOT a principle from the Agile Manifesto?

Correct	Choice
	Our highest priority is to satisfy the customer through early and continuous delivery of valuable software.
	Business people and developers must work together daily throughout the project.
	Working software is the primary measure of progress.
X	Continuous creation of technical debt and good design enhances agility.

Feedback when incorrect: Continuous creation of technical debt and good design enhances agility is NOT a principle of the Agile Manifesto. The real one is, "Continuous attention to technical excellence and good design enhances agility."

20. In Agile, _____ is the primary measure of progress:

Correct	Choice
	A Burndown chart
	Increased customer satisfaction
X	Working software
	Reduced risk

Feedback when incorrect: Agile Manifesto Principle: Working software is the primary measure of progress.

21. Which of the following is NOT a characteristic of an Adaptive PMLC Model?

Correct	Choice
	Iterative Structure
	JIT Planning
X	Clear up front requirements
	Mission Critical Projects

Feedback when incorrect: Adaptive models have minimal information at the beginning of the project.

22. What Scrum event or artifact is the set of items that the Team selects to work on during a Sprint?

Correct	Choice
	Product Backlog
	Definition of Done
X	Sprint Backlog
	Burndown Chart

Feedback when incorrect: The Sprint Backlog is the set of Product Backlog items selected for the Sprint, plus a plan for delivering the product Increment and realizing the Sprint Goal.

23. The Agile Manifesto states we value some items over others. Match the items in the columns below so each item on the left is valued over the corresponding item on the right.

Correct	Choice
Individuals and Interactions	Processes and Tools
Customer Collaboration	Contract Negotiation
Responding to Change	Following a Plan
Working Software	Comprehensive Documentation

Feedback when incorrect: Individuals and interactions over processes and tools

Working software over comprehensive documentation

Customer collaboration over contract negotiation

Responding to change over following a plan

24. In Agile project management, responding to change is valued over _____.

Correct	Choice
	Contract negotiation
	Customer collaboration
	Processes and tools
X	Following a plan

Feedback when incorrect: Agile Manifesto Value: Responding to change over following a plan.

That is, while there is value in the items on the right, we value the items on the left more.

25. Every Project Management Life Cycle (PMLC) has a sequence of processes that include these phases:

Scoping

Planning

Launching

Monitoring & Controlling

Closing

Correct	Choice	
X	True	
	False	

Feedback when incorrect: Every valid project management life cycle must include each of these processes one or more times.

Module 2-2 Knowledge Check

Answers

1. Which is NOT a Scrum Role?

Correct	Choice
	Product Owner
	Team Member
	Scrum Master
X	Project Manager

Feedback when incorrect: Project Manager is not a Scrum Role

2. In which meeting do you capture lessons learned?

Correct	Choice
	Sprint Planning
	Sprint Review
	Daily Status Meeting
X	Sprint Retrospective

Feedback when incorrect: The Sprint Retrospective is an opportunity for the Scrum Team to inspect itself and create a plan for improvements to be enacted during the next Sprint.

3. What Scrum event or artifact is the set of items selected for the Sprint, plus a plan for delivering the product Increment and realizing the Sprint Goal?

Correct	Choice
	Sprint Planning
	Definition of Done
X	Sprint Backlog
	Increment

Feedback when incorrect: The Sprint Backlog is the set of Product Backlog items selected for the Sprint, plus a plan for delivering the product Increment and realizing the Sprint Goal.

4. What Scrum event or artifact supports daily inspection and adaptation?

Correct	Choice
X	Sprint Planning
	Daily Scrum
	Sprint Review
	Sprint Retrospective

Feedback when incorrect: The Development Team uses the daily Scrum to inspect progress toward the Sprint Goal and to inspect how progress is trending toward completing the work in the Sprint Backlog

5. How long is the time-box for the daily Scrum?

Correct	Choice
	It depends
	5 minutes per person on the Development Team
	Whatever the Team decides
X	15 minutes

Feedback when incorrect: The maximum length of the daily Scrum is 15 minutes.

6. Pick which 3 activities are the responsibilities of the Scrum Master in Scrum.

Correct	Choice
	Provide Estimates
	Commit to the Sprint
	Perform user acceptance
X	Facilitate meetings
	Volunteer for tasks
	Make technical decisions
X	Remove impediments
X	Champion Scrum
	Prioritize the backlog

Feedback when incorrect: The Scrum Master facilitates meetings, champions scrum and removes impediments.

7. Which one is NOT a Pillar of Scrum?

Correct	Choice
	Transparency
	Inspection
X	Empiricism
	Adaptation

Feedback when incorrect: Transparency, Adaptation, Inspection are the pillars of Scrum.

8. What is the purpose of the Sprint Review? (Choose three)

Correct	Choice
X	To collaborate with stakeholders
	To provide status on the Sprint
X	To demonstrate what is "Done"
X	To inspect and adapt

Feedback when incorrect: Inspect and Adapt, collaborate with stakeholders, and demonstrate "Done" are performed during the Sprint Review.

9. Select the statements that are TRUE about the Product Owner. (Choose two)

Correct	Choice
	The Product Owner defines the Sprint Goal before the Sprint Planning meeting
X	The Product Owner prioritizes the Product backlog
X	The Product Owner can clarify the backlog during the Sprint
	The Product Owner estimates the size of the Sprint backlog

Feedback when incorrect: The Product Owner is responsible for the ordering of the product backlog and can provide clarification during the Sprint. He or she does not estimate the work, nor should he have the Sprint goal defined before the Sprint Planning meeting.

10. Pick which 4 activities are the responsibilities of the Product Owner in Scrum.

Correct	Choice
	Provides Estimates
X	Create User Stories
	Commit to the Sprint
X	Perform user acceptance
	Champion Scrum
X	Perform release planning
	Design software
	Facilitate meetings
X	Prioritize the backlog

Feedback when incorrect: The Product Owner prioritizes the backlog, creates User Stories, and performs user acceptance and release planning.

11. If the Development Team doesn't like the time of the daily Scrum, what should the Scrum Master do?

Correct	Choice
	Ask the Team to try the existing time for one Sprint
	Tell them that Scrum is immutable and that they need to stick to it
X	Let the Development Team come up with a new time
	Find a time that is open on everyone's calendar

Feedback when incorrect: Let the Development Team come up with a new time since they are self-organized.

12. Your team is running three-week Sprints. How much time should you schedule for Sprint Review sessions?

Correct	Choice
	45 minutes
X	3 hours
	6 hours
	1 hour, 15 minutes

Feedback when incorrect: 3 weeks. Allow one hour per week of Sprint.

13. In Scrum, who is responsible for managing the team?

Correct	Choice
	Scrum Master
	Project Manager
	Product Owner
X	Development Team

Feedback when incorrect: The Development Team is responsible for self-management.

14. Match each of the following items with its associated time-boxed duration for a one-month Sprint.

Correct	Choice
Sprint Review	4 hours
Sprint Retrospective	3 hours
Daily Scrum	15 minutes
Sprint Planning	8 hours

Feedback when incorrect: Sprint Review = 4 hours, Sprint Retrospective = 3 hours, Sprint Planning = 8 hours, Daily Scrum = 15 minutes

15. During which meeting do team members synchronize their work and progress and report any impediments to the Scrum Master for removal?

Correct	Choice
	Sprint Planning meeting
	Sprint Retrospective
	Weekly Status meeting
X	Daily Scrum

Feedback when incorrect: In the daily Scrum team members synchronize their work and progress and report any impediments to the Scrum Master for removal.

16. Who is responsible for change management in Scrum projects?

Correct	Choice
	Project Manager
	Scrum Master
X	Product Owner
	Project Sponsor

Feedback when incorrect: The Product Owner is solely responsible for change management in Scrum.

17. Match the activity (on the right) to the Scrum event (on the left).

Correct	Choice
Sprint Planning	Sprint Goal creation
Sprint Retrospective	Create Improvement Plans
Sprint Review	Demonstrate Functionality
Daily Scrum	Inspect and adapt

Feedback when incorrect: Sprint Planning = Sprint Goal, Sprint Retrospective = Create Improvement Plans, Daily Scrum = Inspect and Adapt, Sprint Review = Demonstrate Functionality

18. When we use the term "container" in Scrum what are we referring to?

Correct	Choice
X	A Sprint or Iteration
	Development team room
	A vertical slice of functionality
	Source code repository

Feedback when incorrect: A container is a closed space where things can get done, regardless of the overall complexity of the problem. In the case of Scrum, a container is a Sprint, an iteration.

19. Who tracks work remaining in the Product Backlog?

Correct	Choice
	The Development Team
	The Scrum Master
	Senior Executives
X	The Product Owner

Feedback when incorrect: The Product Owner tracks work remaining on the Product Backlog.

20. Who is responsible for managing ROI in Agile projects?

Correct	Choice
	The Project Sponsor
	The Agile Project Manager
	The Scrum of Scrums Master
X	The Product Owner

Feedback when incorrect: In Scrum, the product owner has full product responsibility, which includes securing funding, managing to ROI objectives, release planning and more.

21. When is a Sprint finished?

Correct	Choice
	When the definition of "Done" is met
	When the Product Owner accepts the increment
	When the work remaining is zero
X	When the time-boxed duration is met

Feedback when incorrect: The only time a Sprint is finished is when the time-boxed duration is met. If the team completes the Sprint backlog, the Product Owner adds more work to the Sprint.

22. Pick 5 activities that are the responsibility of the development team in Scrum.

Correct	Choice
X	Provides estimates
	Creates User Stories
X	Commits to the Sprint
	Performs user acceptance
	Champions Scrum
X	Volunteers for tasks
X	Makes technical decisions
X	Designs software
	Facilitates meetings
	Prioritizes the backlog

Feedback when incorrect: The Development Team provides estimates, commits to the Sprint, volunteers for tasks, makes technical decisions and designs the software

23. When does Adaptation occur in Scrum?

Correct	Choice
	At the Sprint Review
	During Sprint Planning
	As Part of the Sprint Retrospective
	In the daily Scrum
X	At all four formal Scrum events

Feedback when incorrect: At all four formal Scrum events

24. A cross-functional team in Scrum consists of which types of team members?

Correct	Choice
	A specialist in QA
	A release manager
X	Anyone with the skills to accomplish the work
	An architect

Feedback when incorrect: Cross-functional teams have all competencies needed to accomplish the work without depending on others not part of the team.

25. The purpose of a Sprint Retrospective is for the Scrum Team to:

Correct	Choice
	Review stories planned for the next Sprint and provide estimates.
	Demonstrate completed User Stories to the Product Owner.
	Individually provide status updates on the User Stories in progress.
X	Determine what to stop doing, start doing, and continue doing.

Feedback when incorrect: The purpose of a Sprint Retrospective is for the Scrum Team to determine, what to stop doing, start doing, and continue doing.

26. What is the best definition of "Done"?

Correct	Choice
	Whatever will please the Product Owner
	It is determined by the Scrum Master
	The product has passed QA and has all of the required release documentation
X	The one that would allow the development work to be ready for a release

Feedback when incorrect: The definition of "Done" is one that would allow development work to be ready for a release.

27. With multiple Scrum teams, you should have a separate product backlog.

Correct	Choice
	True
X	False

Feedback when incorrect: Incorrect. There is only one product backlog when multiple Scrum teams are working on the same product.

28. Which one of the following is NOT a Scrum Event?

Correct	Choice
	Sprint
	Daily Scrum
X	Weekly Status
	Sprint Review

Feedback when incorrect: Weekly Status meetings are not a Scrum Event

29. The optimum size of the Scrum Team is:

Correct	Choice
	It depends
X	Between 3 and 9
	5
	7

Feedback when incorrect: Less than 3 may not be an efficient team and greater than 9 makes coordination difficult. Any number in within the range of 3 - 9 is acceptable.

30. The product owner should spend at least 3 hours per day with the development team?

Correct	Choice
X	True
	False

Feedback when incorrect: The product owner should spend at least 3 hours per day with the development team.

31. Match the following roles on the right to the RASCI on the left:

Correct	Choice
Responsible	Team Members
Accountable	Product Owner
Supportive	Scrum Master
Consulted	Subject Matter Experts
Informed	Stakeholders and Business Owner

Feedback when incorrect:

Responsible = Team members

Accountable = The Product Owner

Supportive = The Scrum Master

Consulted = Subject Matters Experts

Informed= External Stakeholders and the Business Owner

32. The behavior where the Scrum Team focuses on one or more stories until they are done is called:

Correct	Choice
	Collaboration
	Sprinting
X	Swarming
	Pair-programming

Feedback when incorrect: Swarming is when the Scrum Team focuses on one or more stories until they are done.

33. Which role is external to the Scrum Team but provides a skills the does not exist on the Team?

Correct	Choice
X	Subject Matter Expert
	Project Manager
	Scrum Master
	Team Member

Feedback when incorrect: The Subject Matter Expert (SME) is external to the Scrum Team but provides a skill that does not exist on the Team.

34. This role champions the products, provides the budget and supports the Scrum Master in removing impediments.

Correct	Choice
	Subject Matter Expert
	Project Manager
X	Business Owner
	Product Owner

Feedback when incorrect: The Business Owner champions the product, provides the budget and supports the Scrum Master in removing impediments.

Module 2-3 Knowledge Check

Answers

1. In Pair Programming, one programmer is responsible for all the coding in an iteration then the programmers switch for the next iteration.

Correct	Choice
	True
X	False

Feedback when incorrect: It is expected in pair programming that the programmers swap roles every few minutes or so.

2. Which of the following is NOT one of the 12 core practices of XP?

Correct	Choice
X	Visualize the flow
	Coding Standards
	System Metaphor
	On-site Customer

Feedback when incorrect: Visualize the flow is a Kanban Practice

3. On XP teams, what is expected from the Project Manager?

Correct	Choice
	Coach the team on Agile practices
X	Help the team work with the rest of the organization
	Design the software
	Provide domain expertise to the team

Feedback when incorrect: A project manager in an XP team ensures that the team works well with the rest of the organization.

4. Which is NOT a role on an XP team?

Correct	Choice
	Coach
	Customer
	Programmer
X	Product Owner

Feedback when incorrect: XP has their own terminology for roles. The similar roles in XP are the XP Customer and XP Tester.

5. Which 5 roles are defined by Extreme Programming?

Correct	Choice
	Scrum Master
X	Coach
	Stakeholder
X	Programmer
X	Tracker
X	Tester
	Product Owner
X	Customer

Feedback when incorrect: Coach, Customer, Programmer, Tracker, Tester are the XP roles,

6. Which XP practice promotes the restriction on overtime?

Correct	Choice
X	Sustainable Pace
	Servant Leadership
	Small Releases
	Pair Programming

Feedback when incorrect: Sustainable pace suggests working no more than 40 hours a week, and never working overtime a second week in a row.

7. In XP, what is the practice of creating a story about a future system that everyone - customers, programmers, and managers - can tell about how the system works?

Correct	Choice
	Extreme persona
X	System metaphor
	Simple design
	Wireframe

Feedback when incorrect: Kent Beck, author of Extreme Programming Explained defines a system metaphor as: "a story that everyone - customers, programmers, and managers - can tell about how the system works."

8. Which of the following is NOT one of the 12 core practices of XP:

Correct	Choice
	Simple Design
X	Vertical Slicing
	Refactoring
	Continuous Testing

Feedback when incorrect: Vertical slicing is taking a backlog item that has a database component, some business logic and a user interface and breaking it down into small stepwise progressions where each step cuts through every slice.

9. What is the role of the XP Coach?

Correct	Choice
	Defines the right product to build
	Determines the order to build
X	Helps the team stay on process
	Ensures the product works

Feedback when incorrect: The XP Coach role helps a team stay on process and helps the team to learn.

10. In XP, the practice that any developer can change any line of code to add functionality, fix bugs, improve designs, or refactor demonstrates:

Correct	Choice
X	Collective Code Ownership
	Pair Programming
	Continuous Integration
	Source Code Control

Feedback when incorrect: Collective Code Ownership is the XP practice that any developer can change any line of code to add functionality, fix bugs, improve designs, or refactor demonstrates.

11. The ultimate goal of _____ is to deploy all but the last few hours of work at any time.

Correct	Choice
X	Continuous Integration
	Synchronous Builds
	Asynchronous Builds
	Collective Code Ownership

Feedback when incorrect: Continuous Integration

12. Extreme Programming (XP) defines four basic activities that are performed during the software development process. These include designing, coding, testing and ...?

Correct	Choice
	Collaborating
	Communicating
X	Listening
	Leveling

Feedback when incorrect: One of the four basic activities of XP is listening to the Customer and also to other development team members.

13. Which of the following is an Agile practice promoted by XP that is often used in conjunction with other Agile methods?

Correct	Choice
	Dynamic Systems Development Method (DSDM)
	Adaptive Software Development (ASD)
X	Test Driven Development (TDD)
	Feature Driven Development (FDD)

Feedback when incorrect: Test-driven development (TDD), also called test-driven design, is a method of software development in which unit testing is repeatedly done on source code.

14. Which of the following describe the roles in pair programming?

Correct	Choice
	Pilot and the navigator
	Coder and the planner
	Leader and the second chair
X	Driver and the navigator

Feedback when incorrect: The programmer at the keyboard is usually called the "driver", the other, also actively involved in the programming task but focusing more on overall direction is the "navigator."

15. Extreme Programming (XP) includes which of the following 3 practices?

Correct	Choice
X	Simple Design
X	Coding standards
	Burndown charts
X	Sustainable Pace

Feedback when incorrect: Burndown charts are not an XP practice.

Kanban for Project Management Knowledge Check

Answers

1. Which is the first step in setting up Kanban?

Correct	Choice
	Place prioritized goals on the left column of the board
X	Map your current workflow
	Lay out a visual Kanban board
	Decide on limits for items in queue and work in progress

Feedback when incorrect: The 5 steps of Kanban are: 1) Map your current workflow 2) Visualize your work 3) Focus on flow 4) Limit your work in process 5) Measure and improve

2. This approach includes a visual process management system and an approach to incremental, evolutionary process changes for organizations.

Correct	Choice
	Extreme programming
	Lean
X	Kanban
	Scrum

Feedback when incorrect: The Kanban approach includes a visual process management system and an approach to incremental, evolutionary process changes for organizations.

3. Kanban means _____ in Japanese?

Correct	Choice
	User Story
	Vertical Slices
	Production Line
X	Signal card

Feedback when incorrect: Kanban in Japanese means signal card

4. At minimum, all Kanban boards should have the following columns:

Correct	Choice
	Backlog, Design, Develop, Unit Test, Acceptance Test, Ready-to-ship
X	The Kanban board columns are determined by the team
	To-Do, Doing, Done
	Analysis, Design, Develop, Test, Deploy

Feedback when incorrect: The Kanban board columns are determined by the team

5. What are the 5 values of Kanban?

Correct	Choice
	Communication, Simplicity, Feedback, Courage, Humility
	Communication, Simplicity, Feedback, Adaptation, Continuous Improvement
X	Respect, Courage, Value, Collaboration, Holistic Approach to Change

Feedback when incorrect: The 5 values of Kanban are: Respect, Courage, Focus on Value, Communication and Collaboration, Holistic Approach to Change

6. Setting up development work in a way that the team can figure out what to do next is called:

Correct	Choice
X	A pull system
	Push system
	Critical path
	Sprint backlog

Feedback when incorrect: A pull system, used in Kanban, presents the development work in such a way that it clearly identifies what should be worked on next.

7. Sequence the core practices of Kanban in order of execution. (drag and reorder)

Correct Order
Visualize the workflow
Limit WIP
Manage the flow
Make process policies explicit
Implement Feedback Loops
Improve collaboratively

Feedback when incorrect: The core practices of Kanban: 1) Visualize the workflow 2) Limit WIP 3) Manage the flow 4) Make process policies explicit 5) Implement Feedback Loops 6) Improve collaboratively

8. The number of days needed between feature specification and production delivery is called:

Correct	Choice
X	Cycle time
	Calendar time
	Ideal time
	Real time

Feedback when incorrect: Cycle time is the number of days needed between feature specification and production delivery.

9. The number of days needed between customer request and production delivery is called:

Correct	Choice
	Cycle time
X	Lead time
	Ideal time
	Real time

Feedback when incorrect: Lead time is the number of days needed between customer request and production delivery.

10. Classes of Services in Kanban are used to:

Correct	Choice
	Support estimation for Kanban Cards
	Prioritize the queue by risk
	Ensure WIP limits are realistic
	All of the above

Feedback when incorrect: Classifying classes of service are typically priorities defined based on business impact and cost of delay.

11. **The purpose of Work in Progress (WIP) limits is to prevent the unintentional accumulation of work, so there isn't a bottleneck.**

Correct	Choice
X	True
	False

Feedback when incorrect: One of the core properties in the Kanban method is that Work in Progress is limited. Limiting WIP is to match team's development capacity and to prevent bottlenecks.

12. **The following is a picture of which of the following Information Radiators?**

Correct	Choice
	Kanban Tracking System
	Burnup Chart
X	Cumulative Flow Diagram
	Burndown Chart

Feedback when incorrect: It is a Cumulative Flow Diagram

13. **The measure of productivity of a Kanban team is:**

Correct	Choice
	Velocity
X	Throughput
	Cycle time
	Lead Time
	Work in Progress

Feedback when incorrect: Through put is the measure of the productivity of a Kanban Team.

14. Kanban cards should always be written using User Stories.

Correct	Choice
	True
X	False

Feedback when incorrect: There are many formats for Kanban Cards. Using User Stories is just one approach.

15. A term used to describe the work that can be delivered which meets the business requirements without exceeding them. (Choose Two)

Correct	Choice
	Epic
X	Minimum Viable Product
	Theme
	User Story
X	Minimum Marketable Features

Feedback when incorrect: Minimum Viable Product (MVP) and Minimum Marketable Features (MMF) are terms used to describe the work that can be delivered which meets the business requirements without exceeding them.

16. Order the 5 focusing steps of the Theory of Constraints.

Correct Order
Identify the System Constraint
Decide How to Exploit the Constraint
Subordinate Everything Else
Elevate the Constraint
Go Back to Step 1, Repeat

Feedback when incorrect:

> Identify the System Constraint
>
> Decide How to Exploit the Constraint
>
> Subordinate Everything Else
>
> Elevate the Constraint
>
> Go Back to Step 1, Repeat

17. Pick the 3 common Kanban Katas.

Correct	Choice
X	Daily Standup Meeting
	Iteration Demo
	Weekly Status
X	Operations Review
	Sprint Retrospective
X	Improvement Kata

Feedback when incorrect:

Common katas for Kanban are as follows:

> Daily Standup Meeting
>
> Improvement Kata
>
> Operations Review

18. In what type of Agile approach would you ask the following questions at the Daily Stand-up?

> **What do we need to do to advance this piece of work?**

> **Is anyone working on anything that is not on the board?**

> **What do we need to finish as a team?**

> **Are there any bottlenecks or blockers to the flow of work?**

Correct	Choice
	Iterative Agile
X	Flow-based Agile
	None of the above

Feedback when incorrect: These are the questions for a flow-based approach as opposed to the typical 3 questions for Scrum and iterative Agile.

Module 2-5 Knowledge Check

Answers

1. Put the following phases of the Agile Unified Process in order:

Correct Order
Inception
Elaboration
Construction
Transition

Feedback when incorrect: The correct order is: Inception, Elaboration, Construction, Transition

2. What are the following:

Focus on the business need
Deliver on time
Collaborate
Never compromise quality
Build incrementally from firm foundations
Develop iteratively
Communicate continuously and clearly
Demonstrate control

Correct	Choice
	None of the Above
X	The principles of DSDM
	The practices of LeSS
	The principles of Agile UP
	The PM Declaration of Interdependence

Feedback when incorrect: They are the 8 principles of DSDM

3. Put the following Crystal properties in order by impact on success:

Correct Order
Frequent Delivery
Osmotic Communication
Reflective Improvement
Personal Safety
Focus
Easy Access to Expert Users
Technical Environment with CI and Automation

Feedback when incorrect:

Correct Order:

> Frequent Delivery
>
> Osmotic Communication
>
> Reflective Improvement
>
> Personal Safety
>
> Focus
>
> Easy Access to Expert Users
>
> Technical Environment

4. Which of the following is NOT considered an enterprise Agile method?

Correct	Choice
	DAD
	SAFe
	LeSS
X	XP

Feedback when incorrect: XP is not considered an enterprise Agile framework without the addition of techniques to support scaling to large projects.

5. Alistair Cockburn created the Crystal Family of Agile Methods, all of whose names contain colors of quartz crystals taken from geology. What two characteristics of an Agile project are used to determine the color of the Crystal method?

Correct	Choice
	Size and duration
	Duration and complexity
X	Size and criticality
	Duration and criticality

Feedback when incorrect: Crystal comes from Alistair Cockburn's characterization of projects along the two dimensions of "size" (meaning the size of the project team) and "criticality" (meaning the damage that will be caused if the developed product or system fails).

6. The technique used to analyze the flow of information and materials through a system to eliminate waste is:

Correct	Choice
	Fishbone diagramming
	Flow charting
X	Value stream mapping
	Pareto analysis

Feedback when incorrect: The value stream map is a Lean tool that practitioners use to analyze the value stream.

7. What of the following is not a step in the Value Stream Mapping process?

Correct	Choice
	Define the current state
	Collect data
X	Amplify Learning
	Depict the future state
	Develop an implementation plan

Feedback when incorrect: Amplify Learning is a Lean development principle.

8. This Agile methodology's properties includes Focus, Osmotic Communication and Project Safety:

Correct	Choice
	Scrum
	Kanban
	Extreme Programming
X	Crystal

Feedback when incorrect: The Crystal family of methodologies focuses on efficiency and habitability as components of project safety. Crystal Clear focuses on people, not processes or artifacts.

9. Which one is not a value of Lean Development?

Correct	Choice
	Pursue perfection
X	Ensure collective code ownership
	Balance long-term improvement and short-term improvement
	After a project flows, keep improving it

Feedback when incorrect: Collective code ownership is an XP principle.

10. What Agile concept expresses delivering value in slices rather than in layers/stages?

Correct	Choice
	Definition of Done
	Value Mapping
X	Sashimi
	Lean Value

Feedback when incorrect: Sashimi is an Agile concept of delivering value in slices rather than in layers/stages.

11. Which is NOT a principle of Lean?

Correct	Choice
	Eliminate waste
X	Time-boxed events
	Deliver fast
	Delay commitment

Feedback when incorrect: Time-boxed events are a practice of Scrum not Lean.

12. Which Agile method goes through the following stages:
   Feasibility Study
   Business Study
   Functional Model
   Design and Build
   Implement

Correct	Choice
X	Dynamic Systems Development Method (DSDM)
	Rational Unified Process (RUP)
	Feature Driven Development (FDD)
	Lean Software Development
	Scrum

Feedback when incorrect: These are the stages of the DSDM project life-cycle

13. Which of the following is not an Agile approach?

Correct	Choice
	Feature Driven Development (FDD)
	Extreme Programming (XP)
	Dynamic Systems Development Method (DSDM)
	Crystal Clear
X	Program Evaluation Review Technique (PERT)

Feedback when incorrect: Program Evaluation Review Technique (PERT) is a traditional project management technique. All of the others are Agile techniques.

14. Match a definition (on the right) to a Lean principle (on the left).

Correct	Choice
Eliminate Waste	Create nothing but value
Create Knowledge	Maintain a culture of constant improvement
Build Quality In	Refactor - eliminate code duplication to zero
Defer Commitment	Schedule irreversible decisions at the last responsible moment
Optimize the Whole	Focus on the entire value stream

Feedback when incorrect:

Eliminate Waste: Create nothing but value

Create Knowledge: Maintain a culture of constant improvement,

Build Quality In: Refactor - Eliminate code duplication to zero

Defer Commitment: Schedule irreversible decisions at the last responsible moment

Optimize the Whole: Focus on the entire value stream

15. When there are multiple Scrum Teams working on one project, what is the approach for integrating the project work?

Correct	Choice
	Maintain a single product backlog
	Manage dependencies via Scrum of Scrums
	Consider a Chief Product Owner role
	Align project teams by technology, feature or location
X	All of the above

Feedback when incorrect: The correct answer is all of the above

16. Pick three items which are considered wastes of Software Development.

Correct	Choice
X	Partially Done Work
	Continuous Integration
X	Task Switching
	Refactoring
X	Defects

Feedback when incorrect: Continuous Integration and Refactoring are not wastes. They provide value. The other three are wastes.

17. One of the major tools and techniques used in Lean Software Development is Value Stream Mapping. What is the primary purpose of value stream mapping?

Correct	Choice
	To improve business processes
X	To identify and eliminate waste
	To ensure product quality
	To Limit WIP

Feedback when incorrect: The single most important goal of using Value Stream Mapping is to identify and eliminate waste.

18. The purpose of the Scrum of Scrums is to perform what function?

Correct	Choice
	To increase knowledge of Agile within the organization
X	To manage cross-team dependencies working on the same project
	To ensure team building and staff development occurs
	To provide dashboard reporting to executives

Feedback when incorrect: When you scale Scrum to more teams, you handle dependencies and coordination among teams working on the product with a Scrum of Scrums

Module 3 Knowledge Check

Answers

1. 80% of the value comes from 20% of the work. Which law is this referring to?

Correct	Choice
	Parkinson's Law
	Moore's Law
X	Pareto's Law
	Jevon's Paradox

Feedback when incorrect: Pareto's law is more commonly known as the 80/20 rule. This means that typically 80% of your results come from only 20% of your efforts.

2. When performing earned value analysis on an Agile project, it is not possible to use story points to calculate the schedule performance index (SPI).

Correct	Choice
	True
X	False

Feedback when incorrect: Completed points per feature divided by actual points per feature is a valid approach for calculating SPI.

3. The following formula can be used to calculate the cost performance index (CPI) on an Agile project.

Correct	Choice
X	True
	False

Feedback when incorrect: Completed feature value divided by actual cost per feature is a valid approach for calculating CPI.

4. What is a Japanese term used in Lean software development is an activity that is wasteful, unproductive, and doesn't add value?

Correct	Choice
	Sashimi
	Kanban
X	Muda
	Kairoshi

Feedback when incorrect: Muda is a term for something that is wasteful and doesn't add value or is unproductive.

5. The backlog is ordered by:

Correct	Choice
X	The needs of the Product Owner
	Risk
	Complexity
	Size

Feedback when incorrect: The backlog is ordered by the needs of the Product Owner.

6. DSDM uses MoSCoW technique to create the prioritized requirements list. In MoSCoW technique, 'M' stands for:

Correct	Choice
	Most useful
X	Must have
	Must not have
	Minimum marketable feature

Feedback when incorrect: MoSCoW is an acronym for: Must Have, Should Have, Could Have, Won't Have

7. In the Kano Model of customer satisfaction, this type of feature makes a product unique from its competitors and contributes 100% to positive customer satisfaction:

Correct	Choice
X	Exciter
	Performance
	Must-have
	Threshold

Feedback when incorrect: Exciter or delighter attributes are for the most part unforeseen by the customer but may yield the most satisfaction.

8. Identify the three components of the Agile Triangle.

Correct	Choice
X	Quality
X	Value
	Cost
X	Constraints
	Scope
	Leadership

Feedback when incorrect: Quality, Value, Constraints

9. In what order do you select requirements to work on in a risk adjusted backlog?

Correct Order
High Risk High Value
Low Risk High Value
Low Risk Low Value
High Risk Low Value

10. The length of time to recover the cost of a project investment is the:

Correct	Choice
	Net Present Value
X	Payback Period
	Earned Value
	ROI

Feedback when incorrect: Payback Period

11. Net present value (NPV) is a ratio that compares the value of a dollar today to the value of that same dollar in the future. An NPV that is negative suggests what?

Correct	Choice
	The project should be rejected
	I don't have enough information
X	The project should be deferred
	The project should be put on hold until the value is 0

Feedback when incorrect: A negative NPV suggests that the project should be deferred over another project that has a positive NPV.

12. Which one is NOT a level of need in the Kano Model?

Correct	Choice
	Basic Needs
	Performance Needs
X	Enabling Needs
	Excitement Needs

Feedback when incorrect: Different categories of customer satisfaction in the Kano model include basic needs, performance needs, and excitement needs.

13. Assuming all projects require the same amount of up-front investment, the project with the highest _____ would be considered the best and undertaken first.

Correct	Choice
	Earned Value Management (EVM)
X	Internal Rate of Return (IRR)
	Payback Period
	Budget at Completion (BAC)

Feedback when incorrect: Generally speaking, the higher a project's internal rate of return (IRR), the more desirable it is to undertake the project.

14. The way that we calculate the number of years it takes to break even from undertaking a project which also takes into account the time value of money is the:

Correct	Choice
	Pay-back period
X	Discounted pay-back period
	NPV
	Cumulative cash flow

Feedback when incorrect: In contrast to an NPV analysis, which provides the overall value of an project, a discounted payback period gives the number of years it takes to break even from undertaking the initial expenditure.

15. Match each component of the Agile Triangle (on the left) to its associated description (on the right).

Correct	Choice
Value	Releasable Product
Quality	Reliable, Adaptable Product
Constraints	Cost, Schedule, Scope

16. A time-boxed period to research a concept and/or create a simple prototype is called a(n):

Correct	Choice
	Sprint
	Iteration
X	Spike
	Retrospective

Feedback when incorrect: A Spike is a time-boxed period to research a concept and/or create a simple prototype.

17. The acronym MoSCoW stands for a form of:

Correct	Choice
	Estimation
	Risk identification
X	Prioritization
	Reporting

Feedback when incorrect: MoSCoW is a simple way to prioritize User Stories. MoSCoW stands for: Must have, Should have, Could have, Won't have.

18. **Project X has an IRR of 12%, and Project Y has an IRR of 10%. Which project should be chosen as a better investment for the organization?**

Correct	Choice
	It depends on the payback period
	Project Y
X	Project X
	Project X or Y, depending on the NPV

Feedback when incorrect: Project X: (IRR) internal rate of return is calculation to compare investment alternatives. A higher value for the internal rate of return is desired.

19. **Which of the following is NOT a prioritization technique?**

Correct	Choice
	User Story Mapping
X	Planning Poker
	Minimally Marketable Features (MMF)
	Kano analysis
	Kitchen Prioritization

Feedback when incorrect: Planning Poker is an estimation technique.

20. **Sequence the steps to User Story Mapping. (drag and drop)**

Correct Order
Product Roadmap Definition
User Story Definition
User Story Decomposition
Release Planning

21. Choose which three statements are true about Approved Iterations:

Correct	Choice
X	Meets the definition of Done
	There is no technical debt
	The Architect has approved it
X	It is communicated to all Team members and stakeholders
X	As a result, the Product Owner updates Roadmaps and Release Plans

Feedback when incorrect: Approved Iterations, Meet the definition of Done, Are communicated to all Team members and stakeholders, The Product Owner updates Roadmaps and Release Plans

22. "Fail Sooner" is a benefit of Incremental Development.

Correct	Choice
X	True
	False

Feedback when incorrect: Incremental Development mitigates the risk of project failure by not meeting the stakeholder's requirements. Deliver in chunks and expect feedback. "Fail Sooner"

Module 4-1 Knowledge Check

Answers

1. Which of the following is the hierarchy of User Story creation.

Correct	Choice
	Task, User Story, Feature, Theme
	Goal, Epic, Activity, User Story
	User Story, Epic, Theme, Feature
X	Theme, Epic, User Story, Task

Feedback when incorrect: A theme is the highest level of the story hierarchy. A Product Owner breaks down a theme into one or more epics. An epic is a group of related User Stories. User stories are then divided into one or more tasks.

2. Non-functional requirements should be written as user stories whenever possible.

Correct	Choice
	True
X	False

Feedback when incorrect: NFRs don't have to be written as User Stories. Instead they are often part of the Definition of Done or part of the Acceptance Criteria

3. Operations and Maintenance staff should not be part of the Agile team.

Correct	Choice
	True
X	False

Feedback when incorrect: The approach of DevOps suggests that Operations and Maintenance staff should be incorporated into Agile Teams.

4. Match the story types on the left to their definition on the right (drag and drop):

Correct	Choice
Spike	Stories that figure out answers to tough technical or design problems
Architecturally Significant	Stories are functional Stories that cause the Team to make architectural decisions
Analysis	Stories that are created to find other stories
Infrastructure	Stories to improve the infrastructure the team is using

Feedback when incorrect:

Spike - An XP term that describes Stories that figure out answers to tough technical or design problems.

Architecturally Significant Stories are functional Stories that cause the Team to make architectural decisions.

Analysis stories exist because they find other stories.

Infrastructure Stories add to or improve the infrastructure the team is using.

5. A common reason a story may not be estimable is the:

Correct	Choice
X	Team lacks domain knowledge.
	The story did not include a role.
	Developers do not understand the tasks related to the story.
	Team has no experience in estimating.

Feedback when incorrect: There are three common reasons why a story may not be estimable: 1) Developers lack domain knowledge 2) Developers lack technical knowledge 3) The story is too big.

6. At completion of iteration planning, the team has finished identifying the tasks they will commit to for the next iteration. Which of the following tools best provides transparency into the progress throughout the iteration?

Correct	Choice
	Hours expended chart
	Management baseline chart
X	Burndown chart
	Gantt chart

Feedback when incorrect: A Sprint Burndown chart will show work completed and working remaining throughout the iteration.

7. Well-written User Stories that follow the INVEST model include which attributes?

Correct	Choice
X	Negotiable, Estimable, Small
	Independent, Valuable, Timely
	Independent, Negotiable, Smart
	Valuable, Easy-to-use, Timely

Feedback when incorrect: A well-written user story follows the INVEST model: Independent, Negotiable, Valuable, Estimable, Small, Testable.

8. Wireframe models help Agile teams:

Correct	Choice
	Test designs
X	Confirm designs
	Configure reports
	Track velocity

Feedback when incorrect: Wireframes help to generate feedback, see potential problems with an interface and confirm designs.

9. A reminder for the developer and Product Owner to have a conversation is:

Correct	Choice
	The Sprint planning meeting
	Backlog grooming
X	A User Story
	An Agile reminder

Feedback when incorrect: A User Story is a reminder for the developer and Product Owner to have a conversation.

10. Match the definitions (on the right) to each of the characteristics of a good User Story (on the left).

Correct	Choice
Negotiable	A story is not a contract
Valuable	If a story does not have discernable value it should not be done
Small	User Stories average 3-4 days of work
Testable	Each story needs to be proven that it is "done"
Independent	Stories can be worked on in any order
Estimable	A story has to be able to be sized so it can be properly prioritized

Feedback when incorrect: Independent stories can be worked on in any order. A Negotiable story is not a contract. If a Valuable story does not have discernable value it should NOT be done. An Estimable story has to be able to be sized so it can be properly prioritized. Small stories average 3-4 days of work. A Testable story needs to be proven that it is "done."

11. Match each Agile requirement type (on the left) to its definition (on the right).

Correct	Choice
Feature	Business solution, capability or enhancement that ultimately provides value to the business.
User Story	Describes the interaction of the users with the system
Story	Any requirement that is NOT a User Story (e.g. technical enabling, analysis, reminder to have conversation)
Task	Fundamental unit of work that must be completed to make a progress on a Story

Feedback when incorrect:

Feature: Business solution, capability or enhancement

User Story: Describes the interaction of the users with the system

Story: Any requirement that is NOT a User Story

Task: Fundamental unit of work

Feature: Business solution, capability or enhancement

12. Suppose your team is working to create a commercial website and is in the process of developing User Stories by role. One team member suggests rather than only thinking about the target user, we should also think of some exceptional users who use the system very differently. What type of user is this team member referring to?

Correct	Choice
	Performance Tester
X	Extreme Persona
	High Risk User
	Admin Role

Feedback when incorrect: An extreme persona is a team-manufactured user that is strongly exaggerated in order to elicit requirements that are non-standard.

13. CRUD is an acronym that defines a way to split stories. What does CRUD stand for:

Correct	Choice
	Create/Replace/Update/Define
	Capture/Replace/Update/Define
X	Create/Read/Update/Delete
	Create/Review/Update/Done

Feedback when incorrect: Create/Update/Delete

14. The definition of an Epic can be written using the acronym CURB. What does CURB stand for.

Correct	Choice
	Create/Update/Replace/Big
X	Complex/Unknown/Risky/Big
	Compound/Unknown/Risky/Basic
	Complicated/Unusual/Really Big

Feedback when incorrect: Complex/Unknown/Risky/Big

15. While developing a story during the iteration, team discovered new tasks that were not identified earlier. A new complicated task is discovered such that the User Story cannot be completed during the Sprint. What should the Team do?

Correct	Choice
	Discuss the situation with the Scrum Master and see if there is still a way to meet the iteration goals.
X	Let the Product Owner decide if there is still a way to meet the iteration goals.
	Modify the scope of other User Stories to allow completion of the Sprint backlog.
	Drop the User Story and inform the Product Owner that it will be delivered in the next iteration.

Feedback when incorrect: Let the Product Owner decide if there is still a way to meet the Sprint goal. The Owner may choose to reduce the functionality of a story or drop one entirely.

16. What can be described as "one or two written sentences; a series of conversations about the desired functionality."

Correct	Choice
	Epic
	Product roadmap
X	User Story
	Story point

Feedback when incorrect: A User Story can be described as "one or two written sentences; a series of conversations about the desired functionality."

17. User Stories are:

Correct	Choice
X	Negotiable
	Created by the Agile Project Manager
	The foundation of the roadmap
	Baselined and not allowed to change

Feedback when incorrect: User Stories are not a contract. They are not meant to be precise, detailed specifications of a feature. They should always be Negotiable.

18. What is the reason to develop personas as part of User Story creation?

Correct	Choice
	When the conversation is centered on the high-level flow of a process
	When trying to capture the high-level objective of a specific requirement
	When communicating what features will be included in the next release
X	When trying to better understand stakeholder demographics and general needs

Feedback when incorrect: Personas are created to better understand stakeholder demographics and general needs.

Module 4-2 Knowledge Check

Answers

1. Suppose your team velocity is 8 story points, and the product backlog items are ordered by priority as shown below. If you are in a Sprint Planning meeting and need to commit to the User Stories for the next iteration, which ones will you select?

Story 1 = 3 Story Points
Story 2 = 4 Story Points
Story 3 = 3 Story Points
Story 4 = 1 Story Points

Correct	Choice
	Story 1 and 2
	Story 2, 3, & 4
	Story 1, 2, & 3
X	Story 1, 2, & 4

Feedback when incorrect: Stories 1, 2, 4: The team only commits to their velocity. They are allowed to take a lower priority story in order (4) to meet their target velocity,

2. Which following statement is the least accurate regarding the Burndown chart?

Correct	Choice
	It is calculated using hours or points
	It is updated by the development team daily
X	It provides insight into the quality of the product
	It reflects work remaining

Feedback when incorrect: The Burndown chart does not measure quality. It measures work completed and work remaining.

3. **Based on the following information, determine the number weeks until the next release:**

   Length of a Sprint = 2 weeks

   Velocity of team = 35 points

   Number of story points assigned to the minimum marketable features (MMF) = 280 points

Correct	Choice
X	16 weeks
	9 weeks
	8 weeks
	12 weeks

Feedback when incorrect: 16 weeks. 280 points divided by 35 points of velocity = 8 Sprints. 8 Sprints of two weeks = 16 weeks.

4. **At completion of iteration planning, the team has finished identifying the tasks they will commit to for the next iteration. Which of the following tools best provides transparency into the progress throughout the iteration?**

Correct	Choice
	Hours expended chart
	Management baseline chart
X	Burndown chart
	Gantt chart

Feedback when incorrect: A Sprint Burndown chart will show work completed and working remaining throughout the iteration.

5. Based upon this Burndown chart, is this project ahead of schedule or behind schedule?

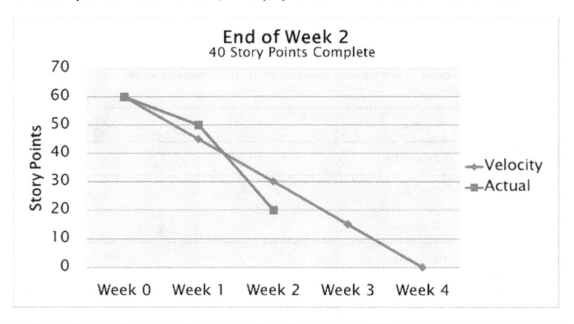

Correct	Choice
	Behind schedule
X	Ahead of schedule

Feedback when incorrect: If the actual line is below the velocity line, the Burndown chart shows that the project is ahead schedule.

6. How do you read a burndown bar chart? Match the phrases below to create instructions.

Correct	Choice
As tasks are completed	the top of the bar is lowered.
When tasks are added to the original set	the bottom of the bar is lowered.
When tasks are removed from the original set	the bottom of the bar is raised.
When the amount of work involved in a task changes	the top of the bar moves up or down.

7. Which of the following is an example of an information radiator?

Correct	Choice
	An email of a status report
X	A whiteboard showing the state of work
	A face-to-face conversation
	A text of a quick question to the Product Owner

Feedback when incorrect: Whiteboards showing state of work. An information radiator is a large, highly visible display used by software development teams to track progress.

8. Which of the following is NOT a KPI (key performance indicator) of Agile?

Correct	Choice
	Actual Stories Completed vs. Committed Stories
	Technical Debt Management
	Team Velocity
	Quality Delivered to Customers
	Team Enthusiasm
X	Team Attendance

Feedback when incorrect: Team Attendance is not a KPI of Agile. Agile teams are self-managing so less focus is spent on micro-managing time in the office, etc.

9. Which of the following is NOT a metric that measures the performance of DevOps in Agile.

Correct	Choice
	Release date adherence percentage
	Percentage increase in the number of releases
X	Business value realized per release
	Defects attributable to platform/support requirements
	Percentage of NFRs met

Feedback when incorrect: Business value metrics are attributed to the business and are captured by the product owner and business owner, not DevOps.

10. When reading a burn-down chart, what does each status measurement say about project performance? Match the items below.

Correct	Choice
Actual Work Line is below the Ideal Work Line	Ahead of Schedule
Actual Work Line is on the Ideal Work Line	On Schedule
Actual Work Line is above the Ideal Work Line	Behind Schedule

11. The trend of work remaining across time in a Sprint, a release, or a product, with work remaining tracked on the vertical axis and the time periods tracked on the horizontal axis is called a _____.

Correct	Choice
	Progress Chart
	Parking Lot Chart
X	Burndown Chart
	Burnup Chart

Feedback when incorrect: A Burndown Chart tracks work remaining on the vertical axis and the time periods on the horizontal axis

12. At the end of first iteration, the team finishes User Stories A, B and 50% of C. What is the team velocity?

The story sizes were:

Story A = 8 Points, Story B = 1 Points, Story C = 5 Points, Story D = 3 Points

Correct	Choice
	11.5
	16
	14
X	9

Feedback when incorrect: 9: Stories are either done or not done. There is no concept of an unfinished story or 50% complete.

13. Typically calculated in story points, this is the rate at which the team converts "Done" items in a single Sprint (drag and drop):

Correct	Choice
	Burndown rate
	Burn-up rate
X	Velocity
	Capacity

Feedback when incorrect: Velocity is calculated in story points. It is the rate at which the team converts "Done" items in a single Sprint.

14. The best description of a Sprint backlog is:

Correct	Choice
	Daily progress for a Sprint over the Sprint's length
	A prioritized list of tasks to be completed during the project
X	A prioritized list of requirements to be completed during the Sprint
	A prioritized list of requirements to be completed for a release

Feedback when incorrect: The Sprint backlog is prioritized list of requirements to be completed during the Sprint

15. Based upon this Burndown chart, is this project trending ahead of schedule or behind schedule?

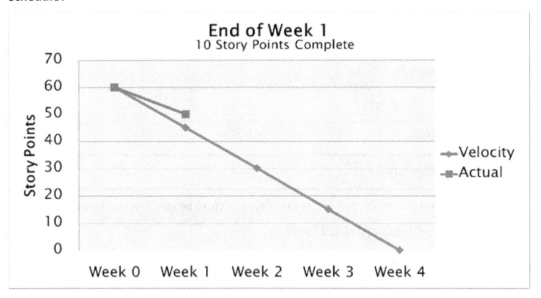

Correct	Choice
	Ahead of schedule
X	Behind schedule

16. Which is a report of all the work that is "done?"

Correct	Choice
X	Burndown chart
	Sashimi
	Kanban chart
	Completion chart

Feedback when incorrect: A Burndown chart shows the work that is done and the work remaining.

17. Product Backlog Items (PBI) described as emergent, are expected to:

Correct	Choice
	Become new technology requirements
	Become the highest priority items
	Be the most recent stories added to the backlog
X	Grow and change over time as software is developed

Feedback when incorrect: Product Backlog items (PBI) described as emergent, are expected to grow and change over time.

18. Which of the following sets of tools is least likely to be utilized by an Agile team?

Correct	Choice
	Digital camera, task board
	Smart board, card wall
X	WBS, PERT charts
	Wiki, planning poker cards

Feedback when incorrect: WBS and PERT charts are tools of traditional project management.

19. Highly visible project displays are called (drag and drop):

Correct	Choice
	Project radiators
	Information refrigerators
X	Information radiators
	Project distributors

Feedback when incorrect: An information radiator is a large, highly visible display used by software development teams to track progress.

20. Which of the following statements is true for measuring team velocity?

Correct	Choice
	Velocity is not accurate when there are meetings that cut into development time.
	Velocity tracking does not allow for scope changes during the project.
X	Velocity measurements account for work done and disruptions on the project.
	Velocity measurements are disrupted when some project resources are part-time.

Feedback when incorrect: Velocity measurements account for work done and disruptions on the project.

Module 5 Knowledge Check

Answers

1. **What does the term "fishbowl" refer to in terms of communication on Agile teams?**

Correct	Choice
X	An all day live video connection with a remote team member
	All team members sharing a common workspace
	All stakeholders in an all-day program review
	A test lab where you watch actual customers test an application
	None of the above

Feedback when incorrect: A fishbowl refers to an all day live video connection with a remote team member

2. **Match the response options to each level of conflict.**

Correct	Choice
Level 1: Problem to Solve	Collaboration or consensus
Level 2: Disagreement	Support and safety
Level 3: Contest	Accommodate, negotiate, get factual
Level 4 : Crusade	Establish safe structures again
Level 5 : World War	Do whatever is necessary

3. There are no project managers on Agile projects.

Correct	Choice
	True
X	False

Feedback when incorrect: There is no "role" of PM on many agile projects, but a well-trained project manager who can embrace the responsibilities of a servant leader can easily play a role such as Scrum Master or coach.

4. Which of the following is NOT an approach to prevent mini-waterfall occurring within an iteration.

Correct	Choice
	Pair Programming
	Mob Programming
	Swarming
	Limit WIP
X	None of the above

Feedback when incorrect: The correct answer is none of the above. All of these approaches support getting work done as quickly as possible on an individual requirement.

5. When we practice active listening, what are the levels through which our listening skills progress?

Correct	Choice
	Self-centered listening, Focused listening, Intuitive listening
X	Internal listening, Focused listening, Global listening
	Global listening, Focused listening, Intuitive listening
	Interested listening, Focused listening, Global listening

Feedback when incorrect: Internal listening, Focused listening, Global listening

6. The Japanese terms for an Agile developmental mastery model is:

Correct	Choice
	Kaizen
X	Shu-Ha-Ri
	Sashimi
	Muda

Feedback when incorrect: Su-Ha-Ri is an Agile development mastery model taken from Japanese martial arts.

7. Which development mastery model of skill acquisition lies in helping the teacher understand how to assist the learner in advancing to the next level?

Correct	Choice
	Tuckman
X	Dreyfus
	Shu-Ha-Ri
	Kaizen

Feedback when incorrect: The Dreyfus Model of skill acquisition lies in helping the teacher understand how to assist the learner in advancing to the next level.

8. Which of the following is NOT one of the 5 common conflict types?

Correct	Choice
X	Compensation anxiety
	Working in silos
	Difference in prioritizing tasks
	Waiting on completion of task dependencies

Feedback when incorrect: Compensation anxiety is not a conflict type. The rest of the list are the common types of conflict.

9. The Project Leader's primary responsibilities are to "move boulders and carry water." What is this an example of?

Correct	Choice
	Command and control leadership
	The leadership metaphor
X	Servant leadership
	Leadership by example

Feedback when incorrect: As a servant leader, the Scrum Master's primary responsibilities are to "move boulders and carry water"-in other words, remove obstacles that prevent the team from delivering business value, and to make sure the team has the environment they need to succeed.

10. Osmotic communication is when team members obtain information from overheard conversations.

Correct	Choice
X	True
	False

Feedback when incorrect: Osmotic communication means that information flows into the background hearing of members of the team, so that they pick up relevant information as though by osmosis.

11. What is the Open Space concept?

Correct	Choice
	When cubicles walls are removed for an Agile team.
X	It is a meeting designed to allow Agile practitioners to meet in self-organizing groups where they can share their latest ideas and challenges.
	It is a core principle of DSDM
	The choice to collocate all team members for the beginning of a project.

Feedback when incorrect: It is a meeting designed to allow Agile practitioners to meet in self-organizing groups where they can share their latest ideas and challenges.

12. Emotional intelligence includes all of the following except:

Correct	Choice
	Perceiving
	Managing
	Influencing
	Achieving
X	Committing
	Decision making

Feedback when incorrect: The 5 factors of Emotional Intelligence are: Perceiving, Managing, Decision making, Achieving, Influencing

13. Suppose you are a Scrum Master on a new Agile team. Which of the following strategies is best way to resolve conflict on the team?

Correct	Choice
	Smooth over
	Ignore
	Use your authority
	Dictate
X	Collaborate

Feedback when incorrect: Collaborate is a formal term for resolving conflict on a team.

14. On Agile teams, conflict is to be avoided at all cost.

Correct	Choice
X	False
	True

Feedback when incorrect: Conflict is a necessary part of team development.

15. Teams of members working in different physical locations are called:

Correct	Choice
	Co-located Teams
	Global Teams
	Outsourced Teams
X	Distributed Teams

Feedback when incorrect: Teams of members working in different physical locations are called distributed teams.

16. What is the sequence of Tuckman's stages of team formation and development progress?

Correct Order
Forming
Storming
Norming
Performing

17. Match each activity on the left to its definition on the right (drag and drop).

Correct	Choice
Coordination	The developer submits code for testing. The UX designer checks that the developer implemented it correctly.
Cooperation	The Product Owner adjusts some story priority to meet the dependency of another team.
Collaboration	Pair programming
Communication	A slide presentation by the Product Owner to stakeholders

18. There are four critical actions that should be embraced by an adaptive leader: improving speed-to-value, having a passion for quality, doing less, and _____.

Correct	Choice
	Facilitating meetings
	Ensuring effective communication
X	Engaging and Inspiring staff
	Managing conflict

Feedback when incorrect: Four critical actions that should be embraced by an adaptive leader are improving speed-to-value, having a passion for quality, doing less, and inspiring staff

19. On an Agile team, the project leader works to remove impediments from blocking the team's progress. This is known as what type of leadership?

Correct	Choice
	Consensus-driven
	Functional management
X	Servant
	Command and control

Feedback when incorrect: A servant leader prioritizes the needs of the team first by removing impediment and resolving issues.

20. When the Agile team works in the same location, the team is said to be_____.

Correct	Choice
X	Co-located
	Functional
	Outsourced
	Distributed

Feedback when incorrect: When the Agile team works in a single location, the team is said to be co-located.

21. All of the following are TRUE about communicating on distributed teams EXCEPT:

Correct	Choice
	Should consider instant messaging tools
	Have a higher need for videoconferencing
	Need to spend more effort communicating
X	Should have an easier Storming phase

Feedback when incorrect: Should have an easier Storming phase

22. A servant leadership role includes:

Correct	Choice
X	Shielding team members from interruptions
	Making commitments to stakeholders
	Determining which features to include in an iteration
	Assigning tasks to save time

Feedback when incorrect: One of the ways that the Scrum Master, as a servant leader, protects the Team is by shielding it from interruptions.

23. High-performing teams feature which of the following sets of characteristics?

Correct	Choice
	Consensus-driven, empowered, low trust
	Consensus-driven, empowered, plan-driven
X	Constructive disagreement, empowered, self-organizing
	Self-organizing, plan-driven, empowered

Feedback when incorrect: High-performing teams support constructive disagreement, are empowered, and self-organizing.

24. Self-organizing teams are characterized by their ability to:

Correct	Choice
	Do their own filing
	Sit where they like
X	Make local decisions
	Make project-based decisions

Feedback when incorrect: Team members are empowered with collective decision making and cross-functional skills, which increases their ability to self-organize and make local decisions.

25. When comparing communication styles, which of the following is true?

Correct	Choice
	Paper-based communication has the lowest efficiency and the highest richness.
	Paper-based communication has the highest efficiency and the lowest richness.
X	Face-to-face communication has the highest efficiency and the highest richness.
	Face-to-face communication has the highest efficiency and the lowest richness.

Feedback when incorrect: Agile manifesto principle: The most efficient and effective method of conveying information to and within a development team is face-to-face conversation.

Module 6 Knowledge Check

Answers

1. Match the contract types on the left to the terms on right:

Correct	Choice
Value delivered:	Payments made upon value-driven deliverables
Fixed Price Increments:	Pay per epic, feature or group of user stories.
Not to Exceed T&M:	Place a cap on cost
Graduated T&M:	Rate increase if delivery is early
Dynamic Scope:	Adjust features to capacity and timing, "Pay for Points" contracting
Team Augmentation:	Highly collaborative T&M model

2. What is a product roadmap?

Correct	Choice
	A list of reports and screens
X	A view of release candidates
	Instructions for deployment
	A backlog prioritization scheme

Feedback when incorrect: A product roadmap allows you to communicate where you want to take your product. You should be able to present at least three release candidates in your roadmap.

3. In Backlog refinement, a "triad" is referring to:

Correct	Choice
	The Product Owner, tester and analyst
X	A developer, tester and analyst
	The Scrum Master developer and tester
	A developer, analyst and Product Owner

Feedback when incorrect: A "triad" is a developer, tester and analyst who work together to discuss an write a story.

4. Which of these statements is NOT correct about Ideal time and Elapsed time?

Correct	Choice
	Ideal time is the time that is actually required to complete the work without any interruptions
	Elapsed time is the amount of time that passes on clock (calendar days)
X	Both of them convey the same meaning
	Normally elapsed days are not equal to ideal days

Feedback when incorrect: Ideal time is not the same as Elapsed time. Elapsed time is the available duration to complete work whereas Ideal time is the time required to complete the work.

5. Which of the following is not part of Agile Discovery?

Correct	Choice
	Document business outcomes that are quantifiable and measurable
X	Define the tasks that the team will perform during an iteration
	Outline a plan for the technical and business architecture/design of the solution
	Describe essential governance and organization aspects of the project and how the project will be managed

Feedback when incorrect: Agile Discovery occurs before the project begins. Task planning occurs with the team during iteration planning.

6. Agile Analysis is a phase in the lifecycle of an Agile project.

Correct	Choice
	True
X	False

Feedback when incorrect: Agile Analysis isn't a phase in the lifecycle of your project. It is an ongoing and iterative activity.

7. Pick the three statements that are true about Agile Analysis.

Correct	Choice
X	It is a highly evolutionary and collaborative process
	It occurs at the beginning and end of a project
X	It is communication rich
	It only includes the project team
X	It explores the problem statement

8. It is not possible to have a fixed price contract in Agile.

Correct	Choice
	True
X	False

Feedback when incorrect: Though a time and materials contract is an easier alternative for an Agile contract, the reality is that fixed-price contracts are necessary but should be limited to Agile discovery, and separate contracts for each iteration.

9. Match the traditional contract model of the left with the Agile alternative on the right.

Correct	Choice
Changes 'controlled' by means of the change control mechanism.	Change is accommodated within the non-contractual product backlog.
Analysis, design, development and testing occur sequentially.	There is concurrent design and development.
Success is measured by reference to conformance with the plans.	Success is measured by reference to the realization of the desired business outcomes.
No value delivered until the entire project has been completed.	Value delivered at the end of every Sprint.
There is no attempt to control the order in which the requirements are tackled.	The highest risk and highest value items are tackled first.

Feedback when incorrect: You did not select the correct response.

10. What is the name of this facilitated process? One or more team members sequence the product backlog from smallest to largest User Story. The rest of the team validates the sequence. The whole team uses a sizing method such as T-shirt size or Fibonacci sequence to group the user stories.

Correct	Choice
	Relative estimation
	Pairwise comparison
	Planning Poker
X	Affinity estimating

Feedback when incorrect: Affinity Estimating is when one or more team members sequence the product backlog from smallest to largest User Story. The rest of the team validates the sequence. The whole team uses a sizing method such as T-shirt size or Fibonacci sequence to group the user stories.

11. What Agile planning artifact is updated minimally once a year by the Product Owner?

Correct	Choice
X	Product Vision
	Product Roadmap
	Release Plan
	Sprint Plan
	Daily Plan

Feedback when incorrect: The Product Vision is updated annually by the Product Owner and stakeholders.

12. What is the order the hierarchy of product definition?

Correct Order
Product Vision
Product Roadmap
Theme
Epic
User Story
Task

13. Wideband Delphi is used by an Agile Project manager to support what activity?

Correct	Choice
	Prioritization
	Scheduling
X	Estimation
	Risk Management

Feedback when incorrect: The Wideband Delphi estimation method is a consensus-based technique for estimating effort.

14. Which Agile estimation technique is based upon relative sizing?

Correct	Choice
	Ideal time
	Bottom up
X	Story points
	Little's Law

Feedback when incorrect: Story points are relative values that do not translate directly into a specific number of hours.

15. What Agile planning artifact should be updated at minimum semi-annually?

Correct	Choice
	Product Vision
X	Product Roadmap
	Release Plan
	Sprint Plan
	Daily Plan

Feedback when incorrect: The Product Roadmap should be updated at least twice a year by the Product Owner.

16. Which is the process of continuously improving and detailing a plan as more detailed and specific information and more accurate estimates become available as the project progresses?

Correct	Choice
	Process Tailoring
	Pareto Analysis
X	Progressive Elaboration
	Open Space Planning

Feedback when incorrect: Progressive Elaboration is the process of continuously improving and detailing a plan as more detailed and specific information and more accurate estimates become available as the project progresses.

17. Product roadmaps are more accurate the closer we get to an actual release.

Correct	Choice
X	True
	False

Feedback when incorrect: Product roadmaps should be updated and made more accurate the closer we get to an actual release.

18. What Agile planning artifact is created by the Product Owner and the development team?

Correct	Choice
X	Product Vision
	Product Roadmap
	Release Plan
	Sprint Plan
	Daily Plan

Feedback when incorrect: The Sprint Plan is created by the Product Owner and the Development Team.

19. When is Planning Poker used?

Correct	Choice
	During backlog prioritization
	As part of Pareto Analysis
X	During User Story sizing and estimating
	As part of the Daily Stand-up

Feedback when incorrect: Planning Poker® is a consensus-based estimating technique. Planning Poker can be used with story points, ideal days, or any other estimating unit.

20. What is the correct sequence of activities in release planning?

Correct Order
Identify features
Prioritize features
Split features using the MMF perspective
Estimate the value of the features
Estimate the cost of the features
Write stories for features
Create release plan by date or scope

21. What type of time estimation excludes non-programming time?

Correct	Choice
X	Ideal Time
	Elapsed time
	Duration
	Real Time

Feedback when incorrect: Ideal Time excludes non-programming time. When a team uses Ideal Time for estimating, they are referring explicitly to only the programmer time required to get a feature or task done, compared to other features or tasks.

22. While managing the Agile Product Lifecycle, match the frequency with which you update the five Agile plans.

Correct	Choice
Product Vision	Annually by Product Owner
Product Roadmap	Semi-Annually by The Product Owner
Release Plan	Quarterly by the Product Owner and teams
Sprint Plan	Each iteration by the team
Daily Plan (Scrum)	Daily by the individual

23. Which of the following is NOT a characteristic of an Agile plan?

Correct	Choice
	Follows rolling wave planning approach
	Are top down
	Easy to change
X	Shows dependencies of one task to others

Feedback when incorrect: Showing dependencies of one task on others is not a characteristic of an Agile plan.

24. _____ an estimate refers to estimating a story based on its relationship to one or more other stories.

Correct	Choice
X	Triangulating
	Triaging
	Aggregating
	Disaggregating

Feedback when incorrect: Triangulating refers to estimating a story based on its relationship to one or more other stories

25. Which of the following is NOT recognized as a "unit" that can be used for estimating the size of the requirements on your Agile project?

Correct	Choice
	Elapsed time
	Relative size
	Ideal time
X	Ideal size

Feedback when incorrect: Real time, relative size and ideal time are all used in Agile estimating.

26. In what activity do the following steps occur:

Removing user stories that no longer appear relevant

Creating new user stories in response to newly discovered needs

Re-assessing the relative priority of stories

Correct	Choice
X	Backlog Grooming
	Progressive Elaboration
	Sprint Planning
	User Story Mapping

Feedback when incorrect: These steps occur in Backlog Grooming or Refinement

27. Agile uses a number sequence for estimating. The series of numbers all begin with 0, 1, 1 and are calculated by adding the previous two numbers to get the next number. This number sequence is called:

Correct	Choice
	Sashimi
	Velocity
	Capacity
X	Fibonacci

Feedback when incorrect: The Fibonacci sequence begins with 0 and 1 and each subsequent number is the sum of the previous two. 0,1,1,2,3,5,8,13,21

28. Team members who are part-time on your project will see at least a 15% reduction in their productivity per hour. The type of resource model in Agile is called:

Correct	Choice
	Collocated
X	Fractional assignments
	Distributed resources
	Over-allocated resources

Feedback when incorrect: Fractional Assignments impact team productivity. Team members who are part-time on your project will see at least a 15% reduction in their productivity per hour.

Module 7 Knowledge Check

Answers

1. When implementing Agile Project Management, risk management that occurs simply by following Agile best practices such as iterative planning and review activities is called:

Correct	Choice
	Adaptive risk management
	Intrinsic risk management
	Inherent risk management
X	Organic risk management

Feedback: Organic risk management is risk management that occurs simply by following Agile best practices such as iterative planning and review activities.

2. Which statement is least accurate when providing a definition of "Done"?

Correct	Choice
	It is the exit criteria to determine whether a product backlog item is complete
	It may vary depending on the project
X	It is defined by the Scrum Master
	It becomes more complete over time

Feedback: The definition of Done is defined by the Development Team and the Product Owner, not the Scrum Master.

3. An iteration prior to a release that includes final documentation, integration testing, training and some small tweaks is called:

Correct	Choice
X	Hardening Iteration
	Buffer Iteration
	Release Iteration
	Integration Iteration

Feedback: A hardening iteration is used for readying the product for production.

4. On a risk map or a risk heat map, the vertical and horizontal axes represent:

Correct	Choice
	Effort and Impact
X	Probability and Impact
	Probability and Exposure
	Impact and Exposure

Feedback: On a risk map or risk heat map the vertical and horizontal axes represent probability and impact.

5. In Agile development, what is the term for the internal things that you choose not to do now, knowing they will impede future development if left undone?

Correct	Choice
	Escaped defects
	Verification and validation results
X	Technical debt
	Intrinsic quality

Feedback: Technical Debt is the development that you choose not to do now, knowing that it will impede future development if left undone.

6. All of the following are attributes of the definition of "Done", EXCEPT:

Correct	Choice
X	It is a static artifact
	Defined by the Product Owner and the Team
	Defines a complete, integrated product by the end of the Iteration
	Can lead to technical debt if not implemented properly

Feedback: The Definition of Done is not static. It should be improved over time.

7. What is the purpose of running a test before you develop the code?

Correct	Choice
	To complete all test cases
X	To ensure it fails
	To ensure it passes
	To be cross-functional

Feedback: You run a test first to ensure it fails. If the test passes before you have written the code then it is a flawed test.

8. Agile development prevents technical debt.

Correct	Choice
	True
X	False

Feedback: Agile development does not prevent technical debt. Technical debt is often more prevalent in Agile due to the urgency to "ship" the software.

9. Refactoring is a key way of preventing technical debt.

Correct	Choice
X	True
	False

Feedback: The key to managing technical debt is to be constantly vigilant, avoid using shortcuts, use simple design, and refactor relentlessly.

10. What is an Agile term for the time period when some or all of the following occur: beta testing, regression testing, product integration, integration testing, documentation, defect fixing.

Correct	Choice
	Spike
	Code Freeze
X	Tail
	Lag

Feedback: Tail is the Agile term for the time period when some or all of the following occur: beta testing, regression testing, product integration, integration testing, documentation, defect fixing.

11. Which one is NOT a reason to perform a Spike?

Correct	Choice
	To perform basic research to familiarize the team with a new technology or domain
	To analyze the expected behavior of a large story so the team can split the story into estimable pieces.
X	To defer a story until a later Sprint while still showing progress to the Product Owner
	To do some prototyping to gain confidence in a technological approach

Feedback: Spikes are used for different reasons: perform research, analyze a story or do prototyping to validate a design approach, not to defer the work.

12. What is a change made to the internal structure of software to make it easier to understand and cheaper to modify without changing its observable behavior?

Correct	Choice
	Pair Programming
	Continuous Improvement
	Test Driven Development
X	Refactoring

Feedback: Refactoring is a change made to the internal structure of software to make it easier to understand and cheaper to modify without changing its observable behavior.

13. Frequent verification and validation is key in Agile but each approach produces a very different result. Verification determines _____ whereas validation determines _____.

Correct	Choice
	if the product is "done" | if the product is "done - done"
X	if I am I building the product right | if I am I building the right product
	if I am I building the right product | if I am I building the product right
	if the product has passed unit testing | if the product has passed acceptance testing

Feedback: Verification: Are we building the product right? Validation: Are we building the right product?

14. Bugs reported by the customer that have slipped by all software quality processes are represented in this metric.

Correct	Choice
	Technical debt
X	Escaped defects
	Risk burndown
	Code quality

Feedback: Escaped defects are bugs that have slipped by all software quality processes.

15. Which of the following are 2 attributes of Exploratory testing?

Correct	Choice
X	It involves minimum planning and maximum test execution
	It is typically automated
X	It is unscripted testing
	It is often the sole testing technique

Feedback: Exploratory testing is manual unscripted testing that has a minimum of planning but a high amount of execution. It is often done in conjunction with other testing.

16. A technique in which a team collaboratively discusses acceptance criteria and then distills them into a set of concrete tests before development begins is called (drag and drop):

Correct	Choice
	Feature Driven Development (FDD)
X	Acceptance Test Driven Development (ATDD)
	Test Driven Development (TDD)
	User Story workshops

Feedback: Acceptance test driven development

17. The _____ the technical debt means the _____ the intrinsic quality?

Correct	Choice
	higher, higher
X	higher, lower
	lower, lower

Feedback: higher, lower. The higher the technical debt means the lower the intrinsic quality.

18. Technical debt is the total amount of less-than-perfect _____ in your project.

Correct	Choice
	Defects
X	Design and implementation decisions
	Code commenting
	Code Sharing

Feedback: Technical debt is the total amount of less-than-perfect design and implementation decisions in your project

19. Testing that often occurs between "Done" and "Done- Done" is:

Correct	Choice
	Acceptance testing
X	Exploratory testing
	Unit Testing
	Test driven development

Feedback: Exploratory testing, unscripted manual testing, is typically done after all of the development iteration are complete and are being made ready for production, sometimes called "Done, Done"

20. Which type of risk analysis does an Agile team use to identify risks on their project?

Correct	Choice
	Risk Burndown Chart
	Pareto Analysis
X	Qualitative Risk Analysis
	Quantitative Analysis

Feedback: Qualitative analysis uses judgment, intuition, and experience in determining risks and potential losses.

Module 8 Knowledge Check

Answers

1. Process tailoring is an iterative approach implementing and improving your SDLC process.

Correct	Choice
X	True
	False

Feedback: Process tailoring is best done in an iterative manner: tailor some, implement some, and then repeat.

2. What is the Japanese business philosophy focused on making constant improvements?

Correct	Choice
	Shu-Ha-Ri
X	Kaizen
	Aikido
	Sashimi

Feedback: Kaizen is the Japanese business philosophy focused on making constant improvements.

3. Match the project factor to the tailoring options:

Correct	Choice
Steady or sporadic delivery	Deliver in a cadence like Scrum or in a flow like Kanban
Immature team	More frequent retrospectives
Frequent project interruptions	Make flow visible with Kanban board to determine impact
Poor quality	Introduce pair programming and other XP practices
Large team or multiple teams	Adopt a scaling framework
Inexperience with Agile	Retrain the team on an Agile framework

4. Which of the following is an Agile improvement technique to address issues continuously, e.g. after daily stand-up?

Correct	Choice
	Retrospectives
	Futurespectives
X	Intraspectives
	Verification Sessions

Feedback: Intraspectives are discussions within the Sprint to address issues typically as a result of issues raised during the daily Scrum

5. Similar to inspect and adapt in Scrum, this can be represented as Build, Measure, Learn.

Correct	Choice
	Six Sigma
X	Agile Learning Cycle
	DMAIC
	Kaizen

Feedback: Learning cycles assume that we are continually engaging in iterative cycles of learning where doing is connected to observing to reflecting to improving and then repeating. In Agile, this can be represented as Build, Measure, Learn.

6. When it the appropriate time to create working agreements?

Correct	Choice
	To set the stage in retrospectives.
	As part of project kick-offs
	Whenever a new team member joins
X	All of the above

7. What is the purpose of practicing asking the "5 Why's"?

Correct	Choice
	To determine the scope of the Sprint
X	To determine the root cause of an issue
	To determine the end result
	To determine the prioritized backlog

Feedback: The 5 Whys is an iterative question-asking technique used to explore the cause-and-effect relationships underlying a particular problem.

8. Your project management office (PMO) has suggested your project could benefit from some self-assessment work at the next retrospective. Which of the following benefits would they most likely be looking to achieve from a self-assessment?

Correct	Choice
	Gain insights for salary performance reviews
X	Improve personal and team practices
	Identify personal traits for human resources counseling
	Assess compatibilities for pair programming assignments

Feedback: The benefits would they most likely be looking to achieve from a self-assessment would be to improve personal and team practices.

9. Question: Which of the following BEST describes ROTI?

Correct	Choice
	Measure of product backlog items (PBI) remaining
	Measure of quality of features delivered in an iteration
	Measure of required effort to complete an iteration
X	Measure of the effectiveness of the retrospective meeting

Feedback: Return on Time Invested (ROTI) is used to measure the effectiveness of the retrospective meetings from the team members' perspective.

10. Sequence the activities that occur in a Retrospective meeting.

Correct Order
Set the Stage
Gather Data
Generate Insights
Decide What to Do
Close the Retrospective

11. You have been asked to review a different project team's recently enhanced methodology to assess its effectiveness and desirable characteristics. The types of characteristics that you should be looking for include evidence of:

Correct	Choice
	A preference for face-to-face communications, significant process weight, recommendations for larger teams to use lighter methods
X	A preference for face-to-face communications, not too much process weight, recommendations for larger teams to use lighter methods
	A preference for face-to-face communications, significant process weight, recommendations for larger teams to use heavier methods
	A preference for face-to-face communications, not too much process weight, recommendations for larger teams to use heavier methods

Feedback: The types of characteristics that you should be looking for include evidence of a preference for face-to-face communications, not too much process weight, recommendations for larger teams to use lighter methods.

12. The retrospective meeting:

Correct	Choice
X	Is intended to promote continuous process improvements
	Is only held at the end of the project
	Is conducted to provide the sponsor with key information on team progress
	Is optional

Feedback: The Sprint Retrospective is intended to promote continuous process improvements

13. **Triple Nickels is a technique used to perform what activity in a retrospective meeting?**

Correct	Choice
	Set the stage
	Generate Insights
X	Gather Data
	All of the above

Feedback: Triple Nickels is used to Gather Data in a retrospective meeting. It is a brainstorming approach where 3 people take 5 minutes to write ideas, then pass to next person to elaborate

14. **Which of the following are TRUE about the retrospective event in Scrum? (Choose 2)**

Correct	Choice
X	It is an opportunity to inspect the people, relationships, process, and tools in the last Sprint
X	It is three hours for a one month Sprint
	It occurs before the Sprint Review
	It is the only time improvements are made during a Sprint

Feedback: It occurs after the Sprint Review. This meeting is one of the opportunities to Inspect and Adapt. The duration is three hours long for a one month Sprint.

15. **Your sponsor is asking about tailoring the company's newly adopted agile methodology. Your advice should be:**

Correct	Choice
	Tailoring it will be a good way to learn the methodology
	Tailoring it will be a good way to ease into the initial adoption process
	We should tailor it first, then consider adopting it
X	We should try it first, then consider tailoring it

16. The purpose of a retrospective is for the team to:

Correct	Choice
	Review stories planned for the next Sprint and provide estimates.
	Demonstrate completed User Stories to the Product Owner.
X	Determine what to stop doing, start doing, and continue doing.
	Individually provide status updates on the User Stories in progress.

Feedback: The purpose of a Sprint Retrospective is for the Scrum Team to determine, what to stop doing, start doing, and continue doing.

17. Which of the following is NOT a technique for continuous improvement?

Correct	Choice
	Self-Assessment
	Process Tailoring
X	Sustainable Pace
	Retrospectives

Feedback: Sustainable pace is not a continuous improvement technique. All of the others are.

18. What is the reason to perform a Force Field analysis with the team?

Correct	Choice
	Decide how to implement a change
X	Generate insights
	Set the stage for the meeting
	Close out the retrospective

Feedback: A Force Field Analysis is a technique to generate insight about what forces are both for and against change.

19. Process tailoring is best undertaken on agile projects when:

Correct	Choice
	Stakeholders want to try a new practice
	The team needs new processes to keep them engaged
X	There are challenges in implementing agile practices
	A boost in team velocity is needed to meet the schedule

Feedback: Process tailoring is best undertaken on agile projects when there are challenges in implementing agile practices.

20. You are engaging in some process analysis and have been advised to watch out for the standard anti-patterns of poor methodology practice. The types of things you should be on the lookout for are processes that display signs of being:

Correct	Choice
	One-of-a-kind, disciplined, heavy, embellished
	One-size-fits-all, disciplined, heavy, embellished
X	One-size-fits-all, intolerant, heavy, embellished
	One-of-a-kind, intolerant, embellished

Cape Project Management, Inc.

Agile Glossary

Agile Contracting	The first lesson we learnt in contracting out agile software development (or anything else for that matter), is to align objectives of the supplier and the customer. It is highly desirable to align supplier success with customer success. The key here is to define the product vision and what must be achieved; foster shared ownership of the goals by treating your supplier as a partner; and consider offering the supplier incentives for meeting key business performance indicators that require partnership with you. http://blog.scrumup.com/2012/11/top-ten-reads-on-agile-contracts.html
Agile Discovery	During the Discovery Phase, designers need to work with the business analyst to capture and define business requirements. This is done by facilitating workshops and interviewing key stakeholders. A lot of sketching, note taking, brainstorming and discussion happen at this stage in order to effectively visualize the early thinking on look and feel, layout and interaction design. It is also worth noting that defining the business model is an evolutionary process. At the end of the discovery and design phases the value proposition needs to map back to real user personas, partnerships, activities, a cost structure, solid business KPIs and have a business mission statement should all clearly defined. https://www.arrkgroup.com/thought-leadership/the-importance-of-getting-the-discovery-phase-right/
Architectural Spike	XP does this while the initial Planning Game is in process. It's not an iteration - it might be longer or shorter, we don't know yet. What it's about is exploring solution elements that seem relevant to the as yet limited knowledge we have about the problem domain, choosing a System Metaphor, putting enough of our build, dbms, and source control tools in place to be able to begin controlled work, and then proceeding until we have something that runs and can be iterated. https://www.linkedin.com/pulse/agile-architecting-practice-architecture-spike-erik-philippus
Active Listening	Active listening is a communication technique used in counselling, training and conflict resolution, which requires the listener to feed back what they hear to the speaker, by way of re-stating or paraphrasing what they have heard in their own words, to confirm what they have heard and moreover, to confirm the understanding of both parties https://en.wikipedia.org/wiki/Active_listening
Adaptive Leadership	Adaptive leadership focuses on team management, from building self-organizing teams to developing a servant leadership style. It is both more difficult, and ultimately more rewarding than managing tasks. In an agile enterprise the people take care of the tasks and the leader engages the people. The facilitative leader works on things like building self-organizing teams, a trusting and respectful environment, collaboration,

| | participatory decision making, and developing appropriate empowerment guidelines (for an excellent discussion of empowerment, see Chapters 6 & 7 in (Appelo, 2011)).

https://www.infoq.com/news/2011/02/highsmith-adaptive-leadership

Appelo, J. (2011). Management 3.0: Leading Agile Developers, Developing Agile Leaders. Upper Saddle River, JN: Addison-Wesley. |
|---|---|
| **Adaptability, Three Components** | Adaptability has three components—**product, process, and people.** You need to have a gung-ho agile team with the right attitude about change. You need processes and practices that allow the team to adapt to circumstances. And you *need* high quality code with automated tests. You can have pristine code and a non-agile team and change will be difficult. All three are required to have an agile, adaptable environment.

http://searchsoftwarequality.techtarget.com/feature/Adaptation-in-project-management-through-agile |
| **Affinity Estimating** | A facilitated process where team members for sequence the product backlog from smallest to largest user story, then the rest of the team validates and finally the user stories are group by a sizing method such as t-shirt size or Fibonacci sequence.

http://www.gettingagile.com/2008/07/04/affinity-estimating-a-how-to/ |
| **Agile Product Lifecycle** | **The Five Agile plans:**
1 – Product Vision: Yearly By Product Owner
2 – Product Roadmap: Bi-Yearly By The Product Owner
3 – Release Plan: Quarterly By The Product Owner And Teams
4 – Iteration Plan: Bi-Weekly By The Teams
5 – Daily Plan (Scrum): Daily By Individual

(EXAM TIP: different authors reference different time periods for updating these plans)
https://www.ramantech.com/implementing-the-5-levels-of-agile-planning/

http://www.romanpichler.com/blog/ |
| **Agile Modeling (AM)** | AM is a collection of values, principles, and practices for modeling software that can be applied on a software development project in an effective and light-weight manner. Values:
1. Communication
2. Simplicity
3. Feedback
4. Courage
5. Humility
Principles/Practices:
• Active Stakeholder Participation. Stakeholders should provide information in a timely manner, make decisions in a timely manner, and be as actively involved in |

	the development process through the use of inclusive tools and techniques. • Architecture Envisioning. At the beginning of an agile project you will need to do some initial, high-level architectural modeling to identify a viable technical strategy for your solution. • Document Continuously. Write deliverable documentation throughout the lifecycle in parallel to the creation of the rest of the solution. • Document Late. Write deliverable documentation as late as possible, avoiding speculative ideas that are likely to change in favor of stable information. • Executable Specifications. Specify requirements in the form of executable "customer tests", and your design as executable developer tests, instead of non-executable "static" documentation. • Iteration Modeling. At the beginning of each iteration you will do a bit of modeling as part of your iteration planning activities. • Just Barely Good Enough (JBGE) artifacts. A model or document needs to be sufficient for the situation at hand and no more. • Look Ahead Modeling. Sometimes requirements that are nearing the top of your priority stack are fairly complex, motivating you to invest some effort to explore them before they're popped off the top of the work item stack so as to reduce overall risk. • Model Storming. Throughout iteration you will model storm on a just-in-time (JIT) basis for a few minutes to explore the details behind a requirement or to think through a design issue. • Multiple Models. Each type of model has its strengths and weaknesses. An effective developer will need a range of models in their intellectual toolkit enabling them to apply the right model in the most appropriate manner for the situation at hand. • Prioritized Requirements. Agile teams implement requirements in priority order, as defined by their stakeholders, so as to provide the greatest return on investment (ROI) possible. • Requirements Envisioning. At the beginning of an agile project you will need to invest some time to identify the scope of the project and to create the initial prioritized stack of requirements. • Single Source Information. Strive to capture information in one place and one place only. • Test-Driven Design (TDD). Write a single test, either at the requirements or design level, and then just enough code to fulfill that test. TDD is a JIT approach to detailed requirements specification and a confirmatory approach to testing. http://www.agilemodeling.com/
Agile Scaling Model	Agile scaling factors are: 1. Team size 2. Geographical distribution 3. Regulatory compliance 4. Domain complexity 5. Organizational distribution

	6. Technical complexity 7. Organizational complexity 8. Enterprise discipline https://www.agilealliance.org/wp-content/uploads/2016/01/Agile-Scaling-Model.pdf
Agile Triangle	The three dimensions critical to Agile performance measurement : • Value, • Quality • Constraints (cost, schedule, scope). Also, simplified to be: • Value • Technical debt • Cost http://jimhighsmith.com/beyond-scope-schedule-and-cost-the-agile-triangle/
APM Delivery Framework	However, if the business objective is reliable innovation, then the process framework must be organic, flexible, and easy to adapt. The APM process framework supports this second business objective through the five phases of: • Envision • Speculate • Explore • Adapt • Close http://www.informit.com/articles/article.aspx?p=174660&seqNum=4
Asynchronous Builds	When you use the integration script discussed earlier, you're using synchronous integration—you're confirming that the build and tests succeed before moving on to your next task. If the build is too slow, synchronous integration becomes untenable. (For me, 20 or 30 minutes is too slow.) In this case, you can use asynchronous integration instead. Rather than waiting for the build to complete, start your next task immediately after starting the build, without waiting for the build and tests to succeed. The biggest problem with asynchronous integration is that it tends to result in broken builds. If you check in code that doesn't work, you have to interrupt what you're doing when the build breaks half an hour or an hour later. If anyone else checked out that code in the meantime, their build won't work either. If the pair that broke the build has gone home or to lunch, someone else has to clean up the mess. In practice, the desire to keep working on the task at hand often overrides the need to fix the build. If you have a very slow build, asynchronous integration may be your only option. If you must use this, a continuous integration server is the best way to do so. It will keep track of what to build and automatically notify you when the build has finished. http://jamesshore.com/Agile-Book/continuous_integration.html

Backlog Grooming/ Refinement	Product Backlog refinement is the act of adding detail, estimates, and order to items in the Product Backlog. This is an ongoing process in which the Product Owner and the Development Team collaborate on the details of Product Backlog items. During Product Backlog refinement, items are reviewed and revised. The Scrum Team decides how and when refinement is done. Refinement usually consumes no more than 10% of the capacity of the Development Team. However, Product Backlog items can be updated at any time by the Product Owner or at the Product Owner's discretion. http://www.scrumguides.org/scrum-guide.html
Brainstorming	A brainstorming session is a tool to generate ideas from a selected audience to solve a problem or stimulate creativity. These meetings are used for solving a process problem, inventing new products or product innovation, solving inter-group communication problems, improving customer service, budgeting exercises, project scheduling, etc. Using these tools can help discussion facilitators and Project Managers with alternative approaches for creative idea generation meetings (aka Brainstorming Sessions). They are particularly useful when previous meetings have gone afoul, are not as effective as they could be or productivity during these exercises is less than it should be. http://www.projectconnections.com/templates/detail/brainstorming-meeting-techniques.html

Burn Down Charts	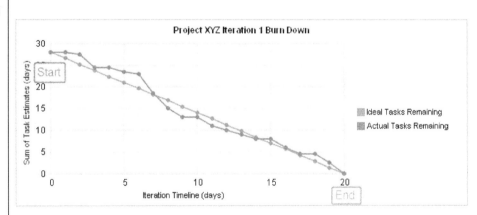 http://en.wikipedia.org/wiki/Burn_down_chart	
	X-Axis	The project/iteration timeline
	Y-Axis	The work that needs to be completed for the project. The time estimates for the work remaining will be represented by this axis.

	Project Start Point	This is the farthest point to the left of the chart and occurs at day 0 of the project/iteration.
	Project End Point	This is the point that is farthest to the right of the chart and occurs on the predicted last day of the project/iteration
	Ideal Work Remaining Line	This is a straight line that connects the start point to the end point. At the start point, the ideal line shows the sum of the estimates for all the tasks (work) that needs to be completed. At the end point, the ideal line intercepts the x-axis showing that there is no work left to be completed.
	Actual Work Remaining Line	This shows the actual work remaining. At the start point, the actual work remaining is the same as the ideal work remaining but as time progresses; the actual work line fluctuates above and below the ideal line depending on how effective the team is. In general, a new point is added to this line each day of the project. Each day, the sum of the time estimates for work that was recently completed is subtracted from the last point in the line to determine the next point.
	Actual Work Line is above the Ideal Work Line	If the actual work line is above the ideal work line, it means that there is more work left than originally predicted and the project is behind schedule.
Burndown Bar Charts	The typical Scrum release burndown bar chart shows a single value--the net change in the amount of work remaining. • As tasks are completed, the top of the bar is lowered. • When tasks are added to the original set, the bottom of the bar is lowered. • When tasks are removed from the original set, the bottom of the bar is raised. • When the amount of work involved in a task changes, the top of the bar moves up or down.	

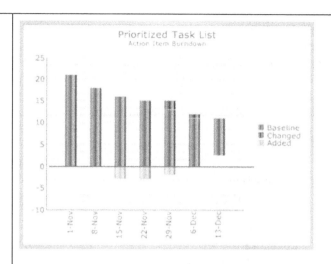

https://www.mountaingoatsoftware.com/agile/scrum/scrum-tools/release-burndown/alternative

Burn Up Charts	The amount of accepted work (that work which has been completed, tested, and met acceptance criteria) is graphed in a burnup chart. The amount of work in an accepted state starts at 0 and continues to grow until it reaches 100% accepted at the end of the Iteration. 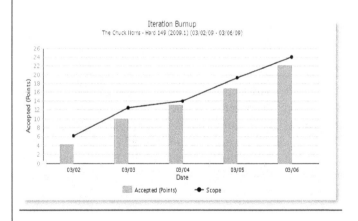 http://www.clariostechnology.com/productivity/blog/whatisaburnupchart
Chartering in Agile	1. **Vision:** The vision defines the "Why" of the project. This is the higher purpose, or the reason for the project's existence. 2. **Mission:** This is the "What" of the project and it states what will be done in the project to achieve its higher purpose. 3. **Success Criteria:** The success criteria are management tests that describe effects outside of the solution itself. https://www.infoq.com/news/2010/05/agile-project-charter

Collaboration	Collaboration is the basis for bringing together the knowledge, experience and skills of multiple team members to contribute to the development of a new product more effectively than individual team members performing their narrow tasks in support of product development. As such collaboration is the basis for concepts such as concurrent engineering or integrated product development. Effective collaboration requires actions on multiple fronts: • Early involvement and the availability of resources to effectively collaborate • A culture that encourages teamwork, cooperation and collaboration • Effective teamwork and team member cooperation • Defined team member responsibilities based on collaboration • A defined product development process based on early sharing of information and collaborating • Collocation or virtual collocation • Collaboration technology (EXAM TIP: There was specifically a question about the difference between coordination and collaboration) http://www.npd-solutions.com/collaboration.html
Collaboration Games	Agile games are activities focused on teaching, demonstrating, and improving Agile and organizational effectiveness using game theory. Using games, we can model complex or time-consuming processes and systems, examine why they work (or don't work), look for improvements, and teach others how to benefit from them. Games can model just the core of a process or model, leaving out unimportant factors. They can involve collaboration, brainstorming, comparing variants, and of course retrospectives. http://tastycupcakes.org/
Collective Code Ownership	The way this works is for each developer to create unit tests for their code as it is developed. All code that is released into the source code repository includes unit tests that run at 100%. Code that is added, bugs as they are fixed, and old functionality as it is changed will be covered by automated testing. Now you can rely on the test suite to watch dog your entire code repository. Before any code is released it must pass the entire test suite at 100%. Once this is in place anyone can make a change to any method of any class and release it to the code repository as needed. When combined with frequent integration developers rarely even notice a class has been extended or repaired. http://www.extremeprogramming.org/rules/collective.html
Collocated And Or Distributed Teams	Collocated Agile is a model in which projects execute the Agile Methodology with teams located in a single room. The methodology requires that the complete team be in close proximity to each other to improve coordination between the members. Collocated Agile teams have proven that the real power of project success lies not in administration, but in the acumen, chemistry, loyalty, and dedication between the collocated teams. Distributed Agile, as the name implies, is a model in which projects execute an Agile

	Methodology with teams that are distributed across multiple geographies. http://www.continuousagile.com/unblock/team_options.html
Compliance	Agile allows faster time to market by deploying working code more quickly. Application of user stories and iterations in a regulated industry can help to keep the team focused for large projects. Compliance regulations or legislation can sometimes change quickly. The opportunity to more easily cater for change gives the business stakeholders value earlier. As requirements change there is an avoidance of waste, due to not designing and detailing all requirements upfront. A successful agile compliance project requires the right people, the right team culture and the right amount of regulation / industry knowledge in the team. A tool may assist in enabling the appropriate levels of communication and reporting – so that the status of the project can be easily visible. Various considerations for agile projects in a regulated industry have been discussed here. Although there may be challenges, for a team with the right focus and frame of mind it is a matter of "where there is a will there is a way". Some areas may need to be adapted – however that merely seems to be in line with the whole essence and concept of what agile is all about – agility and responsiveness. https://www.planittesting.com/us/Insights/2012/Agile-and-Regulatory-Compliance
Conflict Resolution	Principles to Remember Do: Set up conflict management procedures before a conflict arises Intervene early when a fight erupts between team members Get the team working together again as soon as possible Don't: Assume your team agrees on its shared purpose, values, or vision Let conflicts fester or go unattended Move on without first talking about the conflict as a team https://hbr.org/2010/06/get-your-team-to-stop-fighting.html
Conflict Levels	**Level 1: Problem to Solve** We all know what conflict at level 1 feels like. Everyday frustrations and aggravations make up this level, and we experience conflicts as they rise and fall and come and go. At this level, people have different opinions, misunderstanding may have happened, conflicting goals or values may exist, and team members likely feel anxious about the conflict in the air. When in level 1, the team remains focused on determining what's awry and how to fix it. Information flows freely, and collaboration is alive. Team members use words that are clear, specific, and factual. The language abides in the here and now, not in talking about the past. Team members check in with one another if they think a miscommunication has just happened. You will probably notice that team members seem optimistic, moving through the conflict. It's not comfortable, but it's not emotionally charged, either. Think of level 1 as the level of constructive disagreement that characterizes high-performing teams.

Level 2: Disagreement

At level 2, self-protection becomes as important as solving the problem. Team members distance themselves from one another to ensure they come out OK in the end or to establish a position for compromise they assume will come. They may talk offline with other team members to test strategies or seek advice and support. At this level, good-natured joking moves toward the half-joking barb. Nastiness gets a sugarcoating but still comes across as bitter. Yet, people aren't hostile, just wary. Their language reflects this as their words move from the specific to the general. Fortifying their walls, they don't share all they know about the issues. Facts play second fiddle to interpretations and create confusion about what's really happening.

Level 3: Contest

At level 3, the aim is to win. A compounding effect occurs as prior conflicts and problems remain unresolved. Often, multiple issues cluster into larger issues or create a "cause." Factions emerge in this fertile ground from which misunderstandings and power politics arise. In an agile team, this may happen subtly, because a hallmark of working agile is the feeling that we are all in this together. But it does happen.

People begin to align themselves with one side or the other. Emotions become tools used to "win" supporters for one's position. Problems and people become synonymous, opening people up to attack. As team members pay attention to building their cases, their language becomes distorted. They make overgeneralizations: "He always forgets to check in his code" or "You never listen to what I have to say." They talk about the other side in presumptions: "I know what they think, but they are ignoring the real issue." Views of themselves as benevolent and others as tarnished become magnified: "I am always the one to compromise for the good of the team" or "I have everyone's best interest at heart" or "They are intentionally ignoring what the customer is really saying." Discussion becomes either/or and blaming flourishes. In this combative environment, talk of peace may meet resistance. People may not be ready to move beyond blaming.

Level 4: Crusade

At level 4, resolving the situation isn't good enough. Team members believe the people on the"other side" of the issues will not change. They may believe the only option is to remove the others from the team or get removed from the team themselves. Factions become entrenched and can even solidify into a pseudo-organizational structure within the team. Identifying with a faction can overshadow identifying with the team as a whole so the team's identity gets trounced. People and positions are seen as one, opening up people to attack for their affiliations rather than their ideas. These attacks come in the form of language rife with ideology and principles, which becomes the focus of conversation, rather than specific issues and facts. The overall attitude is righteous and punitive.

Level 5: World War

"Destroy!" rings out the battle cry at level 5. It's not enough that one wins; others must lose. "We must make sure this horrible situation does not happen again!" Only one option at level 5 exists: to separate the combatants (aka team members) so that they don't hurt one another. No constructive outcome can be had.

	http://agile.dzone.com/articles/agile-managing-conflict
Conflict Types	**#1 - Lack of Role Clarity** The project manager is responsible for assigning tasks to each project team member. In addition, they often assume that team members understand what is being asked of them. This assumption can be incorrect, leading to team members being unclear on what needs to be accomplished. A good project manager takes the time to explain the tasks, their expectations and timeframes around completion. **#2 - Difference in Prioritizing Tasks** Just because the project manager thinks the task is a milestone, the team member completing the task may not. Team members may be working simultaneously on multiple projects and cannot differentiate the priority of one project's tasks from another. The project manager should try to explain the importance of the overall project to the **#3 - Working in Silos** Often, project team members work independently. They may work remotely or in a different location from other project team members. Conflict arises when team members are not aware of what others are doing and are not communicating with one another. The project manager needs to bring the team together to discuss project status and barriers to getting the project completed promptly. If team members working in silos can envision how they are a part of the bigger picture, they will be more motivated and feel like a part of the team. **#4 - Lack of Communication** Project managers must foster a clear line of communication between project team members. In order to minimize duplication of efforts, the project manager should communicate expectations to all team members. The project manager needs to be easily accessible to project team members at all times during the project. If team members cannot reach their project manager or other team members, they may spin in circles needlessly. **# 5 - Waiting on Completion of Task Dependencies** Some tasks cannot be started until other tasks are completed. Team members need to understand the impact of their role on others. For example if one team member is responsible for ordering equipment and another for installing the equipment, one task is dependent on the other. Conflict can occur if the first team member is delayed in completing their tasks. http://www.brighthub.com/office/project-management/articles/95971.aspx
Container	A container is a closed space where things can get done, regardless of the overall complexity of the problem. In the case of Scrum, a container is a Sprint, an iteration. We put people with all the skills needed to solve the problem in the container. We put the highest value problems to be solved into the container. Then we protect the container from any outside disturbances while the people attempt to bring the problem to a solution. We control the container by time-boxing the length of time that we allow the problem to be worked on. We let the people select problems of a size that can be brought to fruition during the time-box. At the end of the time-box, we open the

	container and inspect the results. We then reset the container (adaptation) for the next time-box. By frequently replanning and shifting our work, we are able to optimize value. http://kenschwaber.wordpress.com/2010/06/10/waterfall-leankanban-and-scrum-2/
Continuous Integration	Continuous Integration (CI) involves producing a clean build of the system several times per day. Agile teams typically configure CI to include automated compilation, unit test execution, and source control integration. Sometimes CI also includes automatically running automated acceptance tests. **Continuous Integration Technique, Tools, and Policy** There are several specific practices that CI seems to require to work well. On his site, Martin Fowler provides a long, detailed description of what Continuous Integration is and how to make it work. One popular CI rule states that programmers never leave anything unintegrated at the end of the day. The build should never spend the night in a broken state. This imposes some task planning discipline on programming teams. Furthermore, if the team's rule is that whoever breaks the build at check-in has to fix it again, there is a natural incentive to check code in frequently during the day. **Benefits of Continuous Integration** When CI works well, it helps the code stay robust enough that customers and other stakeholders can play with the code whenever they like. This speeds the flow of development work overall; as Fowler points out, it has a very different feel to it. It also encourages more feedback between programmers and customers, which helps the team get things right before iteration deadlines. Like refactoring, continuous integration works well if you have an exhaustive suite of automated unit tests that ensure that you are not committing buggy code. http://www.versionone.com/Agile101/Continuous_Integration.asp http://www.martinfowler.com/articles/continuousIntegration.html
Control Limits	Control limits, also known as natural process limits, are horizontal lines drawn on a statistical process control chart, usually at a distance of ±3 standard deviations of the plotted statistic from the statistic's mean. Used in Agile Control charts https://en.wikipedia.org/wiki/Control_limits
Cumulative Flow Diagrams	The Cumulative Flow diagram is very similar to a Burnup Chart. It shows how much of our work (i.e., the effort associated with User Stories) is in different states, such as Completed or In Progress. The Total and Completed curves shows the Release scope and Burnup of completed work, while the In Progress curve shows how much work is associated with Stories currently in development. The primary difference from the standard Burnup and Cumulative Flow diagrams is that the latter shows how much of the work is currently in progress.

	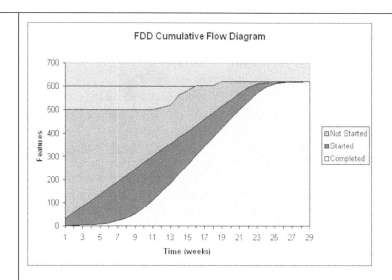 https://www.cprime.com/resource/templates/cumulative-flow-diagram-burnup-chart/
Customer-Valued Prioritization	Agile development is about the frequent delivery of high-value, working software to the customer/user community. Doing so requires the prioritization of user stories and the continuous monitoring of the prioritized story backlog. The primary driver for prioritization is customer value. However, it is insufficient to simply say that the highest-value stories are the highest priority. Product owners must also factor in the cost of development. An extremely valuable feature quickly loses its luster when it is also extremely costly to implement. Additionally, there are other secondary drivers such as risk and uncertainty. These should be resolved early. There may also be experimental stories that are worth developing early to find out whether customers see value in further development along those lines. There may be other prioritization drivers, but business value should always be foremost. 1. Complete the high-value, high-risk stories first if the cost is justified. 2. Complete the high-value, low-risk stories next if the cost is justified. 3. Complete the lower-value, low-risk stories next. 4. Avoid low-value, high-risk stories. http://www.scribd.com/doc/111905434/Agile-Analytics-a-Value-Driven-Approach-Ken-Collier
Cycle Time	Cycle time for software development is measured in the number of days needed between feature specification and production delivery. This is called: Software In Process (SIP). A shorter cycle indicates a healthier project. A Lean project that deploys to production every 2-weeks has a SIP of 10 working days. Some Lean projects even deploy nightly. https://jaymeedwards.com/2012/04/09/cycle-time-the-important-statistic-you-probably-arent-measuring/
Daily	Time-boxed 15 minutes meetings whose purpose is the providing of a concise team

Scrums/Daily Stand-Ups	status. Scrum has each team member asked by the ScrumMaster the following questions: • What did you do yesterday? • What are you doing today? • Are there any impediments that need resolution? (EXAM TIP: I had a couple of questions relating to the purpose of this meeting) http://www.mountaingoatsoftware.com/scrum/daily-scrum
Declaration Of Interdependence	The **PM Declaration of interdependence** is a set of six management principles initially intended for project managers of Agile Software Development projects We are a community of project leaders that are highly successful at delivering results. To achieve these results: ▪ We **increase return on investment** by making continuous flow of value our focus. ▪ We **deliver reliable results** by engaging customers in frequent interactions and shared ownership. ▪ We **expect uncertainty** and manage for it through iterations, anticipation, and adaptation. ▪ We **unleash creativity and innovation** by recognizing that individuals are the ultimate source of value, and creating an environment where they can make a difference. ▪ We **boost performance** through group accountability for results and shared responsibility for team effectiveness. ▪ We **improve effectiveness and reliability** through situationally specific strategies, processes and practices. http://pmdoi.org/
D.E.E.P.	• **Detailed Appropriately.** User stories on the product backlog that will be done soon need to be sufficiently well understood that they can be completed in the coming sprint. Stories that will not be developed for awhile should be described with less detail. • **Estimated.** The product backlog is more than a list of all work to be done; it is also a useful planning tool. Because items further down the backlog are not as well understood (yet), the estimates associated with them will be less precise than estimates given items at the top. • **Emergent.** A product backlog is not static. It will change over time. As more is learned, user stories on the product backlog will be added, removed, or reprioritized. • **Prioritized.** The product backlog should be sorted with the most valuable items at the top and the least valuable at the bottom. By always working in priority order, the team is able to maximize the value of the product or system being developed. http://www.mountaingoatsoftware.com/blog/make-the-product-backlog-deep

Definition Of Done	Definition of Done (DoD) is a simple list of activities (writing code, coding comments, unit testing, integration testing, release notes, design documents, etc.) that add verifiable/demonstrable value to the product. Focusing on value-added steps allows the team to focus on what must be completed in order to build software while eliminating wasteful activities that only complicate software development efforts. Note – the DoD is defined by the Product Owner and committed to by the team. http://www.scrumalliance.org/articles/105-what-is-definition-of-done-dod
Defect Rate	The defect detection rate is the amount of defects detected per sprint. Assuming that developers produce defects at a more or less constant rate, it is correlated with the velocity; the more story points are delivered, the more defects should be found and fixed as well. Teams tend to be pretty consistent in the quality of the software they deliver, so a drop in velocity combined with a rise in the defect detection rate should trigger the alarm. Something's cooking and you need to find out what it is. My personal opinion is that a lower defect detection rate isn't necessarily better than a higher one. A defect more found in one of the development and test environments is a defect less that makes it into production. From that perspective, you could support the statement, the more defects the better. http://theagileprojectmanager.blogspot.com/2013/05/agile-metrics.html
Discounted Pay-Back Period	A capital budgeting procedure used to determine the profitability of a project. In contrast to an NPV analysis, which provides the overall value of a project, a discounted payback period gives the number of years it takes to break even from undertaking the initial expenditure. Future cash flows are considered are discounted to time "zero." This procedure is similar to a payback period; however, the discounted payback period measures how long it take for the initial cash outflow to be paid back, including the time value of money. http://accountingexplained.com/managerial/capital-budgeting/discounted-payback-period

Dreyfus Model of Skill Acquisition	**1. Novice**
	    • "rigid adherence to taught rules or plans"
	    • no exercise of "discretionary judgment"
	2. Advanced beginner
	    • limited "situational perception"
	    • all aspects of work treated separately with equal importance
	3. Competent
	    • "coping with crowdedness" (multiple activities, accumulation of information)
	    • some perception of actions in relation to goals
	    • deliberate planning
	    • formulates routines
	4. Proficient
	    • holistic view of situation
	    • prioritizes importance of aspects

	• "perceives deviations from the normal pattern" • employs <u>maxims</u> for guidance, with meanings that adapt to the situation at hand **5. Expert** • transcends reliance on rules, guidelines, and maxims • "intuitive grasp of situations based on deep, tacit understanding" • has "vision of what is possible" • uses "analytical approaches" in new situations or in case of problems https://en.wikipedia.org/wiki/Dreyfus_model_of_skill_acquisition
DRY	Software must be written expecting for future change. Principles like **D**on't **R**epeat **Y**ourself (DRY) are used to facilitate this. In agile development, changes to the software specifications are welcome even in late stages of development. As clients get more hands-on time with iterative builds of the software, they may be able to better communicate their needs. Also, changes in the market or company structure might dictate changes in the software specifications. Agile development is designed to accommodate these late changes. https://code.tutsplus.com/tutorials/3-key-software-principles-you-must-understand--net-25161
Earned Value Management (EVM)	Agile EVM is now all about executing the project and tracking the accumulated EV according to the simple earning rule. Because Agile EVM has been evolving for many years the following practices are well-established: • EV is accumulated at fixed time intervals (i.e. Timebox, Iteration or Sprint) of 1–4 weeks; • PV and EV is graphically tracked & extrapolated as remaining value in a Release Burndown Chart as shown in figure 6; • Rather than a S-shaped curve the PV in Agile EVM is a straight line because an Agile project has no distinct phases and corresponding variances in the rate of value delivery; • The EV in Story Points done in one fixed time interval is known as the Velocity of a team; • In Agile scope change is embraced and the amount of added (removed) scope in Story Points is added (removed) to the Velocity or Scope Floor. The latter is shown in Figure 6 where several scope increases have lowered the Scope Floor below the x-axis. The advantage of using a Scope Floor is that any scope changes can easily be separated from Velocity variances; • The intersection between the Remaining Value and Scope Floor lines indicates the expected release date and the corresponding Remaining Budget. (EXAM TIP –There was a question on the exam that asked when was the best time to measure EVM) http://en.wikipedia.org/wiki/Earned_value_management#Agile_EVM
Emotional	**Self Awareness**

Intelligence	Awareness of one's own feelings and the ability to recognize and manage these feelings in a way which one feels that one can control. This factor includes a degree of self-belief in one's ability to manage one's emotions and to control their impact in a work environment.
	Emotional Resilience
	The ability to perform consistently in a range of situations under pressure and to adapt one's behavior appropriately. The facility to balance the needs and concerns of the individuals involved. The ability to retain focus on a course of action or need for results in the face of personal challenge or criticism.
	Motivation
	The drive and energy to achieve clear results and make an impact: and to balance both short and long term goals with an ability to pursue demanding goals in the face of rejection or questioning.
	Interpersonal Sensitivity
	The facility to be aware of, and take account of, the needs and perceptions of others when arriving at decisions and proposing solutions to problems and challenges. The ability to build from this awareness and achieve 'buy-in' to decisions and ideas for action.
	Influence
	The ability to persuade others to change a viewpoint based on the understanding of the position and the recognition of the need to listen to this perspective and provide a rationale for change.
	Intuitiveness
	The ability to arrive at clear decisions and drive their implementation when presented with incomplete or ambiguous information using both rational and 'emotional' or insightful perceptions of key issues and implications.
	Conscientiousness
	The ability to display clear commitment to a course of action in the face of challenge and to match 'words and deeds'; in encouraging others to support the chosen direction. The personal commitment to pursuing an ethical solution to a difficult business issue or problem.
	http://businessagile.blogspot.com/2005/02/emotional-intelligence-key-element-of.html
Empirical Process Control	**Empirical Process Control**
	The word "empirical" denotes information gained by means of observation, experience, or experiment. The empirical process control constitutes a continuous cycle of inspecting the process for correct operation and results and adapting the process as needed. There are three legs that hold up every implementation of empirical process control: **transparency, inspection, and adaptation**. The first leg is transparency. It means that those aspects of the process that affect the outcome must be visible to those controlling the process. The second leg is inspection. The various aspects of the process must be inspected frequently enough that unacceptable variances in the process can be detected. The third leg of empirical process control is adaptation. The process or the material being processed must be adjusted if one or more aspects of the process are outside acceptable limits and the resulting product will be unacceptable.

	http://www.scrumstudy.com/scrum-empirical-process-control.asp
Escaped Defects	Escaped Defects are those defects reported by the Customer that have escaped all software quality processes are represented in this metric. Escaping defects should then be treated as ranked backlog work items, along with other project work items. They should be prioritized high enough to resolve them within the next sprint or two and not accumulate a growing backlog. Watch the defect backlog as part of the project metrics. A growing defect backlog is a key indicator that the team is taking on more new work than it can handle. It may also be a key indicator that the team is operating as a "mini-waterfall" project, rather than a agile project, requiring more collaboration between Dev and Quality Engineers and early testing. Drop the number of new items the team works on until the escaping defects are well managed or eliminated. http://qablog.practitest.com/process-quality-feedback-and-escaping-defects/
Exploratory Testing	Exploratory Testing is a technique for finding surprising defects. Testers use their training, experience, and intuition to form hypotheses about where defects are likely to be lurking in the software, then they use a fast feedback loop to iteratively generate, execute, and refine test plans that expose those defects. It appears similar to ad-hoc testing to an untrained observer, but it's far more rigorous. Some teams use exploratory testing to check the quality of their software. After a story's been coded, the testers do some exploratory testing, the team fixes bugs, and repeat. Once the testers don't find any more bugs, the story is done. (EXAM TIP: This is also referred to as testing performed between Done and Done-Done) http://jamesshore.com/Blog/Alternatives-to-Acceptance-Testing.html

Extreme Programming	Extreme Programming (or XP) is a set of values, principles and practices for rapidly developing high-quality software that provides the highest value for the customer in the fastest way possible. XP is extreme in the sense that it takes 12 well-known software development "best practices" to their logical extremes.
	
	The 12 core practices of XP are:
	1) **The Planning Game**: Business and development cooperate to produce the maximum business value as rapidly as possible. The planning game happens at various scales, but the basic rules are always the same:
	   a) Business comes up with a list of desired features for the system. Each feature is written out as a **User Story**, which gives the feature a name, and describes in broad strokes what is required. User stories are typically written on 4x6 cards.
	   b) Development estimates how much effort each story will take, and how much effort the team can produce in a given time interval (the iteration).
	   c) Business then decides which stories to implement in what order, as well as when and how often to produce a production releases of the system.
	2) **Small Releases**: Start with the smallest useful feature set. Release early and often, adding a few features each time.

	3) **System Metaphor**: Each project has an organizing metaphor, which provides an easy to remember naming convention.
	4) **Simple Design**: Always use the simplest possible design that gets the job done. The requirements will change tomorrow, so only do what's needed to meet today's requirements.
	5) **Continuous Testing**: Before programmers add a feature, they write a test for it. When the suite runs, the job is done. Tests in XP come in two basic flavors. a) **Unit Tests** are automated tests written by the developers to test functionality as they write it. Each unit test typically tests only a single class, or a small cluster of classes. Unit tests are typically written using a unit testing framework, such as JUnit. b) **Acceptance Tests** (also known as **Functional Tests**) are specified by the customer to test that the overall system is functioning as specified. Acceptance tests typically test the entire system, or some large chunk of it. When all the acceptance tests pass for a given user story, that story is considered complete. At the very least, an acceptance test could consist of a script of user interface actions and expected results that a human can run. Ideally acceptance tests should be automated, either using the unit testing framework, or a separate acceptance testing framework.
	6) **Refactoring**: Refactor out any duplicate code generated in a coding session. You can do this with confidence that you didn't break anything because you have the tests.
	7) **Pair Programming**: All production code is written by two programmers sitting at one machine. Essentially, all code is reviewed as it is written.
	8) **Collective Code Ownership**: No single person "owns" a module. Any developer is expect to be able to work on any part of the codebase at any time.
	9) **Continuous Integration**: All changes are integrated into the codebase at least daily. The tests have to run 100% both before and after integration.
	10) **40-Hour Work Week**: Programmers go home on time. In crunch mode, up to one week of overtime is allowed. But multiple consecutive weeks of overtime are treated as a sign that something is very wrong with the process.
	11) **On-site Customer**: Development team has continuous access to a real live customer, that is, someone who will actually be using the system. For commercial software with lots of customers, a customer proxy (usually the product manager) is used instead.
	12) **Coding Standards**: Everyone codes to the same standards. Ideally, you shouldn't be able to tell by looking at it who on the team has touched a specific piece of code. (EXAM TIP: Lots of questions about Lean, XP and Scrum principles) http://www.jera.com/techinfo/xpfaq.html
Feature Breakdown Structure (FBS)	During detailed planning, agile development favors a feature breakdown structure (FBS) approach instead of the work breakdown structure (WBS) used in waterfall development approaches. Feature breakdown structures are advantageous for a few reasons: 1. They allow communication between the customer and the development team in terms both can understand. 2. They allow the customer to prioritize the team's work based on business value.

	3. They allow tracking of work against the actual business value produced. It is acceptable to start out with features that are large and then break them out into smaller features over time. This allows the customer to keep from diving in to too much detail until that detail is needed to help facilitate actual design and delivery. http://www.versionone.com/agile-101/agile-feature-estimation/
Fishbone diagram	The fishbone diagram identifies many possible causes for an effect or problem. It can be used to structure a brainstorming session. It immediately sorts ideas into useful categories. http://asq.org/learn-about-quality/cause-analysis-tools/overview/fishbone.html
The Five Whys	A technique for identifying the exact root cause of a problem to determine the appropriate solution. Made popular in the 70s by the Toyota Production System, the 5 whys is a flexible problem solving technique. http://businessanalystlearnings.com/ba-techniques/2013/2/5/root-cause-analysis-the-5-whys-technique
Fractional Assignments	All of the team members should sit with the team full-time and give the project their complete attention. This particularly applies to customers, who are often surprised at the level of involvement XP requires of them. Some organizations like to assign people to multiple projects simultaneously. This fractional assignment is particularly common in matrix-managed organizations. (If team members have two managers, one for their project and one for their function, you're probably in a matrixed organization.) Fractional assignment is dreadfully counterproductive. If your company practices fractional assignment, I have some good news. You can instantly improve productivity by reassigning people to only one project at a time. Fractional assignment is dreadfully counterproductive: fractional workers don't bond with their teams; they often aren't around to hear conversations and answer questions and they must task switch, which incurs a significant hidden penalty. "The minimum penalty is 15 percent... Fragmented knowledge workers may look busy, but a lot of their busyness is just thrashing." [DeMarco 2002] (p.19-20) That's not to say that everyone needs to work with the team for the entire duration of the project. You can bring someone in to consult on a problem temporarily. However, while she works with the team, she should be fully engaged and available. http://www.jamesshore.com/Agile-Book/the_xp_team.html Tom DeMarco and Barry Boehm. 2002. The Agile Methods Fray. *Computer* 35, 6 (June 2002)
Frequent Verification And	The terms Verification and Validation are commonly used in software engineering to mean two different types of analysis. The usual definitions are:

Validation	**Validation**: Are we building the right system? **Verification**: Are we building the system right? In other words, validation is concerned with checking that the system will meet the customer's actual needs, while verification is concerned with whether the system is well-engineered, error-free, and so on. Verification will help to determine whether the software is of high quality, but it will not ensure that the system is useful. The distinction between the two terms is largely to do with the role of specifications. Validation is the process of checking whether the specification captures the customer's needs, while verification is the process of checking that the software meets the specification. Verification includes all the activities associated with the producing high quality software: testing, inspection, design analysis, specification analysis, and so on. It is a relatively objective process, in that if the various products and documents are expressed precisely enough, no subjective judgements should be needed in order to verify software. http://www.easterbrook.ca/steve/2010/11/the-difference-between-verification-and-validation/
Ideal Time	Like Work Units, Ideal Time excludes non-programming time. When a team uses Ideal Time for estimating, they are referring explicitly to only the programmer time required to get a feature or task done, compared to other features or tasks. Again, during the first few iterations, estimate history accumulates, a real velocity emerges, and Ideal Time can be mapped to real, elapsed time. Many teams using Ideal Time have found that their ultimate effort exceeds initial programmer estimates by 1-2x, and that this stabilizes, within an acceptable range, over a few iterations. On a task by task basis the ratio will vary, but over an entire iteration, the ratios that teams develop have proven to remain pretty consistent. For a given team, a known historical ratio of Ideal Time to real time can be especially valuable in planning releases. A team may quickly look at the required functionality and provide a high level estimate of 200 ideal days. If the team's historical ratio of ideal to real is about 2.5, the team may feel fairly confident in submitting an estimate of 500 project days. In fixed-bid scenarios, this kind of estimate can be reliable. https://www.versionone.com/agile-101/agile-management-practices/agile-feature-estimation/
Information Radiator	An information radiator is a large display of critical team information that is continuously updated and located in a spot where the team can see it constantly. The term "information radiator" was introduced extensively with a solid theoretical framework in Agile Software Development by Alistair Cockburn. Information radiators are typically used to display the state of work packages, the condition of tests or the progress of the team. Team members are usually free to update the information radiator. Some information radiators may have rules about how they are updated. Whiteboards, flip charts, poster boards or large electronic displays can all be used as the

| | base media for an information radiator. For teams new to adopting agile work practices the best medium is usually a poster board on the wall with index cards and push pins. The index cards have a small amount of information on each of them and the push pins allow them to be moved around.

Information radiators help amplify feedback, empower teams and focus a team on work results. Too many information radiators become confusing to understand and cumbersome to maintain. If an information radiator is not being updated it should be reconsidered and either changed or discarded.

Robert McGeachy recommended a list of information radiators to be a part of every team room. Apart from the standard Scrum Artifacts, his list included,
<ul>
<li>Team structure with who's on the team</li>
<li>Client Organization structure</li>
<li>High Level and Mid Level plans</li>
<li>Client Phase exit criteria</li>
<li>Team performance survey results</li>
<li>Risks</li>
<li>Recognition awards</li>
<li>Ground Rules</li>
</ul>

http://www.agileadvice.com/archives/2005/05/information_rad.html |
|---|---|
| **Internal Rate Of Return (IRR)** | Internal rates of return are commonly used to evaluate the desirability of investments or projects. The higher a project's internal rate of return, the more desirable it is to undertake the project. Assuming all projects require the same amount of up-front investment, the project with the highest IRR would be considered the best and undertaken first. A firm (or individual) should, in theory, undertake all projects or investments available with IRRs that exceed the cost of capital. Investment may be limited by availability of funds to the firm and/or by the firm's capacity or ability to manage numerous projects.

In more specific terms, the IRR of an investment is the discount rate at which the net present value of costs (negative cash flows) of the investment equals the net present value of the benefits (positive cash flows) of the investment.

http://en.wikipedia.org/wiki/Internal_rate_of_return |
| **Iteration And Release Planning** | Release planning is the process of transforming a product vision into a product backlog. The release plan is the visible and estimated product backlog itself, overlaid with the measured velocity of the delivery organization; it provides visual controls and a roadmap with predictable release points.

http://www.netobjectives.com/files/Lean-AgileReleasePlanning.pdf |
| **I.N.V.E.S.T.** | Attributes of an effective user story: |

	Independent	The user story should be self-contained, in a way that there is no inherent dependency on another user story.
	Negotiable	User stories, up until they are part of a Sprint, can always be changed and rewritten.
	Valuable	A user story must deliver value to the end user.
	Estimable	You must always be able to estimate the size of a user story.
	Sized appropriately or Small	User stories should not be so big as to become impossible to plan/task/prioritize with a certain level of certainty.
	Testable	The user story or its related description must provide the necessary information to make test development

http://www.agileforall.com/2009/05/new-to-agile-invest-in-good-user-stories/

Kaizen	Kaizen is the practice of continuous improvement. Kaizen was originally introduced to the West by Masaaki Imai in his book Kaizen: The Key to Japan's Competitive Success in 1986. Today Kaizen is recognized worldwide as an important pillar of an organization's long-term competitive strategy.

http://www.kaizen.com/about-us/definition-of-kaizen.html |
| **Kanban Boards** | A Kanban means a ticket describing a task to do. A Kanban Board shows the current status of all the tasks to be done within this iteration. The tasks are represented by cards (Post-It Notes), and the statuses are presented by areas on the board separated and labeled with the status. This Kanban Board helps the team understand how they are doing well as well as what to do next and makes the team self-directing.

http://www.infoq.com/articles/agile-kanban-boards
http://blog.brodzinski.com/2009/11/kanban-story-kanban-board.html |
| **Kano Model** | The Kano model offers some insight into the product attributes which are perceived to be important to customers. The purpose of the tool is to support product specification |

and discussion through better development team understanding. Kano's model focuses on differentiating product features, as opposed to focusing initially on customer needs. Kano also produced a methodology for mapping consumer responses to questionnaires onto his model. The model involves two dimensions:

- Achievement (the horizontal axis) which runs from *the supplier didn't do it at all* to *the supplier did it very well*.
- Satisfaction (the vertical axis) that goes from *total dissatisfaction* with the product or service to *total satisfaction* with the product or service.

Dr. Noriaki Kano isolated and identified three levels of customer expectations: that is, what it takes to positively impact customer satisfaction. The figure below portrays the three levels of need: expected, normal, and exciting.

Expected Needs Fully satisfying the customer at this level simply gets a supplier into the market. The entry level expectations are the *must* level qualities, properties, or attributes. These expectations are also known as the *dissatisfiers* because by themselves they cannot fully satisfy a customer. However, failure to provide these basic expectations will cause dissatisfaction. Examples include attributes relative to safety, latest generation automotive components such as a self-starter, and the use of all new parts if a product is offered for sale as previously unused or new. The *musts* include customer assumptions, expected qualities, expected functions, and other *unspoken* expectations.

Normal Needs These are the qualities, attributes, and characteristics that keep a supplier in the market. These next higher level expectations are known as the *wants* or the *satisfiers* because they are the ones that customers will specify as though from a list. They can either satisfy or dissatisfy the customer depending on their presence or absence. The *wants* include *voice of the customer* requirements and other *spoken* expectations (see table below).

Exciting Needs The highest level of customer expectations, as described by Kano, is termed the *wow* level qualities, properties, or attributes. These expectations are also known as the *delighters* or *exciters* because they go well beyond anything the customer might imagine and ask for. Their absence does nothing to hurt a possible sale, but their presence improves the likelihood of purchase. *Wows* not only excite customers to make on-the-spot purchases but make them return for future purchases. These are *unspoken* ways of knocking the customer's socks off. Examples include heads-up display in a front windshield, forward- and rear-facing radars, and a 100,000 mile warranty. Over time, as demonstrated by the arrow going from top left to bottom right in the Kano model, *wows*

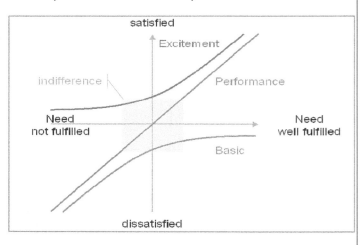

become *wants* become *musts*, as in, for example, automobile self-starters and

	automatic transmissions. http://asq.org/learn-about-quality/qfd-quality-function-deployment/overview/kano-model.html http://en.wikipedia.org/wiki/Kano_model
KPIs in Agile	1. **Actual Stories Completed vs. Committed Stories** – the team's ability to understand and predict its capabilities. To measure, compare the number of stories committed to in sprint planning with the stories identified as completed in the sprint review. 2. **Technical Debt Management** – the known problems and issues delivered at the end of the sprint. It is usually measured by the number of bugs, but may also include deliverables such as training material, user documentation and delivery media. 3. **Team Velocity** – the consistency of the team's estimates from sprint to sprint. Calculate by comparing story points completed in the current sprint with points completed in the previous sprint; aim for +/- 10 percent. 4. **Quality Delivered to Customers** – Are we building the product the customer needs? Does every sprint provide value to customers and become a potentially releasable piece of the product? It's not necessarily a product ready to release but rather a work in progress, designed to solicit customer comments, opinions and suggestions. This can best be measured by surveying the customers and stakeholders. 5. **Team Enthusiasm** – a major component for a successful scrum team. If teammates aren't enthusiastic, no process or methodology will help. Measuring enthusiasm can be done by observing various sprint meetings or, the most straightforward approach, simply asking team members "Do you feel happy?" and "How motivated do you feel?" 6. **Retrospective Process Improvement** – the scrum team's ability to revise its development process to make it more effective and enjoyable for the next sprint. This can be measured using the count of retrospective items identified, the retrospective items the team committed to addressing and the items resolved by the end of the sprint. 7. **Communication** – how well the team, product owner, scrum master, customers and stakeholders are conducting open and honest communications. Through observing and listening you will get indications and clues about how well everyone is communicating. 8. **Team's Adherence to Scrum Rules and Engineering Practices** – Although scrum doesn't prescribe engineering practices—unlike XP—most companies define several of their own for their projects. You want to ensure that the scrum team follows the rules your company defines. This can be measured by counting the infractions that occur during each sprint. 9. **Team's Understanding of Sprint Scope and Goal** – a subjective measure of how well the customer, product team and development team understand and focus on the sprint stories and goal. The goal is usually aligned with the intended customer value to be delivered and is defined in the acceptance criteria of the stories. This is best determined through day-to-day contact and interaction with the team and customer feedback.

	http://pragmaticmarketing.com/resources/9-scrum-metrics-to-keep-your-team-on-track
Lead Time	Lead time is a term borrowed from the manufacturing method known as Lean or Toyota Production System, where it is defined as the time elapsed between a customer placing an order and receiving the product ordered. http://guide.agilealliance.org/guide/leadtime.html
Lean Development	Lean software development is a translation of lean manufacturing and lean IT principles and practices to the software development domain. 1. **Eliminate Waste** • Provide market and technical leadership - your company can be successful by producing innovative and technologically advanced products but you must understand what your customers value and you know what technology you're using can deliver • Create nothing but value - you have to be careful with all the processes you follow i.e. be sure that all of them are required and they are focused on creating value • Write less code - the more code you have the more tests you need thus it requires more work and if you're writing tests for features that are not needed you are simply wasting time 2. **Create Knowledge** • Create design-build teams - leader of the development team has to listen to his/her members and ask smart questions encouraging them to look for the answers and to get back with encountered problems or invented solutions as soon as possible • Maintain a culture of constant improvement - create environment in which people will be constantly improving what they are working on - they should know that they are not and should not be perfect - they always have a field to improve and they should do it • Teach problem-solving methods - development team should behave like small research institute, they should establish hypotheses and conduct many rapid experiments in order to verify them 3. **Build Quality In** • Synchronize - in order to achieve high quality in your software you should start worrying about it before you write single line of working code - don't wait with synchronization because it will hurt • Automate - automate testing, building, installations, anything that is routine, but do it smartly, do it in a way people can improve the process and change anything they want without worrying that after the change is done the software will stop working • Refactor - eliminate code duplication to ZERO - every time it shows up refactor the code, the tests, and the documentation to minimize the complexity 4. **Defer Commitment** • Schedule Irreversible Decisions at the Last Responsible Moment - you should

	know where you want to go but you don't know the road very well, you will be discovering it day after day - the most important thing is to keep the right direction • Break Dependencies - components should be coupled as loosely as possible to enable implementation in any order • Maintain Options - develop multiple solutions for all critical decisions and see which one works best 5. **Optimize the Whole** • Focus on the Entire Value Stream - focus on winning the whole race which is the software - don't optimize local inefficiencies, see the whole and optimize the whole organization • Deliver a Complete Product - teams need to have great leaders as well as great engineers, sales, marketing specialists, secretaries, etc. - they together can deliver great final products to their customers 6. **Deliver Fast** • Work in small batches - reduce projects size, shorten release cycles, stabilize work environment (listen to what your velocity tells you), repeat what's good and eradicate practices that creates obstacles • Limit work to capacity - limit tasks queue to minimum (one or two iterations ahead is enough), don't be afraid of removing items from the queue - reject any work until you have an empty slot in your queue • Focus on cycle time, not utilization - put in your queue small tasks that cannot clog the process for a long time - reduce cycle time and have fewer things to process in your queue 7. **Respect People** • Train team leaders/supervisors - give team leaders the training, the guidance and some free space to implement lean thinking in their environment • Move responsibility and decision making to the lowest possible level - let your people think and decide on their own - they know better how to implement difficult algorithms and apply state-of-the-art software frameworks • Foster pride in workmanship - encourage passionate involvement of your team members to what and how they do (EXAM TIP: Lots of questions about Lean, XP and Scrum principles) http://www.disciplinedagiledelivery.com/lean-principles/
Learning Cycles	The Build–Measure–Learn loop emphasizes speed as a critical ingredient to product development. A team or company's effectiveness is determined by its ability to ideate, quickly build a minimum viable product of that idea, measure its effectiveness in the market, and learn from that experiment. In other words, it's a learning cycle of turning ideas into products, measuring customers' reactions and behaviors against built products, and then deciding whether to persevere or pivot the idea; this process repeats as many times as necessary. The phases of the loop are: Ideas –> Build –> Product –> Measure –> Data –> Learn https://en.wikipedia.org/wiki/Lean_startup

Minimally Marketable Feature (MMF)	Start by identifying your product's most desirable features. Prioritize their value, either through a formal technique or by subjectively ranking each one against the others. Once you've done so, plan your releases around the features. Release the highest-value features first to maximize their return. To accelerate delivery, have your entire team collaborate on one feature at a time and perform releases as often as possible. http://jamesshore.com/Articles/Business/Software%20Profitability%20Newsletter/Phased%20Releases.html
Minimal Viable Product (MVP)	A Minimum Viable Product is that version of a new product which allows a team to collect the maximum amount of validated learning about customers with the least effort. http://leanstack.com/minimum-viable-product/
MoSCoW	The MoSCoW approach to prioritization originated from the DSDM methodology (Dynamic Software Development Method), which was possibly the first agile methodology (?) – even before we knew iterative development as 'agile'. MoSCoW is a fairly simple way to sort features (or user stories) into priority order – a way to help teams quickly understand the customer's view of what is essential for launch and what is not. MoSCoW stands for: • **M**ust have (or Minimum Usable Subset) • **S**hould have • **C**ould have • **W**on't have (but Would like in future) http://www.allaboutagile.com/prioritization-using-moscow/
Multistage Integration Builds	Multi-stage Continuous Integration (MSCI) is an extension of the common practice of shielding others from additional changes by only checking-in when individual changes have been tested and only updating an individual workspace when it's ready to absorb other people's changes. With MSCI, each team does a team-based continuous integration first and then cross-integrates the team's changes with the mainline on success. This limits project-wide churn and allows continuous integration to scale to large projects. https://en.wikipedia.org/wiki/Multi-stage_continuous_integration
Net Present Value (NPV)	The difference between the present value of cash inflows and the present value of cash outflows. NPV is used in capital budgeting to analyze the profitability of an investment or project. NPV compares the value of a dollar today to the value of that same dollar in the future, taking inflation and returns into account. If the NPV of a prospective project is positive, it should be accepted. However, if NPV is negative, the project should probably be rejected because cash flows will also be negative. **Formula**

	Each cash inflow/outflow is <u>discounted</u> back to its present value (PV). Then they are summed. Therefore NPV is the sum of all terms, $$\frac{R_t}{(1+i)^t}$$ where t - the time of the cash flow i - the <u>discount rate</u> (the <u>rate of return</u> that could be earned on an investment in the financial markets with similar risk.); the opportunity cost of capital R_t - the net cash flow (the amount of cash, inflow minus outflow) at time t. For educational purposes, R_0 is commonly placed to the left of the sum to emphasize its role as (minus) the investment. http://en.wikipedia.org/wiki/Net_present_value
Negotiation	Negotiation, meaning "discussion intended to produce agreement", is fundamental to every software project. (And other projects too – my examples just happen to come from the software industry.) Developers and customers must reach agreement on what the system is supposed to do. A wise agreement will define achievable goals and meet the users' real needs. In Fisher and Ury's book, *Getting to Yes,* they call their approach "principled negotiation". It contains four key elements: • Separate People from the Problem • Focus on Interests, not Positions • Invent Options for Mutual Gain • Use Objective Criteria Both parties would be better served to engage in dialog about their underlying interests. Such dialog is encouraged by agile processes. They promote discussion, provide better opportunities to explore interests, and avoid premature "lock in" of positions. Fisher and Ury's style of negotiation is not about winning and losing. It's about *everybody winning*. http://www.agilekiwi.com/peopleskills/the-power-of-negotiation/ Fisher, Roger and William Ury. Getting to Yes: Negotiating Agreement Without Giving In. New York, NY: Penguin Books, 1983.
Open Space Meetings	**Opening**: 1. Show the timeline (agenda), how the event breaks down into Opening, Marketplace of ideas, Break-out sessions, Closing. 2. Sponsor introduces the theme. Briefly. One or two minutes max. Long openings drain the energy of the meeting quickly. Get participants to work ASAP. 3. Facilitators introduce the principles and the format. Explain how the marketplace of ideas works.

	Marketplace of ideas: 1. Participants write 'issues' on pieces of paper. Preferably with bold markers, so they are easy to read from a distance. 2. Participants choose a timeslot for their topic on the agenda wall. 3. One by one, participants explain their issue to the others, with the aim of drawing the right people to their break-out-session. http://www.chriscorrigan.com/parkinglot/planning-an-open-space-technology-meeting/
Osmotic Communications	Osmotic communication means that information flows into the background hearing of members of the team, so that they pick up relevant information as though by osmosis. This is normally accomplished by seating them in the same room. Then, when one person asks a question, others in the room can either tune in or tune out, contributing to the discussion or continuing with their work. When osmotic communication is in place, questions and answers flow naturally and with surprisingly little disturbance among the team. http://alistair.cockburn.us/Osmotic+communication
Pareto Principle	Pareto's law is more commonly known as the 80/20 rule. The theory is about the law of distribution and how many things have a similar distribution curve. This means that *typically* 80% of your results may actually come from only 20% of your efforts! Pareto's law can be seen in many situations – not literally 80/20 but certainly the principle that the majority of your results will often come from the minority of your efforts. http://www.allaboutagile.com/agile-principle-8-enough-is-enough/
Parking Lot Charts	Parking Lot Charts summarize the top-level project status. A parking-lot chart contains a large rectangular box for each **theme** (or grouping of user stories) in a release. Each box is annotated with the name of the theme, the number of stories in that theme, the number of story points or ideal days for those stories, and the percentage of the story points that are complete. http://www.change-vision.com/en/visualizingagileprojects.pdf
Payback Period	The length of time required to recover the cost of an investment. http://www.investopedia.com/terms/p/paybackperiod.asp
Personas	A persona, first introduced by Alan Cooper, defines an archetypical user of a system, an example of the kind of person who would interact with it. The idea is that if you want to design effective software, then it needs to be designed for a specific person. For the bank, potential personas for a customer could be named Frances Miller and Ross Williams. In other words, personas represent fictitious people which are based on your knowledge of real users

	(EXAM TIP: Specific exam question on why use "extreme" personas) http://www.agilemodeling.com/artifacts/personas.htm
Planning Poker	The idea behind Planning Poker is simple. Individual stories are presented for estimation. After a period of discussion, each participant chooses from his own deck the numbered card that represents his estimate of how much work is involved in the story under discussion. All estimates are kept private until each participant has chosen a card. At that time, all estimates are revealed (the card is played) and discussion in differences between the estimates begins. The goal is to keep discussing until variance on the estimate only varies by 1. They highest final number is used for the product backlog. http://store.mountaingoatsoftware.com/pages/planning-poker-in-detail
Pre-mortem	Also called a Futurespective: The pre-mortem activity is great for preparing for an upcoming release or challenge. With a different perspective, the activity guides the participants to talk about all that could go wrong. Then the conversation switches to a mitigation and action plan. http://riskology.co/pre-mortem-technique/
Process Tailoring	You can decide to tailor up, or tailor down. This is up to each organization to decide based on its own business needs. You just need to state your approach in your guidelines and then follow it.. Always tailor up if you want to increase control on your project, simplify your planning/ tailoring process, and run projects with appropriate agility, efficiency, and discipline. http://www.enterpriseunifiedprocess.com/essays/softwareProcessImprovement.html
Product Roadmap	Product/Portfolio planning is a key activity for the Agile Product Manager, which usually consists of planning and management of existing product sets, and defining new products for the portfolio. Now, in order to define the portfolio, the product manager has to develop a **product roadmap** in collaboration with her stakeholders that consists of new upcoming products and existing product plan updates based on the their current status. The product roadmap thus enables identifying future release windows and drives planning for tactical development. http://www.agilejournal.com/articles/columns/column-articles/2650-product-road-mapping-using-agile-principles
Progressive Elaboration	Progressive elaboration is defined by The PMBOK® Guide as continuously improving and detailing a plan as more detailed and specific information and more accurate estimates become available as the project progresses, and thereby producing more accurate and complete plans that result from the successive iterations of the planning process. 1. Decide on a release timebox for the project. This may be one week, two weeks, one month. Whatever your team is comfortable with. 2. Look at the requirements on a high level and have the team decide approximately what you can release in each release cycle. Since this is a high

	level, approximate estimate, you don't need to be too detailed. It's just there to provide a rough idea about how the releases will develop. 3. At every iteration planning meeting, sit with the customer/product owner and decide what you are going to do in that iteration. At this stage, you can ask for more details, and the team can come up with a more accurate estimate based on the details that you now know. 4. At the end of the iteration, update the high level overview with any new information that you now have. 5. Repeat steps 3 and 4 for every iteration. https://projectmanagementessentials.wordpress.com/2010/04/07/progressive-elaboration-moving-from-the-unknown-to-the-known/
Refactoring	Refactoring (noun): a change made to the internal structure of software to make it easier to understand and cheaper to modify without changing its observable behavior. http://martinfowler.com/bliki/DefinitionOfRefactoring.html
Relative Prioritization and Ranking	You use planning, ranking, and priority to specify which work the team should complete first. If you rank user stories, tasks, bugs, and issues, all team members gain an understanding of the relative importance of the work that they must accomplish. Ranking and priority fields are used to build several reports. You rank and prioritize work items when you review the backlog for a product or iteration. http://www.processimpact.com/articles/prioritizing.html
Relative Sizing using Story Points	Your team collaboratively estimates each user story in story points. In his book "Agile Estimation and Planning," Mike Cohn defines story points this way: "Story points are a unit of measure for expressing the overall size of a user story, feature or other piece of work." Story points are relative values that do not translate directly into a specific number of hours. Instead, story points help a team quantify the general size of the user story. These relative estimates are less precise so that they require less effort to determine, and they hold up better over time. By estimating in story points, your team will provide the general size of the user stories now and develop the more detailed estimation of hours of work later, when team members are about to implement the user stories. https://www.excella.com/insights/sizing-agile-stories-with-the-relative-sizing-grid Mike Cohn. 2005. Agile Estimating and Planning. Prentice Hall PTR, Upper Saddle River, NJ, USA
Research Story	Sometimes programmers won't be able to estimate a story because they don't know enough about the technology required to implement the story. In this case, create a story to research that technology. An example of a research story is "Figure out how to estimate 'Send HTML' story". Programmers will often use a spike solution (see Spike Solutions) to research the technology, so these sorts of stories are often called spike stories.

	Programmers can usually estimate how long it will take to research a technology even if they don't know the technology in question. If they can't even estimate how long the research will take, timebox the story as you do with bug stories. I find that a day is plenty of time for most spike stories, and half a day is sufficient for most. http://jamesshore.com/Agile-Book/stories.html

Retrospectives	The meeting performed at the end of an iteration or Sprint in which the project team identifies opportunities for improvement in the next iteration, or in their Agile Process in its entirety.
	Approach
	 1. Set the Stage
	    • Lay the groundwork for the session by reviewing the goal and agenda. Create an environment for participation by checking in and establishing working agreements.
	 2. Gather Data
	    • Review objective and subjective information to create a shared picture. Bring in each person's perspective. When the group sees the iteration from many points of view, they'll have greater insight.
	 3. Generate Insights
	    • Step back and look at the picture the team created. Use activities that help people think together to delve beneath the surface.
	 4. Decide What to Do
	    • Prioritize the team's insights and choose a few improvements or experiments that will make a difference for the team.
	 5. Close the Retrospective
	    • Summarize how the team will follow up on plans and commitments. Thank team members for their hard work. Conduct a little retrospective on the retrospective, so you can improve too.
	
	http://www.estherderby.com/tag/retrospectives
	Esther Derby and Diana Larsen. 2006. *Agile Retrospectives: Making Good Teams Great.* Pragmatic Bookshelf.

Return On Investment (ROI)	A performance measure used to evaluate the efficiency of an investment or to compare the efficiency of a number of different investments. To calculate ROI, the benefit (return) of an investment is divided by the cost of the investment; the result is expressed as a percentage or a ratio. If an investment does not have a positive ROI, or if there are other opportunities with a higher ROI, then the investment should be not be undertaken. The return on investment formula: $$ROI = \frac{(Gain\ from\ Investment - Cost\ of\ Investment)}{Cost\ of\ Investment}$$ (EXAM TIP: The only finance question that I had was on one how the Product Manager manages ROI) http://www.investopedia.com/terms/r/returnoninvestment.asp

Risk Areas	Tom DeMarco and Tim Lister identified five core risk areas common to all projects in their book, Waltzing with Bears: • Intrinsic Schedule Flaw (estimates that are wrong and undoable from day one, often based on wishful thinking) • Specification Breakdown (failure to achieve stakeholder consensus on what to build) • Scope Creep (additional requirements that inflate the initially accepted set) • Personnel Loss • Productivity Variation (difference between assumed and actual performance) http://leadinganswers.typepad.com/leading_answers/2007/04/the_top_five_so.html Tom DeMarco and Timothy Lister. 2003. Waltzing with Bears: Managing Risk on Software Projects. Dorset House Publ. Co., Inc., New York, NY, USA
Risk Adjusted Backlog	Risk Adjusted Backlog focuses on where investment needs to be undertaken, based on risk. The normal risk assessment database process will provide a decreasing list of priorities from the risk calculation: Potential Consequence x Likelihood. It may be necessary to make decisions on which of these should be dealt with first within each of the risk bands. Ideally one would fund and rectify all high and significant risks within the current financial year. However, constraints on both funding and the time to prepare and complete work may cause this ideal to be delayed. https://refinem.com/essential-agile-processes-part-8-risk-adjusted-backlog/
Risk Based Spike	Spikes, another invention of XP are a special type of story used to drive out risk and uncertainty in a user story or other project facet. Spikes may be used for a number of reasons: 1. Spikes may be used for basic research to familiarize the team with a new technology of domain 2. The story may be too big to be estimated appropriately and the team may use a spike to analyze the implied behavior so they can split the story into estimable pieces. 3. The story may contain significant technical risk and the team may have to do some research or prototyping to gain confidence in a technological approach that will allow them to commit the user story to some future timebox. 4. The story may contain significant functional risk, in that although the intent of the story may be understood, it is not clear how the system needs to interact with the user to achieve the benefit implied. http://www.scaledagileframework.com/spikes/
Risk Burn Down Graphs	Risk Burndown graphs are very useful for seeing if the total project risk is increasing or decreasing over time. It allows stakeholders to see instantly if we are reducing project risk.

	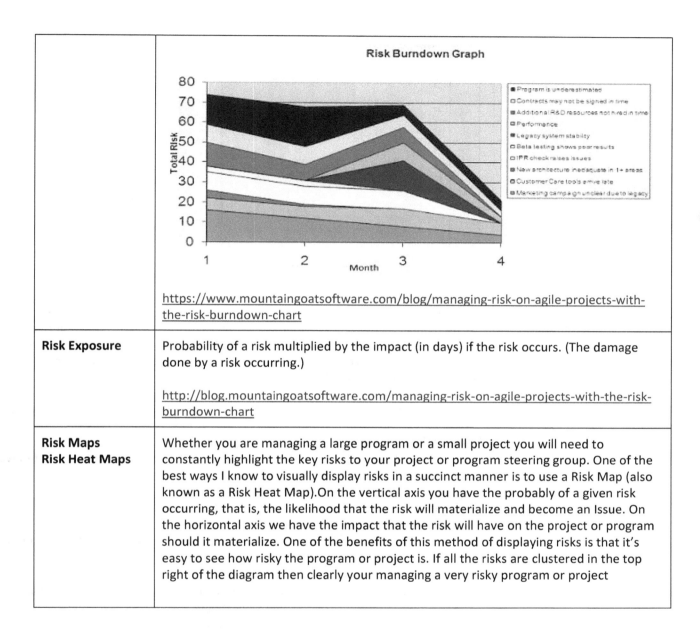 **Risk Burndown Graph** https://www.mountaingoatsoftware.com/blog/managing-risk-on-agile-projects-with-the-risk-burndown-chart
Risk Exposure	Probability of a risk multiplied by the impact (in days) if the risk occurs. (The damage done by a risk occurring.) http://blog.mountaingoatsoftware.com/managing-risk-on-agile-projects-with-the-risk-burndown-chart
Risk Maps **Risk Heat Maps**	Whether you are managing a large program or a small project you will need to constantly highlight the key risks to your project or program steering group. One of the best ways I know to visually display risks in a succinct manner is to use a Risk Map (also known as a Risk Heat Map).On the vertical axis you have the probably of a given risk occurring, that is, the likelihood that the risk will materialize and become an Issue. On the horizontal axis we have the impact that the risk will have on the project or program should it materialize. One of the benefits of this method of displaying risks is that it's easy to see how risky the program or project is. If all the risks are clustered in the top right of the diagram then clearly your managing a very risky program or project

http://www.expertprogrammanagement.com/2009/06/visualise-risks-using-a-risk-map/

Risk Multipliers	Risk multipliers account for common risks, such as turnover, changing requirements, work disruption, and so forth. These risk multipliers allow you to set a date, estimate how many story points of work you'll get done, and be right. It's a simpler version of the risk curves you'll see in good books on estimating and project management. http://jamesshore.com/Blog/Use-Risk-Management-to-Make-Solid-Commitments.html
Scrum Ceremonies	There are four ceremonies • Sprint planning: the team meets with the product owner to choose a set of work to deliver during a sprint • Daily scrum: the team meets each day to share struggles and progress • Sprint reviews: the team demonstrates to the product owner what it has completed during the sprint • Sprint retrospectives: the team looks for ways to improve the product and the process (EXAM TIP: We did not go deeply into the Scrum Roles or Ceremonies in this Guide since this is the most commonly trained and well documented material. If you have not already attended a Scrum training, you should read Ken Schwaber's *Agile Project Management with Scrum*, or minimally, the latest Scrum guide: http://www.scrumguides.org
Servant Leadership	There are several differences between Traditional projects and true Agile projects that—from a project management perspective—can best be summed up by the concept of self organization. In traditional projects, the project manager not only provides the vision of the team, but also directs and manages the team on the more detailed daily tasks by maintaining an up to date project plan. This usually results in a leadership style perhaps best described as "command and control." Agile projects on the other hand, still include the concepts of planning, managing the work, and providing status, but these activities are addressed collectively by the team,

	because at the end of the day they are the ones most familiar with what actually needs to happen to accomplish the project's goals. In this case, the Project Leader is in more of a support and facilitation role, similar in concept to Robert Greenleaf's idea of the Servant Leader. As Mike Cohn puts it in his Certified Scrum Master Class, the Project Leader's primary responsibilities are to "move boulders and carry water"—in other words, remove obstacles that prevent the team from providing business value, and make sure the team has the environment they need to succeed. One model often used to describe the leadership style needed on agile projects is the Collaborative Leadership model suggested by Pollyanna Pixton: • Make sure you have the **right people** on the project team. The right people are defined as those individuals who have passion about the goal of the project, have the ability to do the project, and are provided with the proper capacity, or time to work on the project. • **Trust First**, rather than waiting for people to prove their trustworthiness. • **Let the team members propose the approach** to make the project a success. After all, they are the ones who best know how to do the work. • **Stand back** and let the team members do their work without hovering over them continuously asking for status or trying to direct their activities, and provide support along the way to make sure nothing gets in the way of their success http://www.projectconnections.com/articles/092806-mcdonald.html Pollyanna Pixton, Niel Nickolaisen, Todd Little, and Kent McDonald. 2009. Stand Back and Deliver: Accelerating Business Agility (1st ed.). Addison-Wesley Professional
Shu Ha Ri	Shu-Ha-Ri is a way of thinking about how you learn a technique. The name comes from Japanese martial arts (particularly Aikido), and Alistair Cockburn introduced it as a way of thinking about learning techniques and methodologies for software development. The idea is that a person passes through three stages of gaining knowledge: ▪ **Shu:** In this beginning stage the student follows the teachings of one master precisely. He concentrates on how to do the task, without worrying too much about the underlying theory. If there are multiple variations on how to do the task, he concentrates on just the one way his master teaches him. ▪ **Ha:** At this point the student begins to branch out. With the basic practices working he now starts to learn the underlying principles and theory behind the technique. He also starts learning from other masters and integrates that learning into his practice. ▪ **Ri:** Now the student isn't learning from other people, but from his own practice. He creates his own approaches and adapts what he's learned to his own particular circumstances. ▪ http://martinfowler.com/bliki/ShuHaRi.html
Signal Card	English translation of the Japanese word, Kanban
Spike Solutions	A spike solution, or spike, is a technical investigation. It's a small experiment to research the answer to a problem. For example, a programmer might not know whether Java throws an exception on arithmetic overflow. A quick ten-minute spike will answer the question.

	http://jamesshore.com/Agile-Book/spike_solutions.html
Sprint Review	At the end of each sprint a sprint review meeting is held. During this meeting the Scrum team shows what they accomplished during the sprint. Typically this takes the form of a demo of the new features. The sprint review meeting is intentionally kept very informal, typically with rules forbidding the use of PowerPoint slides and allowing no more than two hours of preparation time for the meeting. A sprint review meeting should not become a distraction or significant detour for the team; rather, it should be a natural result of the sprint. Participants in the sprint review typically include the Product Owner, the Scrum team, the ScrumMaster, management, customers, and developers from other projects. During the sprint review the project is assessed against the sprint goal determined during the Sprint planning meeting. Ideally the team has completed each product backlog item brought into the sprint, but it is more important that they achieve the overall goal of the Sprint. http://www.mountaingoatsoftware.com/scrum/sprint-review-meeting
Story Maps	User story mapping offers an alternative for traditional agile planning approaches like the Scrum product backlog. Instead of a simple list, stories are laid out as a two dimensional map. The map provides both a high level overview of the system under development and of the value it adds to the users (the horizontal axis), and a way to organize detailed stories into releases according to importance, priority, etc. (the vertical axis). The map shows how every user story fits in the full scope. Releases are defined by creating horizontal slices of user stories, each slice is a release. For the first release, it is recommended to build a minimal set of user stories covering all user goals, so that you build a minimal but complete system to validate functionality and architecture early. https://www.thoughtworks.com/insights/blog/story-mapping-visual-way-building-product-backlog
Sustainable Pace	To set your pace you need to take your iteration ends seriously. You want the most completed, tested, integrated, production ready software you can get each iteration. Incomplete or buggy software represents an unknown amount of future effort, so you can't measure it. If it looks like you will not be able to get everything finished by iteration end have an iteration planning meeting and re-scope the iteration to maximize your project velocity. Even if there is only one day left in the iteration it is better to get the entire team re-focused on a single completed task than many incomplete ones. Working overtime sucks the spirit and motivation out of your team. When your team becomes tired and demoralized they will get less work done, not more, no matter how many hours are worked. Becoming over worked today steals development progress from the future. You can't make realistic plans when your team does more work this month and less next month. Instead of pushing people to do more than humanly possible use a release planning meeting to change the project scope or timing. Fred Brooks made it clear that adding more people is also a bad idea when a project is already late. The contribution made by many new people is usually negative. Instead ramp up your development team slowly well in advance, as soon as you predict a release

	will be too late. A sustainable pace helps you plan your releases and iterations and keeps you from getting into a death march. Find your team's perfect velocity that will remain consistent for the entire project. Every team is different. Demanding this team increase velocity to match that team will actually lower their velocity long term. So whatever your team's velocity is just accept it, guard it, and use it to make realistic plans. http://www.extremeprogramming.org/rules/overtime.html
Tail Length	The tail is the time period from "code slush" (true code freezes are rare) or "feature freeze" to actual deployment. This is the time period when companies do some or all of the following: beta testing, regression testing, product integration, integration testing, documentation, defect fixing. http://www.allaboutagile.com/shortening-the-tail/
Task Boards	Similar to Kanban Boards, a task board tracks the progress of work that is part of an overall story. https://realtimeboard.com/blog/scrum-kanban-boards-differences/
Team Development Stages	**Tuckman's Group Development Model** **Forming** In the *first stages* of team building, the *forming* of the team takes place. The individual's behavior is driven by a desire to be accepted by the others, and avoid controversy or conflict. Serious issues and feelings are avoided, and people focus on being busy with routines, such as team organization, who does what, when to meet, etc. But individuals are also gathering information and impressions - about each other, and about the scope of the task and how to approach it. This is a comfortable stage to be in, but the avoidance of conflict and threat means that not much actually gets done. The team meets and learns about the opportunities and challenges, and then agrees on goals and begins to tackle the tasks. Team members tend to behave quite independently. They may be motivated but are usually relatively uninformed of the issues and objectives of the team. Team members are usually on their best behavior but very focused on themselves. Mature team members begin to model appropriate behavior even at this early phase. Sharing the knowledge of the concept of "Teams - Forming, Storming, Norming, Performing" is extremely helpful to the team. Supervisors of the team tend to need to be directive during this phase. The forming stage of any team is important because, in this stage, the members of the team get to know one another, exchange some personal information, and make new friends. This is also a good opportunity to see how each member of the team works as an individual and how they respond to pressure. **Storming** Every group will next enter the *storming* stage in which different ideas compete for consideration. The team addresses issues such as what problems they are really supposed to solve, how they will function independently and together and what leadership model they will accept. Team members open up to each other and confront

	each other's ideas and perspectives. In some cases *storming* can be resolved quickly. In others, the team never leaves this stage. The maturity of some team members usually determines whether the team will ever move out of this stage. Some team members will focus on minutiae to evade real issues. The *storming* stage is necessary to the growth of the team. It can be contentious, unpleasant and even painful to members of the team who are averse to conflict. Tolerance of each team member and their differences should be emphasized. Without tolerance and patience the team will fail. This phase can become destructive to the team and will lower motivation if allowed to get out of control. Some teams will never develop past this stage. Supervisors of the team during this phase may be more accessible, but tend to remain directive in their guidance of decision-making and professional behavior. The team members will therefore resolve their differences and members will be able to participate with one another more comfortably. The ideal is that they will not feel that they are being judged, and will therefore share their opinions and views. **Norming** The team manages to have one goal and come to a mutual plan for the team at this stage. Some may have to give up their own ideas and agree with others in order to make the team function. In this stage, all team members take the responsibility and have the ambition to work for the success of the team's goals. **Performing** It is possible for some teams to reach the *performing* stage. These high-performing teams are able to function as a unit as they find ways to get the job done smoothly and effectively without inappropriate conflict or the need for external supervision. By this time, they are motivated and knowledgeable. The team members are now competent, autonomous and able to handle the decision-making process without supervision. Dissent is expected and allowed as long as it is channeled through means acceptable to the team. Supervisors of the team during this phase are almost always participative. The team will make most of the necessary decisions. Even the most high-performing teams will revert to earlier stages in certain circumstances. Many long-standing teams go through these cycles many times as they react to changing circumstances. For example, a change in leadership may cause the team to revert to *storming* as the new people challenge the existing norms and dynamics of the team. http://en.wikipedia.org/wiki/Tuckman's_stages_of_group_development
Team Space	William Pietri put together a list of rules for great development spaces. Amongst the well documented suggestions like putting the team together, room for daily standup, enough whiteboards and information radiators other suggestions included, • Get collaboration-friendly desks – William suggested this as one of the big pitfalls. He mentioned that many companies would like to foster collaboration but end up having furniture which is hostile to it. • Minimize distractions – The recommended rules to minimize distractions for the development stations include no phones, no email or IM, no off-topic conversation, less foot traffic and executives stay on mute. • Only direct contributors sit in the room – No chickens and certainly not the

	receptionist nor the sales people who would mostly be on the phone. • Pleasant space – Good lighting, decent air, plants, decorations and snacks. http://www.infoq.com/news/2010/02/agile-team-spaces
Technical Debt Management	It's all "those *internal* things that you choose not to do now, but which will impede future development if left undone" [Ward Cunningham]. On the surface the application looks to be of high quality and in good condition, but these problems are hidden underneath. QA may even tell you that the application has quality and few defects, but there is still debt. If this debt isn't managed and reduced, the cost of writing/maintaining the code will eventually outweigh its value to customers. In addition, it has a real financial cost: The time developers spend dealing with the technical debt and the resulting problems takes away from the time they can spend doing work that's valuable to the organization. The hard-to-read code that underlies technical debt also makes it more difficult to find bugs. Again, the time lost trying to understand the code is time lost from doing something more valuable. http://www.infoq.com/articles/technical-debt-levison **Managing technical debt** • **Starting captured debt.** Even if it is just by encouraging developers to note issues as they are writing code in the comments of that code, or putting in place more formal peer review processes where debt is captured it is important to document debt as it accumulates. • **Start measuring debt.** Once captured, placing a value / cost to the debt created enables objective discussions to be made. It also enables reporting to provide the organization with transparency of their growing debt. I believe that this approach would enable application and product end of life discussions to be made earlier and with more accuracy. • **Adopt standard architectures and open source models.** The more people that look at a piece of code the more likely debt will be reduced. The simple truth of many people using the same software makes it simpler and less prone to debt. http://theagileexecutive.com/2010/09/01/forrester-on-managing-technical-debt/
Test First Development	Test-First programming involves producing automated unit tests for production code, before you write that production code. Instead of writing tests afterward (or, more typically, not ever writing those tests), you always begin with a unit test. For every small chunk of functionality in production code, you first build and run a small (ideally very small), focused test that specifies and validates what the code will do. This test might not even compile, at first, because not all of the classes and methods it requires may exist. Nevertheless, it functions as a kind of executable specification. You then get it to compile with minimal production code, so that you can run it and watch it fail. (Sometimes you expect it to fail, and it passes, which is useful information.) You then produce exactly as much code as will enable that test to pass. http://www.versionone.com/Agile101/Test-First_Programming.asp

Test-Driven Development	Test-Driven Development (TDD) is a special case of test-first programming that adds the element of continuous design. With TDD, the system design is not constrained by a paper design document. Instead you allow the process of writing tests and production code to steer the design as you go. Every few minutes, you refactor to simplify and clarify. If you can easily imagine a clearer, cleaner method, class, or entire object model, you refactor in that direction, protected the entire time by a solid suite of unit tests. The presumption behind TDD is that you cannot really tell what design will serve you best until you have your arms elbow-deep in the code. As you learn about what actually works and what does not, you are in the best possible position to apply those insights, while they are still fresh in your mind. And all of this activity is protected by your suites of automated unit tests.
	You might begin with a fair amount of up front design, though it is more typical to start with fairly modest design; some white-board UML sketches often suffice in the Extreme Programming world. But how much design you start with matters less, with TDD, than how much you allow that design to diverge from its starting point as you go. You might not make sweeping architectural changes, but you might refactor the object model to a large extent, if that seems like the wisest thing to do. Some shops have more political latitude to implement true TDD than others.
	http://www.versionone.com/Agile101/Test-First_Programming.asp
Throughput	Throughput is the amount of work items delivered in a given period of time (e.g. week, month, quarter).
	http://old.berriprocess.com/en/todas-las-categorias/item/62-analiticas-lean-kanban-rendimiento
Timeboxing	Timeboxing is a planning technique common in planning projects (typically for software development), where the schedule is divided into a number of separate time periods (timeboxes, normally two to six weeks long), with each part having its own deliverables, deadline and budget. Timeboxing is a core aspect of rapid application development (RAD) software development processes such as dynamic systems development method (DSDM) and agile software development.
	Scrum Timeboxes:
	• Sprint Planning – 2 sessions, 1 hour per week of sprint
	• Sprint Duration – 1-4 weeks
	• Daily Scrums – 15 mins/day
	• Sprint Review – 1 hours per week of sprint, 1 hour prep
	• Sprint Retrospective – 3 hours per sprint
	https://daymoframework.wordpress.com/2010/08/21/a-crash-course-in-time-boxing/
Trade-Off Matrix	Balancing the four constraints – compliance, cost, schedule, and scope – is not a trivial task. However, just like the Agile Triangle, the Tradeoff Matrix used in Agile software development applies to IT. In its software development variant, the Tradeoff matrix is an effective tool to decide between conflicting constraints, as follows:

		Fixed	Flexible	Accept
Scope				X
Schedule		X		
Cost			X	

Rules:

- *Fixed* trumps *Flexible* trumps *Accepts*
- Each column can contain only one check mark
- Two check marks can't have the same priority

Note: The specific check marks in Table 1 are merely illustrative. Any three check marks that adhere to the rules above are legitimate. In fact, the three check marks represent the organization's policy decision as to what really matters.

http://theagileexecutive.com/tag/tradeoff-matrix/

Transition Indicator	A transition indicator is a notification that a risk (i.e., something that will have a negative impact on the cost/schedule of the project *if* it occurs) has materialized and is in need of attention. http://www.informit.com/articles/article.aspx?p=2123314&seqNum=3
Usability Testing	Usability testing is a long-established, empirical and exploratory technique to answer questions such as "how would an end user respond to our software under realistic conditions?" It consists of observing a representative end user interacting with the product, given a goal to reach but no specific instructions for using the product. (For instance, a goal for usability testing of a furniture retailer's Web site might be "You've just moved and need to do something about your two boxes of books; use the site to find a solution.") http://guide.agilealliance.org/guide/usability.html
Use Cases	Use cases are sometimes used in heavyweight, control-oriented processes much like traditional requirements. The system is specified to a high level of completion via the use cases and then locked down with change control on the assumption that the use cases capture everything.

	Use cases attempt to bridge the problem of requirements not being tied to user interaction. A use case is written as a series of interactions between the user and the system, similar to a call and response where the focus is on how the user will use the system. In many ways, use cases are better than a traditional requirement because they emphasize user-oriented context. The value of the use case to the user can be divined, and tests based on the system response can be figured out based on the interactions. Use cases usually have two main components: Use case diagrams, which graphically describe actors and their use cases, and the text of the use case itself. http://en.wikipedia.org/wiki/Use_case
User Stories	A good way to think about a user story is that it is a reminder to have a conversation with your customer (in XP, project stakeholders are called customers), which is another way to say it's a reminder to do some just-in-time analysis. In short, user stories are very slim and high-level requirements artifacts. User stories are one of the primary development artifacts for Scrum and Extreme Programming (XP) project teams. A user story is a very high-level definition of a requirement, containing just enough information so that the developers can produce a reasonable estimate of the effort to implement it. http://www.agilemodeling.com/artifacts/userStory.htm
Value Stream Mapping	Value Stream Maps exist for two purposes: to help organizations identify and end wasteful activities. Finding problems and creating a more efficient process isn't easy; even the best organization can be made more efficient and effective. But bringing about substantive organizational change that actually eliminates waste is a tall order. It's comparatively easy to identify waste, but it's another matter entirely to stop waste from happening in the first place. Value Stream Maps can both sharpen an organization's skills in identifying waste and help drive needed change. But first things first: What a Value Stream Map is and how one can be intelligently produced. The examples and concepts that follow are based on applying a Value Stream Map to a software engineering organization, but these concepts are applicable to a wide range of settings. Value Stream Maps help us bring about organizational improvement, progress in our processes and methods, and most importantly, better software. Value Stream Maps can help both identify and stop waste in an organization http://www.ibm.com/developerworks/rational/library/10/howandwhytocreatevaluestreammapsforswengineerprojects/index.html?ca=drs-
Velocity	Velocity is an extremely simple, powerful method for accurately measuring the rate at which teams consistently deliver business value. To calculate velocity, simply add up the estimates of the features (user stories, requirements, backlog items, etc.) successfully delivered in an iteration. There are some simple guidelines for estimating initial velocity prior to completing the first iteration but after that point teams should use proven, historical measures for planning features. Within a short time, velocity typically stabilizes and provides a tremendous basis for improving the accuracy and reliability of both near-term and longer-term project planning. Agile delivery cycles are very small so

	velocity emerges and can be validated very early in a project and then relied upon to improve project predictability. http://www.versionone.com/agile-101/agile-scrum-velocity/
Wide Band Delphi	Estimation method is a consensus-based technique for estimating effort 1. Coordinator presents each expert with a specification and an estimation form. 2. Coordinator calls a group meeting in which the experts discuss estimation issues with the coordinator and each other. 3. Experts fill out forms anonymously. 4. Coordinator prepares and distributes a summary of the estimates 5. Coordinator calls a group meeting, specifically focusing on having the experts discuss points where their estimates vary widely 6. Experts fill out forms, again anonymously, and steps 4 to 6 are iterated for as many rounds as appropriate. http://en.wikipedia.org/wiki/Wideband_delphi
WIP Limits	Limiting work in process (WIP) to match your team's development capacity helps ensure the traffic density does not increase the capacity of your team. The Kanban board will help you get to the right WIP limit as you become better at it. Without WIP limits you will continue to pile up partially completed work in the pipe thereby creating the phantom traffic jam. Adding to your WIP without completing anything just increases the duration of all tasks in the queue. If you are a product development shop, having a large duration (lead time) can significantly affect your company's profitability. http://www.kanbanway.com/importance-of-kanban-work-in-progress-wip-limits
Wireframes	A wireframe is a "low fidelity" prototype. This non-graphical artifact shows the skeleton of a screen, representing its structure and basic layout. It contains and localizes contents, features, navigation tools and interactions available to the user. The wireframe is usually: • black and white, • accompanied by some annotations to describe the behavior of the elements (default or expected states, error cases, values, content source...), their relationships and their importance, • often put in context within a storyboard (a sequence of screens in a key scenario) • refined again and again • used as a communication tool serving as an element of conversation and confirmation of "agile" user stories http://www.agile-ux.com/tag/wireframe/

Agile Roles	
Scrum Roles	
Product Owner	The **product owner** decides what will be built and in which order. • Defines the features of the product or desired outcomes of the project • Chooses release date and content • Ensures profitability (ROI) • Prioritizes features/outcomes according to market value • Adjusts features/outcomes and priority as needed • Accepts or rejects work results • Facilitates scrum planning ceremony http://www.scrumguides.org
Scrum Master	The ScrumMaster is a facilitative team leader who ensures that the team adheres to its chosen process and removes blocking issues. • Ensures that the team is fully functional and productive • Enables close cooperation across all roles and functions • Removes barriers • Shields the team from external interferences • Ensures that the process is followed, including issuing invitations to daily scrums, sprint reviews, and sprint planning • Facilitates the daily scrums http://www.scrumguides.org
Team	• Is cross-functional • Is right-sized (the ideal size is seven -- plus/minus two -- members) • Selects the sprint goal and specifies work results • Has the right to do everything within the boundaries of the project guidelines to reach the sprint goal • Organizes itself and its work • Demos work results to the product owner and any other interested parties. http://www.scrumguides.org
Extreme Programming (XP) Roles	
XP Coach	The XP Coach role helps a team stay on process and helps the team to learn. A coach brings an outside perspective to help a team see themselves more clearly. The coach will

	help balance the needs of delivering the project while improving the use of the practices. A coach or team of coaches supports the Customer Team, the Developer Team, and the Organization. The decisions that coaches make should always stem from the XP values (communication, simplicity, feedback, and courage) and usually move toward the XP practices. As such, familiarity with the values and practices is a prerequisite. The coach must command the respect required to lead the respective teams. The coach must possess people skills and be effective in influencing the actions of the teams. http://epf.eclipse.org/wikis/xp/xp/roles/xp_coach_60023190.html
XP Customer	The XP Customer role has the responsibility of defining what is the right product to build, determining the order in which features will be built and making sure the product actually works. The XP Customer writes system features in the form of user stories that have business value. Using the planning game, he chooses the order in which the stories will be done by the development team. He also defines acceptance tests that will be run against the system to prove that the system is reliable and does what is required. The customer prioritizes user stories, the team estimates them. http://epf.eclipse.org/wikis/xp/xp/roles/xp_customer_6D7CB91B.html
XP Programmer	The XP Programmer is responsible for implementing the code to support the user stories http://epf.eclipse.org/wikis/xp/xp/roles/xp_programmer_D005E927.html-
XP Programmer (Administrator)	The XP Programmer (Administrator) role includes most of the traditional software development technical roles, such as designer, implementer, integrator, and administrator. In the administrator role, the programmer deals with establishing the physical working environment http://epf.eclipse.org/wikis/xp/xp/roles/xp_system_administrator_92735060.html
XP Tracker	The three basic things the XP Tracker will track are the release plan (user stories), the iteration plan (tasks) and the acceptance tests. The tracker can also keep track of other metrics, which may help in solving problems the team is having. A good XP Tracker has the ability to collect the information without disturbing the process significantly. http://epf.eclipse.org/wikis/xp/xp/roles/xp_tracker_AD8A6C9F.html
XP Tester	The primary responsibility of the XP Tester is to help the customer define and implement acceptance tests for user stories. The XP Tester is also responsible for running the tests frequently and posting the results for the whole team to see. As the number of tests grow, the XP Tester will likely need to create and maintain some kind of tool to make it easier to define them, run them, and gather the results quickly. Whereas knowledge of the applications target domain is provided by the customer, the XP Tester needs to support the customer by providing:

	<ul><li>Knowledge of typical software failure conditions and the test techniques that can be employed to uncover those errors.</li><li>Knowledge of different techniques to implement and run tests, including understanding of and experience with test automation</li></ul> http://epf.eclipse.org/wikis/xp/xp/roles/xp_tester_44877D41.html

The Agile Manifesto

In February 2001, 17 software developers met at the Snowbird, Utah resort, to discuss lightweight development methods. They published the *Manifesto for Agile Software Development* to define the approach now known as agile software development. Some of the manifesto's authors formed the Agile Alliance, a nonprofit organization that promotes software development according to the manifesto's principles.

The Agile Manifesto reads, in its entirety, as follows:

We are uncovering better ways of developing software by doing it and helping others do it. Through this work we have come to value:

> **Individuals and interactions** over processes and tools
>
> **Working software** over comprehensive documentation
>
> **Customer collaboration** over contract negotiation
>
> **Responding to change** over following a plan

That is, while there is value in the items on the right, we value the items on the left more.

The meanings of the manifesto items on the left within the agile software development context are described below:

- Individuals and Interactions – in agile development, self-organization and motivation are important, as are interactions like co-location and pair programming.
- Working software – working software will be more useful and welcome than just presenting documents to clients in meetings.
- Customer collaboration – requirements cannot be fully collected at the beginning of the software development cycle, therefore continuous customer or stakeholder involvement is very important.
- Responding to change – agile development is focused on quick responses to change and continuous development.

Twelve principles underlie the Agile Manifesto, including:

1. Our highest priority is to satisfy the customer through early and continuous delivery of valuable software.
2. Welcome changing requirements, even late in development. Agile processes harness change for the customer's competitive advantage.
3. Deliver working software frequently, from a couple of weeks to a couple of months, with a preference to the shorter timescale.
4. Business people and developers must work together daily throughout the project.
5. Build projects around motivated individuals. Give them the environment and support they need, and trust them to get the job done.
6. The most efficient and effective method of conveying information to and within a development team is face-to-face conversation.

7. Working software is the primary measure of progress.

8. Agile processes promote sustainable development. The sponsors, developers, and users should be able to maintain a constant pace indefinitely.

9. Continuous attention to technical excellence and good design enhances agility.

10. Simplicity--the art of maximizing the amount of work not done--is essential.

11. The best architectures, requirements, and designs emerge from self-organizing teams.

12. At regular intervals, the team reflects on how to become more effective, then tunes and adjusts its behavior accordingly.

http://agilemanifesto.org/

www.ingramcontent.com/pod-product-compliance
Lightning Source LLC
Chambersburg PA
CBHW082107070326
40689CB00052B/3746